1984

Comparative Development
in Social Welfare

Comparative Development in Social Welfare

EDITED BY E. W. MARTIN

London · George Allen & Unwin Ltd
Ruskin House   Museum Street

ISBN 0 04 361014 5

Printed in Great Britain
in 11 point Plantin type
by Unwin Brothers Limited
Woking and London

Contents

page

1 The History of Changing Approaches
to Social Welfare *Asa Briggs* 9

2 From Parish to Union: Poor Law
Administration, 1601–1865 *E. W. Martin* 25

3 The Unreformed Workhouse, 1776–1834
James S. Taylor 57

4 Speenhamland in Berkshire *Mark Neuman* 85

5 Public Assistance in the United States:
Colonial Times to 1860 *Blanche D. Coll* 128

6 The American Historian and Social Welfare:
From the Civil War to World War II
Milton D. Speizman 159

7 Victorian Social Provision: Central and Local
Administration *E. C. Midwinter* 191

8 The History of Medical Care *Brian Abel-Smith* 219

Notes on Contributors 241

Index 242

I

The History of Changing
Approaches to Social Welfare

ASA BRIGGS

The essays in this volume all pivot on a central theme—the development of public provision for social welfare. Yet they range widely over time and place. They all point to the difficulties of generalization. What one generation has taken to be axiomatic, a matter of common sense, has often seemed to later generations to be far from self-evident. Sometimes, indeed, it has seemed to be not so much over-simplified as absurd. For this reason, if for no other, the historian must concern himself with shifts in values, whether sudden and dramatic or slow and unspectacular. His time-span must encompass many centuries. Nor can he rest content with the currently fashionable tendency to generalize easily about 'pre-industrial' and 'industrial' society or, to complete the triad, 'industrial' and 'post-industrial' society. Industrial societies were faced with common 'problems', which were identified as 'problems' independently in different places, and often the same 'solutions' emerged, but there were significant variations in the timing, in the style and, not least, in the form of response. There were frequent carry-overs from earlier periods, and during the earlier 'pre-industrial' periods themselves, there were diversities of experience which were expressed in different ways of thinking and feeling about change. The difficulties in generalizing persist. In the confused present, it is difficult for any sensitive traveller around England, historian or not, to think of it as either a post-industrial society or as a society where either inequalities in the provision of social welfare resources or attitudes towards them have been fully ironed-out.

To argue along these lines is not to imply that it is impossible to generalize, but rather that there is a danger in premature generalization. Before adequate comprehensive histories of public provision for social welfare can be written—about England, Europe or the world—we must have more essays of the kind represented in this collection. We must build up from the local or regional detail—the detail of experience—rather than employ the detail at secondhand to illustrate established propositions. Further and deeper understanding will then depend on our ability to relate and to compare.

There are several ways in which this ability can be extended. First, we can explore the language used in different generations, borrowing perhaps from anthropologists who have turned to the use of words and their collection in clusters, taking as some of the obvious key words in this context 'community', 'rank', 'class', 'masses', 'problem', 'system', 'welfare', 'state' and, not least, 'society' itself. The role of abstraction in the evolution of attitudes must be examined at different levels. The word 'system', for example, sometimes used, particularly in its origins, with pejorative popular undertones, has always been a difficult word for experts to employ in relation to almost all aspects of the history of social policy in England, including the history of education. They have usually resorted, therefore, to qualifying clauses like 'the English system if it may be called a system'.[1] Several other favourite examples of abstraction almost universally applied, not least the word 'class', have often confused rather than assisted specialized researchers or have led them into over-simplification. For most people, there are more profound difficulties. Thinking about society is thinking about the unthinkable. There is an habitual resort, therefore, to clichés. It was a Leeds clergyman, R. W. Hamilton, who said feelingly of the term 'masses' as long ago as 1845 that 'our judgments are distorted by the phrase. We unconsciously glide into a prejudice. We have gained a total, without thinking of the parts. It is a heap, but it has strangely become indivisible'.[2]

Second, therefore, we must try to get behind words to the human relationships which make up the stuff of social history. In this connection, it is impossible to leave out power relationships, although these never tell us the whole story. Social history cannot be separated from political and economic history in any period. For centuries it cannot be separated off from religious history, since 'charity' itself was institutionalized. The concept of 'social policy', central to modern history, is related to changing approaches to the efficacy and scope of government and administration. So, too, is the more recent concept of 'social work'; not surprisingly in recent years there have been sharp reactions against 'traditional' ways of thinking about it and organizing it. The very word 'welfare' itself has often carried with it the same pejorative undertones as the word 'system'.

Third, we can identify cross-influences from one place to another in the history of social welfare, the processes making for communication and convergence. The communication may be direct, leading to rapid identification, or oblique and incomplete. The convergence may be from 'parish to union', from local to national—a main theme in the social history of England, which for centuries was a history of 'sub-cultures'—or from national to international. The concept of a 'welfare state' has crossed most frontiers since 1945, more often perhaps as a slogan than as a set of ideas.[3] In the twentieth century, through bodies like the International Labour Organization, there may even be international initiative. Yet for all the interchange and the initiative we are far from living in one world, and the gulf between 'underdeveloped' and 'developing' countries—a conceptual dichotomy which itself demands critical scrutiny—is at least as great as that between 'rich' and 'poor' in the earlier history of 'developed' societies and which often leads to somewhat similar reactions. There is an element of parallelism which is itself worthy of further study. One of the weaknesses of a latter-day 'Whig' interpretation of the history of public provision of social welfare has been willingness to rest content with linear explanations and to devote more attention to chains of cause and effect, national or international, in recent history than to aspects of human attitudes and relationships which require to be considered across time.

Given recent developments in the study of history—and of those related subjects, like demography, sociology and psychology, with which historians are increasingly concerned—this is a good moment for re-assessment. The writing of local history has been transformed in recent years, with attention being devoted to variations of local economic and social structures, to mobility and class, to political and social control and the role of élites, to residential patterns and the formulation of civic policies.[4] Since local action has so frequently preceded national action in the making of English social policy and since local variation continues to be important, even basic, in concerns like education and, to a lesser extent, health, the new approach to local history should illuminate the making of social policies. In particular, it should enable us to examine continuities and discontinuities, to identify individuals and groups who directed attention locally to social 'issues' and mobilized opinion, and to explore the changing 'matrix' or 'matrices' at critical times like the early and late years of the nineteenth century. The treatment of such subjects was often cursory and conventional in such standard works as *The Victoria County History*, but as local history has moved from the manor to the council and from the village to the city, perspectives have changed at least as much as historical techniques.

As things stand—and they are not standing still—we know more, though still not enough, about the early nineteenth century in relation, for example, to poor law policies, than we do about the late nineteenth and early twentieth centuries. We have begun, too, seriously to consider the history of the family, using new evidence and new techniques. It already seems clear that during the late 1880s and 1890s there was a second social 'transformation' which must be studied locally—first in towns and cities—before it can be understood nationally. It was then that voluntary action, for all its Victorian vigour, seemed in many fields to be increasingly inadequate to cope with many of the problem areas of life, which its sponsors had identified, that new forms of organization and leadership emerged not simply within the growing labour movement (which was itself part of the matrix); and that, even more significantly, local public provision began to seem both inadequate and patchy. The demand for central intervention needs to be related both chronologically and functionally not only to cumulative administrative processes at the centre—a topic of recent historical research and controversy[5]—or to the rise of 'experts' in particular social fields,[6] but to contested judgments about the efficacy and coverage of local intervention.

In this connection statistical studies of provincial poverty, notably Rowntree's study of York, were more influential than Booth's study of London, and they need to be 'placed' in national history with as much care for context and impact as earlier theories of poverty, pre- and post-industrial, which influenced legislation. The latter have recently been studied in detail with emphasis rightly being placed on the fact that 'the debate on poor relief [before 1834] was concerned as much with government as it was with poverty'.[7] Early twentieth-century reformers might be willing to accept the existence of primary poverty in London as a shocking 'fact' which required further investigation, but when a similar proportion of primary poverty was revealed in a very different kind of community like York, the case for national action was reinforced with a sense of urgency, even of priority. As C. F. G. Masterman put it, there was a kind of 'thunderclap'. Booth's nine bulky volumes, for all their 'science', left a 'general impression of something monstrous, grotesque, inane; something beyond the power of individual synthesis; a chaos resisting all attempts to reduce it to orderly law'. Rowntree's 'definite and limited material' was manageable enough and comprehensible enough to guide policy, and, we can add in retrospect, to guide it towards the peculiarly English twentieth-century balance between the urban and the national.[8]

A study along these lines provides a necessary prelude to Bentley Gilbert's admirable monograph on the Edwardian period which is based on a meticulous study of primary central sources and which evaluates the influence on English social policy of a quite different foreign 'model'—that of Germany, where the 'state' was conceived of in a quite different way.[9] The importance of such comparative studies is obvious, though they are still in their infancy. 'When an analyst cannot experiment with his subject through replication, establishment of controls, and the manipulation of variables,' an American historian has written recently, 'then he resorts to the comparative method in the hope of achieving the same explanatory results.'[10] The work of those English social historians who have produced new insights into the range and variety of local processes must be followed through by social historians who are willing and able to compare English national experience with that of other countries. In both cases, they will point to what is common and to what is distinctive, producing in the process new versions of national history.

A second recent development in the study of history has been the scholarly examination of words in their different and changing meanings. Efforts have also been made to push behind verbal screens and to separate 'rhetoric' (perhaps an overworked word) and argument. The task is not easy, least of all in relation to national history. Consider, for example, the analysis of the following passage from Nathaniel Woodard, the founder of a well-known group of public schools in the middle years of the nineteenth century:

> It is the glory of a Christian State that it regards all its children with an eye of equal love and our institutions place no impossible barrier between the cottage and the front of the throne; but still parity of rights does not imply equality of power or capacities, or natural or accidental advantages.
>
> Common sense forbids that we should lavish our care on those least able to profit from it while we withhold it from those by whom it would be most largely repaid. The class compelled to give the greater part of each day to the toilsome earning of its daily bread may be as richly endowed as that which is exempt from this necessity but it is manifest that those who are subject to such a pressure must, as a body, enjoy less opportunities of cultivating their natural endowments.[11]

A number of familiar concepts freely employed in debates about social welfare can be picked out of this passage at once: 'rights', 'power', 'class', 'opportunities', 'endowments'—concepts which were part of the scaffolding of educational controversy long before 1851 when Woodard wrote and which are still a part of the scaffolding in current controversy. Yet we are immediately affronted or amused in the present period of history by Woodard's appeal to 'common sense' and his employment in the last sentence of the word 'manifest'; and, if we wish to probe more deeply into the circumstances as well as the psychology of the man, we now require a careful exegesis of the term 'Christian State' which was the premiss not only of Woodard's argument but of his energetic activities. It was not just a rhetorical lead-in like the word 'glory', and we would not understand mid-Victorian society if we were to treat it as such. Increasingly we know that the pattern of attitudes in that society cannot simply be explained in terms of the logic of industrialization.[12]

Quantitative history, booming across the Atlantic at the present time, is a rewarding subject and we can profit greatly both by asking questions about the flow and distribution of resources devoted to social ends in relation to other ends (either through charity, the propensity to give, or through local or national public provision),[13] but we must also look both to ideas and to motives. In this connection, a novelist may tell us more than a sociologist. In her great novel *Middlemarch*, George Eliot, grappling with the Victorian preoccupation with public health, 'the sanitary idea', wrote perceptively of Lydgate and Dorothea that they embodied 'the mixed result of young and noble impulse struggling amid the conditions of an imperfect social state, in which great feelings will often take the aspect of error, and great faith the aspect of illusion. For there is no creature whose inward being is so strong that it is not greatly determined by what lies outside of it'.[14] The comment is an invitation to explore more than one aspect of social motivation.

The analysis of particular passages—and they can be chosen from any epoch and from sermons, often extremely useful, and pamphlets as much as from novels or plays—can be supplemented by more comprehensive studies of communication (or the lack of it) between whole groups of people and the effects that this had on what we might call the language or languages of society. There remains much of general interest in Margaret Simey's pioneering study of Liverpool which was published in 1951 and still remains the only local study of its kind. As early as 1829, the founders of the District Provident Society in Liverpool recognized that

it is very difficult, humanly speaking, to preach Christianity with any effect, to men and women who have no comforts, and seemingly no desire for any. . . . It seems an almost hopeless attempt to argue with people respecting the wants of a future life, when they never think of providing that of the following day.[15]

Much writing on social welfare in the nineteenth century was influenced by conceptions of the family rather than by deductions about 'economic man' derived from the 'science' of political economy or the different versions of 'utilitarianism'. Recent studies by Bernstein and others of the language of schoolchildren are relevant in this connection, and they have a significance in a bigger context than that of the present or that of the history of education.[16] The texture of social policy even before the industrial revolution can be fully appreciated only if we bear in mind that we know less about the language, and attitudes, of recipients than about the language and attitudes of donors. The epitaphs and the memorials with their talk of 'benevolence' and 'sensibility' speak to posterity; we still know too little about the relationship between what George Eliot thought of as 'inside' and 'outside'.[17]

In the nineteenth century, we approach a world of words which is sometimes deceptively familiar, yet the problems of interpretation persist. The relationship between 'education' and 'class', to take only one example, was usually posed in England during the mid-nineteenth century not in terms of relationships between the 'working class' and the rest, as it is now, but in terms of the relationships between 'aristocracy' and 'middle classes'. If we now find it difficult, without a leap of the imagination, to listen attentively to unfamiliar voices, particularly when, like those of Woodard, they are uncongenial, we should remember that for those 'in authority' during the nineteenth century, old or new men of power, the ways of thinking and feeling of the 'lower classes in society', urban proletariat or rural labourers, were difficult to understand, except perhaps when they shared the same 'respectable' values (not necessarily for the same reasons) as the 'middle classes' or when there were natural if not always acknowledged affinities between the 'idle' in high and low estate. In a fascinating minute of 1845, Henry Moseley, one of the first inspectors of schools (five of the first seven full-time inspectors were Anglican clergymen whose attitudes belonged essentially to pre-industrial society) wrote bluntly:

> The fact is that the inner life of the classes below us in society is never penetrated by us. We are profoundly ignorant of the springs of public opinion, the elements of thought and the principles of action among them—these things which we recognize at once as constituting our own social life.[18]

The views of inspectors, major figures in the making of nineteenth-century English social policy, have been studied in considerable detail in recent years,[19] and there were few of them who would have taken as a 'fact' what Moseley, a scientist as well as a clergyman, treated as fact. Yet the most percipient historian of twentieth-century social policy has made the same point as Moseley in writing at a distance about the poor law which for generations encompassed almost every aspect of social welfare. In his remarkable inaugural lecture of 1951, Richard Titmuss emphasized that

> the poor law, with its oppressive disciplinary functions, rested on assumptions about how people ought to behave. It only went into action if people behaved in a certain way, and the services it provided were based on conditions that people should thereafter behave in a certain way.

The means of policy even at a later date, he generalized, not least in the Edwardian period between 1906 and 1914, when the 'foundations of the welfare state' were laid, were commonly derived from norms of behaviour expected by one class from another and founded on outer rather than inner observation.

> Insight was lacking partly because the structure of society then did not encourage those who influenced social policy to understand the lives of those for whom the services were intended.[20]

The term 'social welfare' itself (like the term 'welfare state') emerges tattered from the studies of Titmuss.

Similar arguments have been advanced with sharp immediate point and pungency in the more recent 'poverty' controversy in the United States, which had not started in 1951.[21] And the new school of practitioners of 'history from below' in England and the United States, seeking to uncover the attitudes of people without power, people whose names have not passed down through history, has already made a number of breakthroughs in interpreting ways of thinking and feeling, particularly in the early stages of industrialization. There is value in itself in the recovery of the sense of immediacy, in listening to lost voices, yet the chief stimulus to new studies of the history of the public provision of social welfare—and it is difficult to do without the term, however tattered—remains as it always was, the desire through social action to effect and direct change in the present. The fact that there is no finality itself encourages shifts in interpretation.

In the light of such considerations, reinforced by a closer examination of 'social structure' and of individual and social psychology, both the detail of the history of the public provision of social welfare and earlier generalizations about it need review. The Webbs, for all their industry and enterprise, expressed in great achievements fully realized, now seem unduly selective in their choice of detail and for reasons of personality as well as upbringing severely limited or blinkered in their capacity to generalize adequately. So, too, do those 'functionalist' historians of a later generation who treated the development of 'social policy' as 'inevitable' in all 'advanced' societies. Karl Polanyi's view, vividly elaborated, that 'the one comprehensive feature' of the history of the nineteenth century was the fact that 'society protected itself against the perils inherent in a self-regulating market system',[22] seems at once too general and too remote. Whether we turn to the history of the poor law, in those countries where it existed, of insurance, of public health or of education, we need a different kind of analysis. In some ways, the work of earlier historians or administrators working behind the scenes, men who took nothing for granted while social policy was in the melting pot, are far more useful than even the best potted surveys.[23]

Such an analysis must not assume that 'necessity' was the mother of all policy, and it must take into full account the controversies, often bitter and protracted, which surrounded all crucial aspects of policy-making. While it is true that the various branches of social policy taken as a whole 'represent social provision against waste of life and resources and against social inefficiency—not concessions',[24] the different steps in the story can be understood only when the interplay of pressures is thoroughly examined at each point. As John Rex has written, we need as underpinning the kind of sociological theory which is 'built around the notions of conflict, imperative coordination and balance of power'.[25] Taking the Education Act of 1902 as an example, Rex rightly insisted that what happened could not be explained in terms of 'orthodox functionalist theory'.

Some sections of the ruling classes were opposed to the idea of secondary education altogether. Those who were in favour of it vied with one another about controlling it, because they had different ideas about the content of education. And the working classes demanded it either in the hope that their children would 'get on' in the existing order, or because they recognized that such education would help them in the establishment of a new social system. The resulting educational system was a compromise between these conflicting pressures.

This approach rightly emphasizes the role of conflict. A similar kind of analysis is necessary, however, to explain 'consensus', since consensus, however short-lived, has been important particularly in the twentieth century when social policies were being reassessed, as they so often were, in the crucible of war.[26] 'Solidarity' and 'universality' were intimately interrelated.

Not all historians of social welfare have been aware of the pitfalls in generalizing retrospectively about the 'trends' or 'movement' of the past, but some pre-war writers on the history of social security, in particular, put the point plainly when they argued (before the term 'welfare state' was coined) that any attempt to trace the historical development of social security in terms of the evolution of 'concepts' alone was exposed to the dangers that attend *ex post facto* judgements.[27] Most of the 'reforms' which had been introduced, they explained, were designed by their authors as remedies for specific evils not as contributions to the growth of a 'movement'. The 'trends' were not perceived at the time. And the inhibitions were great. Take, for example, the well-known comment of the Select Committee on Old Age Pensions in 1899 that

> if the State is to provide the means for the cost of the pensions, the State, it seems to us must necessarily administer the scheme, and that is a proposition which we are unable to support.

In the inter-war years had there been any real awareness of 'trend', the history of unemployment policy would have been quite different and it was through changes in attitudes towards involuntary unemployment that some of the biggest general changes in attitudes to social welfare as a whole emerged. The basic point about 'trend' and 'movement' has been well made by a distinguished reviewer of Maurice Bruce's useful textbook *The Coming of the Welfare State* (1961). Gertrude Williams wrote:

> Most of us in reality so take for granted the world in which we grow up that it requires a great effort of the imagination to realize the conflict of ideas and ideals, the prejudices and sectional interests and pressures of which it is the outcome. . . . The fundamental principles on which the social services are based, as well as their financial and administrative structure, were matters on which there were great diversities of opinion, and there is still no unanimity.[28]

There were often minority and majority reports, and not only in 1909, the landmark year of the publication of the two Reports of the Royal Commission on the Poor Laws.

It is easier in 1971, perhaps, to appreciate that history does not move in straight lines than it was in the aftermath of World War II when new social policies were being translated into legislation and when, despite the frequent roughness of the in-fighting, there was a sense that the term 'welfare state' was 'now a socio-political category deemed generally descriptive of the States of our time'.[29] Indeed, since Titmuss's lecture of 1951, published in the year of the fall of the post-war Labour government, there have been changes of ideas on both sides of the Atlantic as well as economic pressures on resources set aside for social welfare. The 'cumulative play' of many different forces has led not only to the application of financial restraints on what were thought to be generally applicable policies but on reactions against those policies. The reaction has come both from left and right, and the atmosphere is now so different from that of 1951 that many of the books published around that time already seem dated. Thus T. H. Marshall's valuable and influential *Citizenship and Social Class* (1950), which traced the development of social policy in stages involving the recognition first of civil, then of political, and finally of social rights, would now need not a supplement but a revision. His argument that within an inegalitarian money economy there was being established an increasingly egalitarian system of 'citizenship', carrying with it full and equal 'membership' in the modern community, needs re-examination as an argument, and in the light of recent statistical studies of continuing deprivation it looks far too stilted.

The historian of social welfare cannot stop at one moment of time and assume 'finality' any more than the social administrator can. In considering the period spanned in this volume, however, which ends before the current ferment, when little is taken for granted and when there are signs not of consensus but of polarization,[30] he will find that the work of certain historians of an older generation remains stimulating and indispensable. H. L. Beales' seminal Hobhouse lecture on *The Making of Social Policy* should still be set alongside the scattered writings of R. H. Tawney which begin with the erosion of the medieval order and end with twentieth-century live issues. In many respects, indeed, Titmuss took over where Tawney left off. The strength of Beales' and Tawney's work lay in the fact that they got beyond legislation and administration to social dynamics without ever forgetting that they were dealing with real people. Tawney, in particular, was explicit about this. In an early essay on education, which interested him more than social security or public health, he wrote simply but directly that

educational problems cannot be considered in isolation from the aspirations of great bodies of men and women for whose sake alone it is that educational problems are worth considering at all.

He went on to show through an analysis of the concepts of 'status' and of 'the career open to the talents' ('ladder' it was then rather than 'lift') how the educational policy of a period reflects its conceptions of human society.[31] Society was not an abstraction; it was a network of relationships between real people. At the same time, it needed to be explored rather than taken for granted, and the exploration was a prelude to action.

In his preface to the second edition of *Equality* (1938), Tawney stated bluntly that

the issue depends, not on the impersonal forces beloved by the sociologists, but on the convictions of common men and their courage in acting upon them.

Neither 'ladders' nor 'lifts' are talked of much these days, yet we are living in a society where the influence of these concepts has changed the composition of governments and of parliaments and profoundly affected the way in which policies are being debated. And it is not only governments which are involved. This is a time when for a combination of reasons some of the oldest ideas in the history of social welfare, notably the idea of 'public service' itself, have shown signs of erosion, and when every longstanding voluntary institution devoted to social welfare (a few of them are celebrating centenaries, more of them fiftieth anniversaries) is being forced to consider not only changes of name but changes of function and approach. In such circumstances, the study of history always comes into its own, and it is with the strongest sense of the value of historical studies that these essays have been assembled.

Notes

1. Cf. Joshua Fitch's important article on education in the supplement to the ninth edition of the *Encyclopaedia Britannica* with the *Robbins Report* (1963). 'The purpose of this article', wrote Fitch, 'is to trace the gradual growth of what may be called the English system.' 'Even today', the Robbins Report commented, 'it would be a misnomer to speak of a system of higher eduction, if by system is meant a consciously coordinated organisation. . . . Higher education has not been planned as a whole or developed within a framework consciously devised to promote harmonious evolution.' The same point has often been made about other branches of social policy, including the provision of social security.

2. R. W. Hamilton, *The Institutes of Popular Education* (1845), p. 8.

3. See Asa Briggs, 'The Welfare State in Historical Perspective' in *Archiv Europ. Sociology*, II (1961), pp. 221–58; there is a useful collection of essays published in India and edited by S. P. Aiyer, *Perspectives of the Welfare State* (Bombay, 1966).

4. See, for example, H. J. Dyos (ed.), *The Study of Urban History* (1968).

5. The research and controversy was greatly stimulated by the work of Oliver MacDonagh; see his article 'The Nineteenth Century Revolution in Government' in *Historical Journal*, I (1958), pp. 52–67, and his book *A Pattern of Government Growth* (1961). Since then there has been a mass of critical writing; for further developments see below pp. 000–000.

6. For reflections on the changing role of 'experts' and professionals, see H. Perkin, *The Origins of Modern English Society* (1969); D. Roberts,

Victorian Origins of the British Welfare State (1960); R. J. Lambert, *Sir John Simon* (1964); and W. J. Reader, *Professional Man* (1966).

7. J. R. Poynter, *Society and Pauperism: English Ideas of Poor Relief, 1795–1834* (1969), p. xxii. See also B. Inglis, *Poverty and the Industrial Revolution* (1971).

8. Review of B. S. Rowntree, *Poverty: A Study of Town Life* (1901).

9. B. S. Gilbert, *The Evolution of National Insurance in Great Britain: The Origins of the Welfare State* (1966); in a second book, *British Social Policy, 1916–1939* (1970), Gilbert draws on pioneering research in the national archives in relation to a period which still requires large-scale research of a monographic kind and about which far too many generalizations are made on the basis of inadequate secondary evidence.

10. R. F. Berkhofer, *A Behavioural Approach to Historical Analysis* (1969), pp. 252–3.

11. N. Woodard, *Public Schools and the Middle Classes: A letter to the Clergy of the Diocese of Chichester* (1851), quoted in W. L. Burn, *The Age of Equipoise* (1964), p. 266.

12. Nor can the act of 1834 which laid the foundations of all nineteenth-century policies. See Poynter, p. xii.

13. For aspects of the approach, see a useful compilation of articles edited by D. K. Rowney and J. Q. Graham, *Quantitative History: Selected Readings in the Quantitative Analysis of Historical Data* (1969); J. M. Price, 'Recent Quantitative Work in History: A Survey of the Main Trends' in *History and Theory*, 9 (1969), pp. 1–14; D. S. Landes and C. Tilly, *History as Social Science* (1971).

14. See Asa Briggs, '*Middlemarch* and the Doctors' in *The Cambridge Journal*, I, 12, (1948), p. 753.

15. J. Shaw, *An Account of the Liverpool District Provident Visiting Society* (1834), quoted in M. B. Simey, *Charitable Effort in Liverpool in the Nineteenth Century* (1951), p. 30.

16. See B. Bernstein and D. Henderson, 'Social Class Differences in the Relevance of Language to Socialisation' in *Sociology*, 3 (1969), and D. Lawton, *Social Class, Language and Education* (1968); for the language of piety and the development of later languages of benefactors, see D. Owen, *English Philanthropy, 1660–1960* (1965).

17. The monumental idea persisted into the twentieth century. See W. S. Churchill's 1908 letter to Asquith, quoted in Gilbert, *The Evolution of National Insurance*, p. 252; 'The Minister who will apply to this country the successful experiences of Germany in Social Organization may or may not be disappointed at the polls, but he will at least have left a memorial which time will not deface of his administration.'

18. Quoted by R. Johnson, 'Educational Policy and Social Control in Early Victorian England' in *Past and Present*, 49 (1970), p. 104.

19. Roberts, *op. cit.*, M. W. Thomas, *The Early Factory Legislation* (1948); E. L. and O. P. Edmonds, *I Was There: the Memoirs of H. S. Tremenheere* (1965).

20. See, for example, A. Downs, 'Alternative Futures for the American Ghetto' in *Daedalus* (1968), pp. 1379–90; W. Bloomberg and H. J. Schmandt (eds.), *Power, Poverty and Urban Policy* (1968).

21. See G. Y. Steiner, *The State of Welfare* (1971).

22. K. Polanyi, *The Great Transformation* (1944), p. 76; see also E. H. Carr, *The New Society* (1951).

23. Books like, for example, F. Adams, *History of the Elementary School Contest in England* (1882); S. H. N. Bunbury (ed.). *Lloyd George's Ambulance Wagon: Being the Memoirs of William J. Braithwaite, 1911–1912* (1957).

24. H. L. Beales, 'The Making of Social Policy' (*Hobhouse Memorial Lecture, 1945*); see also M. Ginsberg (ed.), *Law and Opinion in the Twentieth Century* (1959), and the very important theoretical study by W. G. Runciman, *Relative Deprivation and Social Justice* (1966).

25. J. Rex, *Key Problems of Sociological Theory* (1961), ch. 4.

26. See A. Marwick, *Britain in the Century of Total War* (1968); P. A. Johnson's *A Land Fit for Heroes* (1968) along with Marwick's *The Deluge* (1965) deal in an interesting way with World War I.

27. See, for example, T. S. Simey, *Social Administration* (1937).

28. *British Journal of Sociology*, XIII, 2 (1962), pp. 177–8.

29. L. Krieger, 'The Idea of the Welfare State' in *Journal of the History of Ideas*, XXIV (1963), p. 556.

30. Titmuss rightly questioned the usefulness of the term 'welfare state', as did Professor Peter Townsend, who played a big part in directing the spotlight on continuing poverty in Britain; his latest assessments of the situation are given in two articles in *The Times*, 9 and 10 March 1971. For the comparative position in the United States, see R. Scott 'The Welfare Farewell' in *The Guardian*, 5 and 6 March 1971. The trend of discussion on the left follows the problem of a 'welfare society'. Questioning from the right about the principle of 'universality' as embodied in wartime and immediate post-war legislation preceded the fall of the Labour government in 1951 and has recently involved a probing both of practice and of principles. Current argument about 'welfare' is wide-ranging. It encompasses the nature of 'social work' and its relationship to social policy; the role of different categories of 'social workers', and their development in a post-Seebohm setting; the effects of taxation policy on benefits and incentives; education, including school education and higher education; housing; and recently, for the first time since the 1930s, the impact of unemployment.

31. R. H. Tawney, 'An Experiment in Democratic Education' originally published in *The Political Quarterly* (1914) and reprinted in R. Hinden (ed.), *The Radical Tradition* (1964), pp. 70–81.

2

From Parish to Union
Poor Law Administration
1601–1865

E. W. MARTIN*

THE MANAGEMENT OF THE POOR

Poverty has always been a stumbling-block to human happiness
and welfare, yet in periods of social optimism philosophers and
others have fostered the illusion that collective wisdom and
individual good sense could even eliminate its toll. For example,
John Stuart Mill said that poverty 'in any sense implying suffering'
could be got rid of by the exercise of care and effort.[1] Any study
of charitable endowment or of poor law deterrence and control
will indicate that this type of simplification needs to be qualified.[2]

A study of the growth of administration forces the mind
toward the poor. A reliable pamphleteer spoke in 1796 of what
has since come to be called a 'culture of poverty'.[3] He referred to
a society of employers and a society of the employed. There were
different kinds of affluence coming from land, industry and
commerce; and different kinds of poverty among the peasants,
paupers and artisans.[4] Administration cannot be understood

* I am grateful to many people for the opportunity to get together these
essays on subjects connected with the problems of poverty and the poor.
I must mention the help and encouragement given to me by members of
the staff of the University of Sussex when I held a Leverhulme Research
Fellowship there from 1965–67. My friends, Professor Asa Briggs,
Stephen Yeo and his wife, Eileen, made life easier for me in my studies
of a complicated theme. Since pursuing the subject much further I am
indebted to the staff of the University of Exeter Library, and in particular
to Mr John Lloyd, MA, FRSL, and to Dr Charles Scott, Librarian and
Deputy Librarian respectively.

apart from historical causes: the why and the wherefore of social ethics and a developing legality. It was the interplay of these factors that led to the practical formulation and application of a poor law as distinct from voluntary relief of the poor. Poor law became a policy of coercion and punishment, of aid and assistance, or a combination of all these aims.

Before the legally compulsive stage was reached (under the Elizabethan code of 1597–1601), poverty had become a basic problem. It challenged and divided the Church fathers and medieval canonists. Some believed then that discrimination in almsgiving was imperative; and that the 'deserving' could be separated from the 'undeserving'.[5] Others felt that charity encompassed everyone. What was a problem for lawmakers in the twelfth century remained so for those who had to work out standards of 'eligibility' in the nineteenth.

One of the main problems facing students of modern history is to determine if the ecclesiastical administration was a public and continuous one. It has been suggested that there was a canonistic theory of public relief[6] because, when the Church used its property to help the poor, this could not be fairly described as private charity. The property was public property used for the general welfare.[7] So it does not seem there was any breakdown of the canonical system. The Church had provided a framework for the secular poor law of Tudor times. That is to say, from the twelfth century up to the final codification of the Elizabethan poor law in 1601, a single tradition can be discerned.[8]

The cry to 'put an end to indiscriminate charity'[9] was loud in the nineteenth century. This word 'indiscriminate' occurs and recurs in poor law history, acting as a sort of verbal boundary mark between expressions of the humane view and the legalistic view, between one kind of intellectual outlook and another.[10] The voluntary or charitable impulse has been strong in England and there is good reason to underline the fact that welfare had a philanthropic origin. But probably it is going too far in the wrong direction to argue flatly that the poor law evolved out of plans to regulate voluntary charity.[11]

It was not Luther[12] or Zwingli[13] who brought a fresh influence into the English system of poor law administration. The Catholic humanist, J. L. Vives[14], was the transplanter of the new compulsive idea. He conceived a system of organized assistance.[15] In 1526—just about the time when there was anxiety regarding the traditional methods of poor relief—secular authorities in Europe were getting to grips with what was truly called either a menace or a scandal.[16] Vives exercised much influence. Although written in England, the work by which he is mainly known was addressed to the senate and consuls of Bruges. He divided the poor into three classes: the unsettled beggars, the poor in hospitals or poorhouses, and the poor living at home. He suggested that two senators be employed to learn about the poor from neighbours: to find out the kind of people they were, how they lived, and what caused their poverty. He understood that poor people tended to be suspicious of each other: 'Information about one poor man shall not be taken from another, for envy is not idle.'[17]

The scheme Vives devised was apparently applied at Ypres; and it had an effect on English poor law administration. It was similar to the kind of municipal charity such as that produced by Bishop Ridley and his City of London committee for the alleviation of destitution, set up in 1553. The poor were classified by Ridley and his advisers into three main categories: the poor by impotency, the poor by casualty, and the thriftless poor.[18] Under that dispensation, St Bartholomew's and St Thomas' hospitals in London were for the caring of the sick; Christ's Hospital for the housing of homeless children; and the Bridewell for the correction of those members of the able-bodied poor who were recalcitrant and would not work. This was a policy very like that adopted in 1601. The basic problem of the poor law authorities was how to deal with the various classes of poor people.

In an introduction to a collection of tracts on poor relief,[19] Sidney Webb drew attention to the fact that the administration of the thousands of local authorities had an important equal to that of national policy. He thought that sporadic almsgiving was not adequate to provide for the impotent or thriftless and said that it was the local authorities of parish and borough, in England and in Europe, that led the way to a more sensible and systematic provision.[20] By 1601 overseers and justices had to think in terms of a new concept—the management of the poor—so that the danger and inconvenience they caused should be reduced to a minimum. It was not to be a matter only of punishment instead of aid, of incarceration instead of freedom to move, or of the failure of Christian concern. It was the effects of many causes which began to bring about a conflict between charity and law. Two sides of the growing dilemma thrust forward into the regions of England, as explosive in their way as a race relations issue now. This was to be true of the poor law struggle in its firmly secular form, which is our concern. By their testimonies, the regions suggest that the decline in charity was not really an overall decline. What slowed down was the indiscriminate distribution of alms in the traditional way.

Responsibility for the support of the sick, the aged and the poor began to devolve on the civil parish and its institutions. When the ubiquitous justices of the peace[21] got fully into their stride as controllers of the overseers and of the poor, their role was constructive. For all their authority, they were not entirely free agents because many of them were landowners and thought in terms not only of property but of the social obligations that went along with it. Poverty and pauperism are variable phenomena and it is not possible to take a general view in the interpretation of regional problems. Local problems demanded local solutions which have to be examined with the national framework in mind. Perhaps Leviathan was beginning, in places, to replace the Good Samaritan. Legality of a kind was taking over from an unsatisfactory and makeshift charity, even if it was at times a corrupt and localized legality derived from parish demands and parish greed. The Church lost its special hold on supplicants, and the poor law was both cause and effect in the decline of personal charity.[22]

There is no doubt about the antiquity and continuity of English poor law policy.[23] Between the binding parochialism of the act of 1601 and the culmination of the new way of things—the Union Chargeability Act of 1865—changes took place slowly. The English poor law in its early stages[24] has been described as more of a growth than a creation,[25] and the statute of 1601[26] is also singled out as by far the most important regulation affecting poor relief until the Poor Law Amendment Act of 1834. In 1900 it was named as still being the practical basis of the poor law system.[27]

This Elizabethan statute firmly laid it down that the parish should find a convenient stock of flax, hemp, wool, thread, and iron, and other ware and stuff to set the poor on work; and also

competent sums of money for and towards the necessary relief of
the lame, impotent, old, blind, and such other among them being
poor and not able to work; and also for the putting out of such
children to be apprentices.[28]

Some authorities have placed emphasis on different facets of the
Elizabethan code. Maurice Bruce[29] has argued that the Tudor
poor law was built up out of compassion and fear and that the
basis of our welfare state was a combination of social amelioration
and police deterrence.[30] G. R. Elton has put forward the view that
when welfare legislation—relief of the poor, provision of work,
and care of the sick—became the inescapable duty of parish
officials, this was really a new departure. The whole poor law,
'the great achievement of the paternal state in action, was in
practice the product of the Elizabethan administration'.[31]

Professor Karl de Schweinitz concentrated his attention on
43 Elizabeth c. 2 and leaves one in no doubt as to his opinion.

> The Act of 1601 usually spoken of as the culminating statute in
> the development of the Poor Law is anticlimactic. It merely
> repeats the Act of 1597–98,[32] having scarcely anything in it that
> is new except the extension of liability to grandparents. What
> has helped to make it a landmark in the relief of distress is the
> fact that it is the last rewriting of the total law. Not until 1662[33]
> is anything of substantial importance added, and that is specifi-
> cally concerned with settlement. . . . The Poor Law has reached
> the form in which it is to influence thought and operation for
> the next three centuries and more. The 43 of Elizabeth is the
> parent of governmental relief in England and in the United
> States. The parent in relation to which our present system of
> social security expresses both development and revolt.[34]

Implicit in de Schweinitz's view of the Elizabethan Act is the
wider assumption that in reforming social welfare legislation the
policy maker must have a proper understanding of his predecessors' motivation. In 1843 a well-informed assistant poor law
commissioner Twistleton,[35] was saying much the same thing in a
lengthy report on the origin and meaning of local Acts of Parliament. Like Sir Samuel Romilly[36] he no doubt deprecated those
departures from the general law 'which make a different state of
the poor laws in each particular parish which chooses to apply for

such a Bill'.[37] Twistleton knew, better than most, that the old poor law contained much that was a product of local motivation. He was anxious to promote a more serious study of the history of ideas and institutions because 'a knowledge of the causes and effects of the various changes which have been made in them from time to time'[38] would insure against the folly of tampering with the main principles of a complex organization. He suggested that the merit of those responsible for the Poor Law Amendment Act of 1834 would be better appreciated by knowing about the errors, hesitancies and perplexities of the earlier legislators.[39]

OPPOSITION TO THE OLD POOR LAW

A principal cause of opposition (in so far as it could be stated at all) would appear to have been that parishes had to find work for destitute able-bodied persons on the basis of inadequate means and an imperfect parochial machinery. This was the main brunt of the attack launched against the old poor law—that is, against outdoor relief for the able-bodied pauper.

The institutionalization of ideas is the history of reform. It is in the rough and tumble of daily work that knowledge about the reliability of theories is acquired. Administration, or the application of a policy, really implies this. What began at parish level as a kind of cooperation between justices and overseers, or as organized assistance on a direct and personalized basis, had to broaden out into assistance based on incorporations of parishes, on poor law unions and counties, until the broadest level of state assistance is reached. Such ideas can be traced back a long way. For instance, the provision of workhouses for the poor was recommended by many reformers. There were the plans of Sir Josiah Child and Henry Fielding for the metropolis; those of Sir Matthew Hale, William Hay, Thomas Alcock, Sir Richard Lloyd and Thomas Gilbert for hundreds or divisions of hundreds; while R. Haines and Lord Hillsborough proposed workhouses for counties, and Dr Davenant and John Bellers 'carried their projects to an extent still more complicated and unmanageable'.[40]

To understand the true meaning of the old poor law, there is need to pay attention to administration rather than legislation.[41] It is undoubtedly true that the history of the poor law is not just the history of legislation. If it were so, its course would be far less difficult to chart. It is the history of administration also. Theory and practice have rarely coincided and the administrative design was always changing. One authority has said that the practical 'administrative genius of a nation is quite infallibly embodied in its working definition of pauperism and in the mechanism in which that definition is, or is not embodied'. He maintains that there are many new poor laws in our history 'and that history is more truly represented as a tidal movement, an ebb and flow between two opposite principle of severity and leniency, than as a steady and progressive achievement of a comprehensive system'.[42]

The philosophy of localism, the harsh dominance, and the suspicious peasant fear, reflecting the two sides of rural society, shaped the old poor law, defying the edicts of central government even after 1834. In the west of England, for example, there is displayed all the paraphernalia of local power dispersed through the vestry, magistrates, churchwardens and overseers. The actual methods devised and the local characteristics developed can be discovered in workhouse accounts, overseers' registers, settlement examinations, and apprenticeship indentures.

PARISH MANAGEMENT OF THE OLD POOR LAW

In the agricultural counties such as Devon and Dorset or Somerset and Wiltshire, there is evidence that the period from 1662 to 1782 was the era of self-government or parish management. The outstanding feature which marks these one hundred and twenty years as a definite landmark in the history of poor relief is its complete parochialism.[43] Parish officials had to work out answers to all kinds of social or economic problems posed by the need to relieve, employ and punish.

The national importance of certain local experiments is afforded by such an example as the development of workhouses or houses of industry where it was intended profitably to employ the poor. A Bristol historian has claimed that when poor law administration was still largely a matter of experiment, it fell to Bristol, by the Act of 1696 'for Erecting Hospitals and Workhouses', to start a method which moved from the city to other areas and created a national structure by the Poor Law Amendment Act of 1834.[44] In 1695 the Bristol reformer, John Cary, had written an *Essay on The State of England in relation to its Trade, its Poor and its Taxes*. Despite the opposition of the wily and formidable Daniel Defoe[45] —who called workhouses and charities 'Mischiefs to the Nation'[46] —these institutions did indeed become the Mecca of the poor law reformer.[47]

The first systematic use of the 'offer of the House' to a pauper applying for relief can be traced to the Workhouse Test Act of 1723.[48] This attempt to deter the poor man from asking for aid originated not from houses of industry established by local acts nor from the pamphlet *College of Industry* (1695) by the idealistic Quaker, John Bellers, but from the experiments of a man named Matthew Marryott, who worked so successfully at his home, Olney in Buckinghamshire, that he was much in demand as one who could reduce the burden of pauperism. He carried out his work between 1714 and 1722.[49]

However it was begun, this discriminatory method did encourage the building of consolidated workhouses for the profitable employment of the poor of a town. Workhouses had been built at Exeter, Crediton and Tiverton in 1698 and at Plymouth in 1708. Sir John Clapham said that the returns of 1776-7 (initiated by the reformer Thomas Gilbert) reported that the counties of the south-west were well endowed with workhouses—Devon having ninety-five and Somerset seventy-five. The Devon houses were mostly in the small and ancient boroughs such as Honiton, Bampton, Axminster and Barnstaple. But there was a house to hold thirty persons in the small village of Sampford Courtenay. Nor was this an isolated case.[50] The line between the workhouse and the poorhouse is not very firm and distinct—at least not until the early years of the nineteenth century when the latter began to disappear.

Under the old poor law, all parishes had to bear the cost of settlements. This was undoubtedly the most punishing feature of localism and the greatest evil of the poor law itself. Important commentators such as Charles Weston,[51] George Coode,[52] and Adam Smith[53] all condemned settlements. The act of 1662 from which all the parochial troubles stemmed appears to have deserved the description 'preposterous law' applied to it by the Webbs.[54]

32

A decisive step forward in the movement away from localism was taken under Gilbert's act of 1782. This measure had great merit in that it showed a humane concern for the poor. It also marked a diminution in the power of overseers in certain areas. Thomas Gilbert thought that poor rates had increased for many reasons; one of these was that 'the opulent and better informed part of the parishioners' did not take on work as parish officers. They left it instead to 'inferior people, who are ignorant and inexperienced, and as unwilling as their betters to give themselves trouble or disoblige their neighbours'.[55] Few politicians of the eighteenth century could have been more aware of the problems arising out of parochial mismanagement than this sinecurist, Member of Parliament for Lichfield. He was a voluminous pamphleteer, a student of poor law methods who was a true policy-maker in the sense that his dogged pursuance of his ideas led to radical changes and to modifications in ways of thinking about the poor and pauperism.[56] Gilbert was a country gentleman, born at Cotton in Staffordshire in 1719 or 1720, and he has gained fame because he was able to turn the minds of legislators away from the self-contained parish and towards the idea of incorporation which, though not new, was thus given a much greater impetus. Country gentlemen did not always lack a persistent idealism in local government and national politics. This was possibly due, in Namier's opinion, to the fact that they were independent people who were indifferent to office.[57] Such an argument would not seem to apply in regard to Gilbert and he was uncharacteristic of his class. There was undoubtedly tension between aristocracy and squirearchy. In south-west England, the country gentry held power; members of the aristocracy were spread very thinly on the ground and in the five counties of Devon, Cornwall, Somerset, Dorset and Wiltshire only one son of a peer ever represented the region between 1707 and 1801.[58]

Gilbert's act (22 George III c. 83) was a permissive one, however. Between 1795 and 1850, about 924 parishes had been grouped into 67 unions. But his act marks a stage in poor law administration and deserves the most careful study in relation to localism and its gradual shrinkage. Gilbert had desired that the parish officer should be controlled by visitors and guardians. He wanted to take away some of powers from the overseers of the

C

33

poor. He was indicting also the simple system of welfare built up in the parishes and boroughs.

THE EFFECTIVENESS OF PARISH ADMINISTRATION

It is not easy to say just how effective the parochial system of welfare was on the whole. It varied greatly. Much can be inferred from records and close scrutiny of them is necessary. A small parish in the English county of Devon, Ashwater, offers the sort of evidence from overseers' accounts that could be duplicated many times. It is not to be called typical, and yet it is not uncharacteristic. In the Ashwater records, one name constantly recurs as a recipient of aid—that of Laurence Dunn.

Here was a man known to those who provided the aid. Their service was a personal service even though they had to spend public money. They would have the necessary facts about his character, health, and general attitude toward neighbours and community. His name first appears in the accounts in 1706. In the year 1715 there is a characteristic entry demonstrating how Dunn was cared for by the parish authorities:

> Paid towards the relief of Laurence Dunn and his family for four weeks, 4s; paid to him for eight weeks at 2s a week according to Justices' order, 16s; 43 weeks at 1s 6d a week £3 4s 6d; pair of shoes for his wife, 2s 6d; 6 yards of linen cloth and thread for Dunn's family, 4s; pair of shoes for his daughter, 1s 6d; 2 yards of linen cloth for his family, 1s 8d; 4 yards of woollen cloth to make his wife a coat, 9s 3d; 4 yards of woollen cloth, canvas and bone for two gowns for his daughters, 11s 5d; pair of shoes for him, 3s 10d; 6 lbs of wool for him, 5s 4d.[59]

In that same year, Dunn's daughter was bound as an apprentice by the parish; the sum of 15s was paid to the man employing her, and 2s 6d for the indenture. Payments had been made quite regularly to this family. In 1734 a kettle and bedstead were bought for 5s 6d; and Dunn was paid 1s a week for 35 weeks and 1s 3d for six weeks, making a total of £2 2s 6d. Then come the last entries in that same year:

Paid for a coffin for Laurence Dunn, 7s; for affidavit and stretching him forth, 2s; for wool, soap and candles, 1s 1d; for making his grave and carrying him to the church, 2s; spent at his burial, 5s; for two years rent for the poor house, 2s; Laurence Dunn buried on February 2nd.[60]

Dunn and his family were sympathetically treated by overseers and this shows how parish welfare could work effectively. Another contributor to this present volume, Professor J. S. Taylor, has suggested in his thesis on rural poverty[61] that the overseer was not an unsatisfactory public servant. He studied the records of over sixty Devon parishes and found that overseers did not innovate without vestry support. The worst abuses were possibly found in towns where parish officers were not connected to family responsibility or the occupation of land.[62]

Taylor did not think that all towns suffered from defective or corrupt administration. He pointed out that between 1808 and 1824 in the borough of South Molton the office of overseer was held by a mercer, a butcher, musician, druggist, wool-stapler, hairdresser, innkeeper, leather dresser, gentleman, linen draper, glazier, printer, and one or two other types. But it should be noted that South Molton was cited in the evidence presented in the 1834 report as an example of a town where elected tradesmen were unfitted for the office they occupied.[63] In fact, this borough's administrative machinery had been ably handled. Also an assistant overseer, a permanent official, had been employed.

After 1819 select vestries were established in Devon. This was an attempt to carry out the views expressed by the Committee of 1817.[64] In 1822 a seventeen-man select vestry was set up at Cheriton Bishop in that county. At the first meeting in September of that year eight allowances were reduced and two cut off altogether. The vestry lasted only a short time (until January 1823); it was not discontinued because of any corruption or inefficiency or struggle for parish power, as the Webbs suspected, but because there was not a 'sufficient saving in money to warrant so many people spending so much time in becoming disliked by their fellow parishioners'.[65]

Personal factors probably did not count quite so much in boroughs or market towns as in the even more isolated rural parishes where the iron law of custom was dominant. The controversial Speenhamland scale or allowance system may or may not have had an effect on the distribution of charity. The late W. E. Tate[66] argued that the 'unfortunate Speenhamland system' was a creation of the Buckinghamshire magistrates at their Epiphany Quarter Sessions. The sessional records for January 1795 do indicate that some sort of relief scale was fixed, but it was apparently not a 'bread scale'. The magistrates did not feel that the industrious labourer was being fairly treated, so they put forward the following proposals:

> When it happens that a labourer and his wife and such of his children as may be able to do so duly and honestly perform the several labours on which they may be employed and yet do not earn the weekly sums after mentioned the same ought to be made up to them by the Parish Officers: For a Man and his Wife not less than 6s. For a Man and his Wife with one or two small children, 7s, and for every additional Child under the age of ten years, 1s.
> It is therefore unanimously agreed to by this Court that allowances at the direction of the Magistrates but not less than the above allowance be made to the families of poor Labourers from this time till further order by this Court.[67]

A copy of the order was sent to churchwardens and overseers of the poor of every parish in Buckinghamshire so that some regulation of parish relief was brought about.

The Speenhamland scale (or the second calculation of it) geared wages to the price of the gallon loaf. This was worked out in May 1795. Under it a labourer and his wife, with one child, would get 6s a week when a loaf cost 1s and 10s when it cost 2s. A labourer and his wife with seven children would get 15s in the first instance and 25s in the second.[68]

Records in the borough of Tiverton show that the select vestry had a longer life in this Devon borough than in many others. The scale of relief drawn up there in June 1822 can be compared with the controversial Speenhamland scale. Devon, of course, was a so-called Speenhamland county, but its scale of relief was of a different type:

Scale of Relief

To be granted to the Poor, as per order of Select Vestry,
June 22, 1822

1. Sick, infirm people confined to their beds and unable to work. Idiots, blind and insane paupers, 3s per week.
2. Infirm persons unable to work, 2s 6d per week.
3. Paupers having more than 3 children and earning but 7s per week shall be allowed 1s per week for the 3rd child and 1s per week for each additional child. If they earn 8s per week they shall maintain 3 children, if 9s four and so on.
4. Base children with their mother 1s 6d per week. Children above one year at nurse, 2s per week, and under one year, 2s 6d per week.[69]

The representative character of the poor law in humane terms has both an ideological and institutional value. R. H. Tawney emphasized this when he wrote about the history of the poor law in the nineteenth century.

There is no touchstone, except the treatment of children which reveals the character of a social philosophy more clearly than the spirit in which it regards the misfortunes of those of its members who fall by the way.[70]

In Devon children and young people suffered under the system of compulsory apprenticeship which was so predominant a feature of the county. Even as early as 1815[71] legislators had spoke out against the method of employment on the grounds that children were separated from their parents too early. Boys and girls from about the ages of five to thirteen were apprenticed to farms and trades. It continued until after 1840.

An investigator reporting to the commission of 1832 stated that the practice of binding children compulsorily—without the consent of child, parents or masters—was very general in Devon, Cornwall and Somerset. He found that farmers approved of the method and did not favour the alternative scheme of voluntary hiring. At Woodbury, near Exeter, the compulsory method was discontinued for a time. But no other way of employing the children was found and they continued to get parish pay:

37

Fifteen children who have been thus treated do not go out to work, and are brought up in idleness. The magistrates have, in consequence, recommended returning to the system, and the parish has been divided into allotments.[72]

The system operating at Hatherleigh in Devon was outlined by a magistrate in 1831. The practice of binding apprentices by lot or ballot was described as 'disgusting tyranny or cruelty';[73] and it was proposed that instead of the long-term binding—up to the age of twenty-one or the time of marriage—there should be substituted useful and decent yearly service.[74]

It was stated in the Poor Law Report of 1834 that the apprenticing of boys to farmers was unknown in the mainly agricultural county of Dorset.[75] This has been shown to be untrue of the county as a whole. A study of 686 indentures from eighteen parishes in the western part of the county revealed that out of 434 of these, only 11 related to children apprenticed outside the parish. The other 252 indentures came from parishes elsewhere in the county and of these 176 concerned children apprenticed to non-parishioners. This demonstrates the fact that in the rural areas of west Dorset a very different policy operated from that which was common elsewhere. In most parts of Dorset, the parish overseers were usually anxious to find a place for the child where he or she could gain a new settlement. In the rural west the policy was to place apprentices within the parish.[76] Areas of Devon showed at times a similar variety.

These local variations are the most daunting and yet the most exhilarating aspects of administration under the old poor law. It is not possible therefore to follow in the wake of the policy-makers of 1832 and indulge in a total and intemperate condemnation of the old welfare methods. We can envisage the parish pauper and the agricultural labourer as creatures of God and 'objects of charity'. They were also creatures of the law. God and the law had this in common: both could be disregarded for the sake of expediency, and often were.

CENTRALIZATION AND THE REFORMS OF 1834

We have seen that the alleged 'principles of 1834'—those of less eligibility and the workhouse test—were not first formulated by members of the Poor Law Commission of 1832. For example, a pamphlet was published in 1801 on the regulation of a workhouse in the Wiltshire parish of Bradford. The burden of the message (and moral) was that while all reasonable comfort would not be denied to the poor within the workhouse, they would not be *'raised to an equality with those that may be acquired by persevering labour'*. Too much encouragement would tend to produce a slothful disposition and depress that spirit of exertion which enables 'the poor to prove the truth of the maxim that the relief that comes from themselves is the best and most effectual'.[77]

The italicized words sum up the principle of less eligibility and the tone of the 1834 report itself. It is also a regional reminder of the sentiments expressed by the Rev. Thomas Chalmers,[78] to whose 'brutal optimism' Kirkman Gray[79] commendably referred. Karl Marx also disliked those labourers in the vineyards of the Lord: the 'Reverends of Protestant theology' such as 'Parson Wallace, Parson Townsend, Parson Malthus and his pupil the arch-parson, Thomas Chalmers'.[80] Marx was inclined to include also within his criticism Jeremy Bentham, the greatest administrative genius of his age. He looked on him as no more than 'a leather-tongued oracle of the ordinary bourgeois intelligence'.[81]

In any comparison of the administrative roles of the old poor law and the new it has to be recognized that the luminaries of the new movement, Edwin Chadwick[82] the forceful administrator, and Nassau William Senior,[83] the theorist, were trying to correct evils, following on from the thought of Bentham, Malthus and Chalmers.

But the administrative pattern does not yield its full meaning unless followed a little further. Legislators in 1832 had a huge task to face. They had to find a workable alternative to the unhelpful Malthusian conclusion that the poor law should be abolished. When the Royal Commission was set up the chairman was the Bishop of London, Dr Blomfield,[84] and Nassau Senior, Sturges Bourne[85] and Frankland Lewis[86] were among the members. Chadwick and Senior appeared to be firm friends. The latter was a man of drive and ambition who had been Bentham's secretary during the sage's later years. Chadwick's career, it has been suggested, provides what is almost a bridge between the eighteenth century and modern ideas about government.[87]

Although described as 'wildly unhistorical'[88] and 'wildly unstatistical'[89] the report of 1834 must nevertheless be classified as a document of primary importance so far as the administration of the poor law is concerned. It has stood as a reminder of the ideas and customs of parochialism and an emergent bureaucracy aiming at wider horizons and more complex, more impersonal relationships. Inspired in part by utilitarianism, classical economics, and Malthusian population doctrine it 'shaped public welfare institutions for nearly a century',[90] and epitomized a punitive attitude towards poverty and pauperism.

The reformers of 1834 tried to make certain that public assistance would not enable people to get away from their responsibilities as productive workers. They endeavoured to apply the utilitarian pleasure-pain principle to charity so that the condition of anyone on public assistance would be less acceptable than that of the lowest paid labourer which was classed as independent. The report did lead on to more centralization on the local and national levels which could be regarded as necessary for the improvement of the existing welfare machinery.[91]

Yet the Commission advocated no new principles of relief. The famous formula that paupers should be less eligible than independent labourers was embodied in the 1601 Act. So it is safe to say that the law as worked out in 1834 was mainly concerned with the organization of relief rather than with the formal introduction of any new principles.[92] The old poor law and the new are usually looked on as being entirely separate systems. Indeed, through the efforts of tireless propagandists the impression was given that the amending Act of 1834 was a major piece of legal surgery or a drastic reformulation of fundamental principles and a total removal of demoralizing and corrupt practices. Would it not be more realistic to regard the savage changes which did occur in 1834 as no more than an extension of an established method, devised and revised from time to time in order to care for and discipline the various classes of poor people. One could hazard the view that so many reformers had given thought to poor law problems over the centuries that there was little new ground to be scrutinized under the umbrella of the poor law.

There was a scientific or Benthamite zeal about this enquiry; even the results were largely predictable because of the political and social bias of the members of the Commission and their assistants and the persons selected from the various regions for interview.[92] Possibly there is some evidence to back up the statement that the inefficiency of local poor law administration and the riots which took place in some agricultural districts following refusal to grant aid of the Speenhamland sort, did create the kind of atmosphere in which reform became an urgent matter.[94] But it is equally doubtful whether the allowance system itself was adopted under the 'double panic of famine and revolution';[95] indeed the word 'revolution' is a dangerous one to employ generally in respect of the isolated rural poor. Under stress and in response to the pangs of hunger, they might revolt sporadically but were always deficient in that kind of organizing power necessary for the carrying out of a sustained revolutionary action. This was true in 1830 as in 1795, although one can see clearly that there were areas of revolt in certain counties such as Wiltshire, Somerset and parts of Devon.

Whatever might have provided the initial impetus under which it began, the Commission was dazzled by the magnitude of its facts. While admitting the possibility of error in the interpretation of great masses of material, and the existence of middle-class prejudice, large claims could be made for the administrative value of this new deal. The evidence assembled in answer to the rural and town queries came from all counties and many thousands of witnesses varying from gentlemen and farmers to artisans and shopkeepers. These people agreed only

in their practical experience as to the matters in question, in their general description both of the mode in which the laws for the relief of the poor are administered and of the consequences which have already resulted from that administration.[96]

So at the time the amendment of the law did appear urgent.

The social analysis drawn from so wide an area and so diverse a section of the population carried weight. It looked then, and if one strives hard for objectivity, it looks now, like the preamble to a new method in the treatment of poverty and pauperism. Can we discern through the Report too powerful an advocacy of deterrence and a persistent undercurrent of propaganda?

In the report there is reference to the 'mischievous ambiguity

41

of the word poor'.[97] It was the opinion of the writer or writers that any diminution in money spent on poor relief 'would be regarded as so much taken from the labouring classes; as if those classes were naturally pensioners on the charity of their superiors'.[98] These words sound as if they were written by Nassau Senior. He has, in fact, claimed that he was the author of much of the report:

> The Report, or at least three-fourths of it was written by me, and all that was not written by me was re-written by me. The greater part of the Act, founded on it, was also written by me; and in fact, I am responsible for the effects good or evil (and they must be one or the other in an enormous degree) of the whole measure.[99]

This seems definite enough, but in his book *The Evils of Disunity in Central and Local Administration*, published in 1885, the other moving spirit of change, Edwin Chadwick, has something to say. He refers to the fact that Lord John Russell thought '*my* report on the Amendment of the Poor laws' had 'saved the country from great social evils, if not absolutely from social revolution'. And he goes on to add that he was charged by his colleagues 'with the preparation of the more full exposition of their general report which I accomplished with some assistance in minor details from Mr Senior'.[100]

In several pamphlets Senior drew attention to what he called the three great sources of human welfare or the great bonds of civilized society: industry, providence and mutual benevolence. Being an advocate of thrift and self-help, the prescribed overall solution to all that ailed the poor, he was critical of the allowance system and especially of outdoor relief to the able-bodied poor. When all is said, the parish chests and regional records do yield enough to show that the Speenhamland-type of social welfare had in it a good deal of practical compassion, whereas the voice of Nassau Senior sounds, at this distance in time, a little like a current contributor to *The Times*.

> It says to the idle and the heedless, your subsistence shall not depend on your exertions or your contrivance; to the young, Marry as soon as you like, your families shall be provided for; to the well-employed, Spend all your earnings, that parish will

support you when they fail; if you do save, the pauper will claim what you lay by; and to the benevolent, What you give is only so much saved to the parish; if you wish to indulge your sympathy do it cheaply, by assessing your neighbours.[101]

In any account of administration, the whole effort of Nassau Senior matters a good deal even though he was less active than Chadwick in the application of ideas. It was when he became retrospective that Senior adopted a critical tone.

The poor laws of southern England are an attempt to unite the irreconcilable advantages of freedom and servitude. The labourer is to be a free agent, but without the hazards of free agency; to be free from the coercion, but to enjoy the assured subsistence of the slave. He is expected to be diligent, though he has no fear of want; provident though his pay rises as his family increases; attached to a master who employs him in pursuance of a vestry resolution; and grateful for the allowance which the magistrates order him as a right.[102]

The man who felt able to class Malthus as 'our most eminent living philosophical writer',[103] was not keen on 'rights' for the poor:

The instant wages cease to be a bargain—the instant the labourer is paid not according to his *value* but his *wants*, he ceases to be a freeman. He acquires the indolence, the improvidence, the rapacity, and the malignity, but not the subordination of a slave. He is told that he has a *right* to wages, but that he is *bound* to work. Who is to decide how hard he ought to work, or how hard he does work? Who is to decide what amount of wages he has a *right* to? As yet the decision has been made by the magistrates. But they were interested parties. The labourer has thought fit to correct that decision.[104]

The inference is that who knows what labourers will ask for next: 'Next year perhaps the labourer will think it *unjust* that he should be paid less than 4s a day in winter and 5s in summer—woe to the tyrants who deny him his *right*.'[105] Senior also referred to rick-burnings, smashing of threshing machines and such forms of luddite action. He lapsed into the expedient role of woeful

43

prophet, arguing that if the feeling among the lower classes continued to prevail, then 'what is extensively prevalent under the present administration *will*, at no remote period, become universal in southern districts'.[106]

The power generated by Senior and Chadwick in the report of 1834 (and it was considerable) had its basis in an underestimation of the manifold problems. It was assumed that what was being attacked, namely the old poor law, had far less social value, less utility in so far as the community was concerned than the new administrative code which was being so eagerly presented and recommended. It is true that the old poor law had used outdoor relief as a device to help the poor and unemployed. It was a way of meeting the problem of surplus labour in the backward rural sector of an expanding society. The Commissioners had deliberately selected and arranged their facts so as to impeach the existing administrative structure on predetermined lines.[107]

The main charge against the allowance system and its form of relief was that it led to demoralization, to a debasing of the moral nature of labouring people. Poverty thus became a public sin and stigma. It is this kind of rooted or fixed belief in the laxity and even criminality of the poor which caused the report to become a reactionary document. Where the attack was directed toward actual administrative problems or to 'magisterial' errors, the position is different because it should always be remembered that it is the administrative side of this new deal which achieved something of lasting value.

Centralization was regarded by Chadwick as an answer to most of the problems affecting poor law administration. The new poor law, however, was founded

> not upon any extensive survey of human character and institutions, but upon the belief that the discipline of the workhouse is the best and most effective test of poverty. Bishop Copleston, writing on poor laws some twenty-five years ago, pronounced these institutions (workhouses), as effective correctives of pauperism, great failures. . . . A despotic and hard centralization is a dead weight; it is only by a division of labour and responsibility between the local and central boards that that species of centralization can be obtained which is truly an animating and

useful principle of action. Take two or three points. A work-house—A board of farmers whose business it is to register the edicts of the poor law commissioners, and to act upon them.— A central power in Somerset House; hard, despotic, unbending; and you have not altogether an unfair outline of the New Poor Law.[108]

That comment was written in 1847, and it was not really a fair summary. On the credit side, the Poor Law Amendment Act of 1834 created for the first time manageable units of local administration more or less alike in size and with uniform powers. This was done by grouping parishes into unions around a market town or urban centre. The Act also created Poor Law Commissioners who were to administer it, thus setting up a new branch of the central government which would handle local affairs, that is, the 600 or so poor law unions which were replacing as administrative units the 15,000 parishes and townships.[109]

OLD POOR LAW SURVIVES 1834

Because the Poor Law Amendment Act of 1834 caused such considerable changes to be made in the poor law method itself there was excuse for the assumption that a 'new poor law' had been introduced. In fact, the actual foundation of the old poor law, the 1601 Act was not repealed in the nineteenth century. It is necessary to underline the fact that a change took place in the administrative method and not in the law itself. So it is helpful to look at the main provisions in the basic Elizabethan act. That is, those which relate to employment for the able-bodied; necessary relief for the sick; and industrial education for the children.[110] Some authorities have put forward similar points of view. Robert Pashley thought that the legislature had attended in 1834 to improvements 'in the mere administration of relief, to the organization of union boards and to the control conferred on a central authority'.[111] An American student suggested that it was not until 1834, two hundred and fifty years after the passage of the Elizabethan statute, that any serious question was raised about the general effectiveness of the poor law. Nor were the fundamentals even then disturbed because the Poor Law Commission of that time paid attention simply to abuses of administration.[112]

45

There was no ready acceptance, regionally, of a mechanism of repression toward which the Select Committee of 1828[113] had inevitably pushed the minds of reformers who had to reinterpret the Elizabethan statute as regards relief and the provision of work. The methods and arguments were rejected by many. Some had listened willingly to the words of William Cobbett in December 1834 when he spoke out against the new system. He asked his parliamentary constituents what they thought would have been their fate if all the powers of government had been vested in those 'who brought in and pushed on the Poor-law Bill, and who had penny-a-line Chadwick and the rest of that crew stuck up in a corner of the House to dictate its proceedings'.[114]

Edwin Chadwick claimed in 1836 that poor rates had been greatly reduced under the new system; and supplied figures to show that there had been a saving of £10,148 in expenditure on the poor during that year. But this did not mean that there was easy cooperation between central and local government. In fact, it was more than a decade before a true equilibrium was built up or a proper system established. Opposition to the new poor law subsided only very slowly; by 1847 when the Poor Law Board came into existence, the move from parish ways to union methods reached a climax. The man largely responsible for the change was C. P. Villiers (1802–98), who served as Member of Parliament for Wolverhampton from 1835 until his death. Villiers was appointed president of the Poor Law Board in 1859 and he helped to accelerate the process of unionization that had been going on intermittently for many years.[115]

Villiers was the man behind the Union Chargeability Act of 1865[116] which can be regarded as a landmark in the history of the poor law. The measure was intended to ensure that the common fund of a union should be used for the maintenance and relief of the poor within that union, irrespective of the parish to which the pauper belonged.[117] In moving a first reading of the bill on 20 February 1865, Villiers was eloquent in pleading for the morals and well-being of the poor. He said the parish system was full of errors and that all kinds of enactments had been evolved to correct them. He reminded his parliamentary colleagues that in 1830 there had been a 'servile insurrection'. There were riots in agricultural districts ascribed to the maladministration of the poor laws. The Commissioners in 1834 did not wish to keep the parochial system, but they did not press ahead with plans to widen the area of chargeability because they felt that the requisite support would not be obtained. There was little doubt among well-informed people that the cost of the poor should be charged not to a single parish but to a common fund of a union.[118] Villiers said that between 1851 and 1861, in 821 agricultural parishes, there had been a decrease of 3,118 in the number of houses while the number of inhabitants had increased by 16,497. So Villiers asked for a repeal of the parochial settlement clause in the Poor Law Amendment Act of 1834:

> The Bill will cast the poor upon the general fund; and, what is extremely important, will transfer the power of removal from the overseers to the guardians.[119]

The point to remember is that even when the union had become the administrative unit, the chargeability remained parochial. In the close parishes controlled by one or two landowners the building of cottages was discouraged so that the poor had to move away to places where rents and rates were high.[120] The Union Chargeability Act made it certain that the charge for maintaining paupers was borne by the Common Fund.[121]

In thinking about the new interpretation, the new method for a sharper control of poor relief, one should not forget the ideas of Bentham and Malthus. Bentham died in 1832 and Malthus in 1834. The influence of Bentham, the great administrator, who had so concerned himself with pauperism and pauper management,[122] lived on in the person of indefatigable Edwin Chadwick; and there is some evidence that Senior went as far as practical realities allowed with the Malthusian idea of the abolition of poor relief. Bentham had provided justification for the political reforms desired by some thinkers. His 'greatest happiness' principle had established deterrence as the first justification of punishment and reformation as a secondary objective.[123] Bentham alone among thinkers of that time had expounded the principle of less eligibility as a justification for relief.[124] He had decided also that outdoor relief was not consistent with that basic principle in the theoretical sense.

The influence of Malthus is more complex. A question arises

47

as to whether Nassau Senior was the natural inheritor of Malthusian notions and a supporter of the abolition of the poor laws? At one stage he was certainly a sympathizer. The doctrine of abolition, though rarely overtly proclaimed, does lie behind the thinking of Senior and his friends. The evidence of an assistant poor law commissioner, J. W. Cowell, is of particular interest here because he was a member of that little 'inner circle' that Senior gathered together in the Political Economy Club.[125] In an account of the parish of Thurgarton in Nottinghamshire, Cowell comes out into the open as a lineal descendant of Malthus and Chalmers—that is, one who does not believe in poor laws and poor relief at all. He said there was nothing specially peculiar or local in Thurgarton to shake his general view that it would have been better if

> the whole body of labourers throughout England had been left alone during the last forty years—had there been no 43 Elizabeth, no scale nor other similar inventions regulating wages—their general condition would be highly flourishing.[126]

That kind of social theory had not worked and never would work. Theorists who became policy-makers had to abandon it. Yet the aims of legislators and administrators at that time had been directed toward an elimination of claimants at the parish table by making the poor law unpleasant and unpopular. Problems facing men such as Senior and Chadwick were not dissimilar to those of earlier (and much later) times. Administrators were still confronted with the unenviable task of discrimination. Writing in 1752, Thomas Alcock came close to stating the whole truth about the primary administrative difficulty, namely, sorting out the 'deserving' from the 'undeserving'. Labourers, he said, had a fear of one day coming to want; and this was a motive for industry and sobriety. But the motive is weakened when 'a Man has the Prospect of Parish Pay to rely on in case of future Wants or Misfortunes'. On this sort of presumption

> the sluggard is tempted to continue in Sloth; the Glutton, as he receives his gains, eats them, and the Drunkard, drinks them. In short, Men labour less and spend more; and the very law that provides for the Poor, makes Poor. A Law to enforce relief,

tends to destroy the Principle it proceeds from, the Principle of Charity . . .[127]

This was the eternal problem of poor law policy or of organized assistance over the whole period of parish and union responsibility; it remains an area of dispute in any analysis of contemporary welfare.

Notes

1. *Utilitarianism*, pp. 21–2; cf. A. L. Macfie, *The Individual in Society* (1967), p. 15: 'John Stuart Mill's dogmatism about the completeness of economic theory in his day is just a reflection of a relatively prosperous environment, a certain middle-class myopia, and a clear cut though superficial theory of ethics and society.'
2. 'Indigence may be provided for, mendicity may be extirpated, but all attempts to extirpate poverty can have no effects but bad ones,' *Edinburgh Review* (July 1836), p. 501. On this point Alfred Marshall wrote: 'I do not regard the problem of pauperism, as distinguished from the problem of poverty, as of so great an importance as it seems to other people to be', *Official Papers*, p. 205.
3. See J. Vancouver, *An Enquiry into Causes and Production of Poverty* (1796). The term 'culture of poverty' has become fashionable. It may also be useful, and is not itself really new. See Oscar Lewis: *Five Families: Mexican Case Studies in the Culture of Poverty* (1959); and same author's *La Vida, A Puerto Rican Family in the Culture of Poverty* (1967). This concept is minutely examined in 'An Evaluation of the Concept "Culture of Poverty" ' by Jack L. Roach and Orville R. Gursslin in *Social Forces*, 41, 3 (March 1967). They draw attention to 'culture as cause' and 'culture as description': 'An important distinction is that between the causal and descriptive conceptions of a culture of poverty. Many students of poverty tend to confuse these conceptions and conclude in effect that the traits of the poor are the cause of the traits of the poor.' Cf. *The Times Literary Supplement*, 21 September 1967, pp. 829–30.
4. *An Enquiry into the Causes and Production of Poverty and the State of the Poor* (1796), p. 3. Vancouver was very definite in his condemnation of the poor laws at a time when they were the subject of much discussion: 'These laws, by long experience, are confessedly proved not only incompetent to the humane design of their original institution, but, on many occasions, totally subversive of the interests they were ordained to promote,' pp. 38–9.
5. 'The Decretists and the "Deserving" Poor', *Studies in History and*

D

Society, I (1958–9). Professor Brian Tierney discusses the problems of the canonists. See also Walter Ullmann, *The Growth of Papal Government in the Middle Ages* (1955), p. 370. For discussion of the influence of medieval thought on institutions, see: Brian Tierney, 'Some Recent Works on the Political Theories of Medieval Canonists', *Traditio* X (1954), pp. 594–625; W. Ullmann, *The Political Theories of the Medieval Canonists* (1949); 'Concerning the Political Theories of the Medieval Canonists', Fr A. M. Stickler, *Traditio* 7, (1949–51), pp. 450–63; 'Intellectual History and Its Neighbours', John Higham, *Journal of the History of Ideas*, 15, (1954), pp. 339–68; and 'The Customary Poor Law of Three Cambridgeshire Manors', F. M. Page, *Cambridge Historical Journal* 3 (1929–31), pp. 125–33.

6. Brian Tierney, *Medieval Poor Law: A Sketch of Canonical Theory and Its Application In England* (University of California Press, 1959).

7. Tierney, p. 43.

8. *ibid.*, p. 132.

9. Sir William Ashley, *An Introduction to Economic History and Theory* (1925), pp. 339–40.

10. For an analysis of what is called the 'sentimental and the legal' methods of dealing with pauperism, see 'Charity, Pauperism and Self-Help', *The Westminster Review* XLVII (1875), pp. 107–42.

11. Ashley, *The Economic Organisation of England* (1914), p. 110.

12. Lutheranism provoked a concern with interior life, a withdrawal from worldliness, and thus produced what Troeletsch called a 'permanent principle' so that 'the whole system of Christian social effort slipped away into the modern policy of social welfare'; Ernst Troeletsch, *The Social Teachings of the Christian Churches* (1931), pp. 566–7; see also F. R. Salter (ed.), *Some Early Tracts on Poor Relief*, p. 87, 'Ordinance for a Common Chest'.

13. Ulrich Zwingli's 'Articles Touching Almsgiving' outlined a scheme introduced at Zurich in 1525, which became 'a guide to the Protestant method of dealing with social problems'; see Salter, *op. cit.*, p. 98.

14. S. and B. Webb, *English Local Government*, vol. VII, pp. 35–6.

15. Vives wrote an account of his methods in *De Subventione Pauperum*, translated in Salter, *op. cit.*; see also *Collection Vives* (1943).

16. R. H. Tawney, *Religion and the Rise of Capitalism* (1964), p. 122.

17. Salter, p. 11.

18. Bishop Ridley preached a sermon before King Edward VI and was asked to form a committee, along with Sir Richard Dobbs, then Lord Mayor of London, and others. The three main types of poor people were each divided into three groups, as follows:

'The poor by impotency: the fatherless poor man's child;
the aged, the blind and the lame;
those diseased by leprosy, etc.

'The poor by casualty: the wounded soldier;
the decayed householder;
sick persons visited by grievous disease.

'The thriftless poor: the rioter that consumeth all;
                         the vagabond that will abide in no place;
                         the idle person, as the strumpet and others.'

from W. Harrison, *A Description of England* (n.d.) edited by J. Lington, p. 123, 'Elizabethan England'.

19. Salter, *op. cit.*

20. *ibid.*, p. viii.

21. Cf. William Lambard, *Eirenarcha, or of the Office of the Justice of the Peace* (1581); Rev. Richard Burn, *The Justice of the Peace and Parish Officer* (1755); Bertram Osborne, *Justice of the Peace, 1361–1848* (1960).

22. Christopher Hill, *Society and Puritanism in Pre-Revolutionary England* (1966), pp. 266–70.

23. Thomas Mackay, *History of the English Poor Law* (1904), vol. III, p.14.

24. E. M. Leonard, *The Early History of English Poor Relief* (1900).

25. *ibid.*, pp. 134–5.

26. *ibid.*

27. *ibid.*

28. Theodore Dodd, *Administrative Reform and the Local Government Board* (1906), p. 89.

29. Maurice Bruce, *The Coming of the Welfare State* (1966).

30. Bruce, p. 23, and W. E. Tate, *The English Village Community and the Enclosure Movements* (1967) p. 124.

31. G. R. Elton, *England under the Tudors* (1955), p. 499.

32. 39 Elizabeth I c. 3.

33. 13 & 14 Charles II c. 12.

34. Karl de Schweinitz, *England's Road to Social Security 1347–1947* (1947), p. 28.

35. Hon. Edward Boyd Twistleton (1809–74), became an assistant poor law commissioner in 1839, and in 1843 was appointed commissioner to enquire into Scottish poor laws. Two years later, he became chief commissioner in Ireland, a post he held until 1849.

36. Sir Samuel Romilly (1757–1818), law reformer.

37. Romilly, *The Life of Sir Samuel Romilly*, 2 vols. (1842), vol. II, p. 241.

38. *Ninth Annual Report of the Poor Law Commissioners* (1843), p. 90.

39. *ibid.*

40. James Baker, *The Life of Sir Thomas Bernard* (1819), p. 147.

41. Dorothy Marshall, 'The Old Poor Law, 1662–1795', *Economic History Review* VIII (1957), p. 295.

42. H. L. Beales, 'The New Poor Law', in E. M. Carus Wilson (ed.), *Essays in Economic History* (n.d.), pp. 179–80.

43. Marshall, *The English Poor in the Eighteenth Century* (1960), p. 6.

44. E. E. Butcher, *Bristol Corporation of the Poor*, 1696–1834 (1932), p. 1.

45. Defoe was a wily and formidable pamphleteer.

46. In this pamphlet ['Giving Alms No Charity'], Defoe also says: 'That 'tis a Regulation of the Poor that is wanted in England, not a setting them to work.' The pamphlet, first published in 1704, was written in

opposition to a bill for the employment of poor people introduced into Parliament by Sir Humphrey Mackworth. Defoe was probably responsible for the ultimate failure of this measure.

47. E. E. Lipson, *The Economic History of England* (1948), vol. III, p. 472. Students of economic history will probably be encouraged to discount Lipson as out-dated, but his work on social welfare still has merit. See also *House of Commons Journals* XXII, pp. 483–4; XXX, p. 38; XXXIII, p. 599; and C. R. Fay, *Great Britain from Adam Smith to the Present Day* (1928), p. 338.

48. 9 George I c. 7.

49. Sir F. Eden, *The State of the Poor*, vol. I, p. 269.

50. Sir John Clapham, *An Economic History of Modern Britain*, 'The Early Railway Age, 1820–50'.

51. Charles Weston was the author of *Remarks on the Poor Laws and on the State of the Poor*, a work published at Brentford in 1802. The Parliamentary expert on the law of settlement, George Coode, said that Weston was 'the best informed of all the writers on poor laws that I have any knowledge of'.

52. Coode's 'Report on the Law of Settlement and Removal' was published in *Parliamentary Papers*, vol. XXVI (1851) and a supplement to it appeared in 1854.

53. *Wealth of Nations* (1817), vol. I, p. 124.

54. *English Local Government*, reprint (1963), vol. 2, p. 407.

55. *A Collection of Pamphlets Concerning the Poor with Observations by the Editor* (1787), pp. 153–4.

56. See A. W. Coats, 'Economic Thought and Poor Law Policy in the Eighteenth Century', *Economic History Review* 13 (1960–1) for an excellent account of Thomas Gilbert. Insufficient work has been done on him as yet. He remains in shadow, as if the things he did (or tried to do) had a greater significance than the character of their elusive originator. Reference is made to Gilbert in Sir Lewis Namier and John Brooke, *House of Commons, 1754–90* (1964), pp. 499–501, and in I. R. Christie, *The End of Lord North's Ministry, 1780–82* (1958), p. 349.

57. Namier, *The Structure of Politics at the Accession of George III* (1957), p. 6.

58. *op. cit.*, p. 70. Namier also said: 'The English political family is a compound of "blood", name and estate, this last, as the dominion of monarchs, being the most important of the three; that is why mansions instead of families are so often the subject of monographs dealing with the history of the English upper classes'; *England in the Age of the American Revolution*, 2nd ed. (1961) pp. 19–20.

59. Unpublished and undeposited poor law accounts in the parish of Ashwater.

60. Ashwater records.

61. *Poverty in Rural Devon, 1780–1840* (dissertation for a Ph.D., Stanford University, 1966).

62. Taylor, p. 29.

63. *ibid.*, p. 30.
64. The Report of this important Select Committee, under the chairmanship of the Rt Hon. William Sturges Bourne, was published in the *Parliamentary Papers*. The Committee was concerned with anything that would 'check or modify the system itself'. For the sake of the paupers themselves it was considered necessary then to find a way 'of setting again into action those motives which impel persons, by the hope of bettering their condition on the one hand, and the fear of want on the other, so to exert and conduct themselves, as by frugality, temperance and industry, and by the practice of those other virtues on which human happiness has been made to depend, to ensure to themselves that condition of existence in which life alone can be otherwise than a miserable burthen; the temptation to idleness, to improvidence, and want of forethought are under any circumstances so numerous and enticing that nothing less than dread of the evils, which are their natural consequences, appears to be sufficiently strong, in any degree to control them.' What this Committee was saying added up to the assertion that the 'labouring classes' would only get more entangled in the net of pauperism if they were constantly provided with sums of money. In order to lend some force and weight to undocumented assertions, they quoted from Edmund Burke's pamphlet *Thoughts and Details on Scarcity* (1795) in which he said that although compassion should be shown to poor people there need be, 'no lamentation of their condition'.
65. Taylor, p. 28.
66. In his book, *The English Village Community and the Enclosure Movements* (1967), p. 85, Tate makes it clear that he thought the Speenhamland method was 'truly disastrous' and he suggests that the decision taken at the Pelican Inn, which is familiar to all students, was a development of the Buckinghamshire decision. This is a possibility, but the proof for it does not appear to exist.
67. Quarter Sessions Records, Buckinghamshire County Record Office, Aylesbury, reference supplied by the County Archivist, E. J. Davis.
68. The Speenhamland justices considered two plans: 'That they should fix the lowest price to be given for labour, as they were empowered to do by the 5th. Eliz. 1, c.4: and 2ndly, that they should act with uniformity in the relief of the *impotent* and *infirm* Poor, by a table of universal practice, corresponding with the supposed necessities of each family. The first plan was rejected, by a considerable majority; but the second was adopted . . .'; Eden, *The State of the Poor*, vol. 1, pp. 576–7; J. L. and B. Hammond in *The Village Labourer* give an account of this method; Miss Dorothy George, *England in Transition* (1953), p. 95 calls it 'a device, purely local in its origin and intended to meet an emergency' which was to become the basis for a general policy; and Karl Polanyi in *Origins of Our Time* (1945), pp. 270–6 gives a note on the system and its literature. Mark Neuman completed a dissertation (University of California in 1967) on *Aspects of Poverty and Poor Law Administration in Berkshire, 1782–1834*. See also his chapter 4 below.

69. Records deposited in the Town Clerk's Office, Tiverton, Devon.

70. Tawney, *op. cit.*

71. *Parliamentary Debates,* XXX. 'Report from the Committee on Parish Apprentices', pp. 534–42.

72. *Parliamentary Papers,* XXVII, Appendix A, p. 432.

73. *The Parish Apprenticeship System* (1831), p. 9.

74. *ibid.,* p. 11.

75. *Parliamentary Papers,* vol. XXVII.

76. G. A. Body, *The Administration of the Poor Laws in Dorset 1760–1834, with special reference to Agrarian Distress,* (Ph.D. thesis, Southampton University 1965).

77. *Regulations relative to Superintending Workhouse in the parish of Bradford in Wiltshire,* pp. 1–2.

78. Rev Thomas Chalmers (1780–1847), a theologian who also wrote about his own unrealistic brand of 'philanthropy' in *Tracts on Pauperism* (1833) and *The Christian and Civic Economy of Our Large Towns* (1821–6).

79. B. Kirkman Gray. *Philanthropy and the State* (1908), p. 88.

80. *Capital* (3 vols.), (1932) vol. I, p. 676. For all its influence on social thought, Malthus' *Essay on Population* (1798), did not impress Marx. 'In its first form', he wrote, 'it is nothing more than a schoolboyish, superficial plagiary of Defoe, Sir James Steuart, Townsend, Franklin, Wallace, etc., and does not contain a single sentence thought out by himself. The great senation this pamphlet caused was due solely to party interest.' Marx, vol. I, p. 265.

81. Bentham had taken the English shopkeeper as the normal man: 'Whatever is useful to this queer normal man, and to his world, is absolutely useful. This yard-measure, then, he applied to the past, present and future. The Christian religion is useful, because it forbids in the name of religion the same fruits that the penal code condemns in the name of the law.' Marx, vol. I, p. 668.

82. For a reliable account of Edwin Chadwick's poor law activities see S. E. Finer, *The Life and Times of Sir Edwin Chadwick* (1952).

83. Much more work needs to be done on the mind and achievement of Nassau Senior. Two works dealing with aspects of his life and thought are: S. L. Levy, *Nassau Senior, The Prophet of Modern Capitalism* (1943) and Marian Bowley, *Nassau Senior and Classical Economics* (1927).

84. Charles James Blomfield (1786–1857), appointed to See of Chester in 1824 and to that of London in 1828. He was a member of the Poor Law Board in 1836.

85. Rt Hon. William Sturges Bourne (1769–1845), an influential politican known mainly because of the act for regulation of parish vestries (59 George III c. 12).

86. Sir Thomas Frankland Lewis (1780–1855), politician and administrator.

87. G. M. Young and W. D. Handcock (eds.), *English Historical Documents, 1833–1874* (1956), vol. XII, p. 684.

88. R. H. Tawney, *Religion and Rise of Capitalism* (1964), p. 272.

89. Blaug, 'The Poor Law Report Re-examined', *Journal of Economic History*, XXIV (1964), p. 243.

90. R. Lubove (ed.), *Social Welfare in Transition* (1966), p. vi.

91. Lubove, *loc. cit.*

92. 'Public Relief and Private Charity in England', C. A. Ellwood in *Modern Methods of Charity*, ed. C. R. Henderson (1904), pp. 165–235.

93. *ibid.*, p. 38.

94. *ibid.*, p. 39.

95. J. R. Pretyman, *Dispauperisation* (1878), p. 27. A world like 'revolution' is one to be used with caution in respect of riots in Speenhamland counties. A German commentator, Baron von Voght, writing in 1796, pointed to one of the roots of rural disturbance: 'When once the history of the poor is well-known it will be seen how large a proportion of the miseries of the lower orders arise *from local errors and prejudices*, from ignorance and want of advice.' 'Account of the Management of the Poor in Hamburgh between the years 1788 and 1794' (1817), reprinted in *The Pamphleteer*, XXII (March 1818), pp. 443–68.

96. *Parliamentary Papers*, vol. XXVII, p. 3.

97. *Parliamentary Papers*, vol. XXVII, p. 156. This reference leads on to the much quoted statement that outdoor relief to the able-bodied poor was the master evil of the system. The greater evil of settlement is thus reduced for the sake of an argument designed to support the abolition of the sort of aid in the home that, in fact, was not (and could not) be abolished.

98. *ibid.*

99. N. Simpson (ed.), *Correspondence and Conversations of Alexis de Tocqueville with Nassau W. Senior from 1834–1859* (1872).

100. E. Chadwick, *The Evils of Disunity in Central and Local Administration* (1885), pp. 107–8.

101. *A Letter to Lord Howick (1832)*, p. 25. To this letter Senior appends, with approval, evidence given by Dr Thomas Chalmers to the select Committee of the House of Commons on the state of the poor in Ireland, part III. Chalmers stated: 'I look upon a compulsory provision to be that which acts as a disturbing force upon certain principles and feelings, which, if left to their own undisturbed existence, would do more for the prevention and alleviation of poverty than can be done by any legal or artificial system whatever.'

102. *Three Lectures on the Rate of Wages* (1830), pp. ix–x.

103. *Two Lectures on Population* (1829), p. 1.

104. *Three Lectures on the Rate of Wages*, p. xxi

105. *ibid.*

106. *ibid.*, p. xiv.

107. M. Blaug, 'The Myth of the Old Poor Law', *Journal of Economic History*, XXIII (June 1963), pp. 176–7.

108. Sir Walter James, *Thoughts upon the Theory and Practice of the Poor Laws* (1847), pp. 7–8.

109. West Midland Study Group, *Local Government and Central Control* (1956), p. 8.

110. *Administrative Reform and the Local Government Board* (1906), p. 5.

111. *Pauperism and Poor Laws* (1852), p. 286.

112. Robert W. Kelso, *The History of Public Relief in Massachusetts* (1922), pp. 20–6.

113. *Report from the Select Committee on that part of the Poor Laws relating to the Employment or Relief of able-bodied Persons from the Poor Rate* (1828).

114. *Policitical Register*, LXXXV–VI, pp. 662–3.

115. References to assist in tracing this process of change are given in Sidney and Beatrice Webb, *English Local Government*, pp. 8, 226.

116. 28 and 29 Victoria c. 79.

117. John J. Clarke, *Social Administration including the Poor Laws* (1927).

118. See S. and B. Webb, pp. 8, 431–2.

119. *Parliamentary Debates*, 3rd series, 178 (1865), pp. 467–86.

120. Thomas Mackay, *Public Relief of the Poor* (1901), pp. 123.

121. See C. P. Villiers, *Parliamentary Debates*, 3rd series (1865).

122. The voluminous writings of Jeremy Bentham on pauperism and pauper management (the Bentham Papers) are housed in the Library of University College, London. See also *Works*, ed. J. Bowring (1833–43); and *Pauper Management Improved* (1812) and *Observations on the Poor Bill, introduced by the Rt Hon. William Pitt*, ed. Edwin Chadwick (1838).

123. B.-S. Rodman, 'Bentham and the Paradox of Penal Reform', *Journal of the History of Ideas*, XXIX, 2 (1968), pp. 200–1.

124. J. R. Poynter, *Society and Pauperism; English Ideas on Poor Relief, 1795–1834* (1969), p. 327.

125. Marian Bowley, *Nassau Senior and Classical Economics* (1937), p. 286.

126. Parliamentary Papers, XXVII, Appendix A, p. 603.

127. Rev T. Alcock, *Observations on the Defects of the Poor Laws* (1752), pp. 10–11.

3
The Unreformed Workhouse 1776 - 1834

JAMES S. TAYLOR

Of the pre-1834 workhouses[1] the Webbs wax eloquent: 'their incredible foulness and promiscuity, their insanitation and utter inadequacy of accommodation, and the demoralizing cruelties and tyrannies of the contractors to whom they were habitually "farmed". . . '.[2] Even a recent defender of the pre-1834 poor law refers to the workhouse as 'invariably an unsanitary and disorderly institution'.[3] Men who lived at that time often had no better opinion. Some of Crabbe's poetry portrayed the workhouse in most dismal hues.[4] Many pamphleteers did no less. C. D. Brereton called them 'stranded hulks' and 'seminaries of crime and the feeders of our houses of correction'.[5] The workhouse, according to the 1834 report of the Poor Law Commissioners, was

> a large almshouse, in which the young are trained in idleness, ignorance and vice; the able-bodied maintained in sluggish sensual indolence; the aged and more respectable exposed to all the misery that is incident to dwelling in such a society, without government or classification. . . .[6]

Although not all contemporaries or later students have been so critical, the notion that workhouses of that time were grim bastilles for the poor is a canon of poor law history. Yet no evaluation of pre-1834 workhouses has been attempted since the Webbs and Dorothy Marshall wrote of them over forty years ago.[7]

What is the evidence? There are, of course, the oft-used pamphleteers, with their catalogues of abuses and remedies, providing a plethora of contradictory and often ill-informed opinion. As one intolerant critic wrote: 'Every man rushes to the press with his small morsel of imbecility; and is not easy till he sees his impertinence stitched in blue covers.'[8] This source, so useful in the study of attitudes, ideas and legislative initiatives, is much less valuable in determining how the poor law actually worked.[9]

Another source is the evidence assembled for Parliament. There are, first of all, quantitative studies—overseers' returns to Parliament covering the years 1776, 1803 and 1813–15—that contain, among other items, statistics on workhouses for all of England and Wales.[10] These are unique. Even the 1834 report's twelve folio volumes of evidence provide no national survey of almost all parishes and places. The returns provide number and capacity of workhouses in 1776 and number of inmates and costs of workhouse relief in 1803 and 1813–15. Yet the returns are most imperfect. What was meant by 'workhouse', the term used in all three surveys, was not made clear to the overseers, with the consequence that some overseers made returns for what were no more than rent-free dwellings where neither work nor regimen were provided. John Rickman, who spent much of his adult life collating population and poor law statistics, complained of 'the *gross amount* of the dulness of all probable Overseers',[11] but the fault lay also in the imprecision in the instructions compilers of information gave overseers. Another difficulty is that intentional misrepresentation by some overseers and even magistrates occurred, caused by suspicion of the use that might be made of the information.[12] Then one must consider that parishes did not always keep separate workhouse accounts, and even those parishes with adequate accounts possessed categories of expense, such as building or repairing workhouses, that some overseers reported and others did not. The 1776 returns are incomplete, for houses under local Acts of Parliament, included in later returns, were omitted, although there are separate returns for many houses of this sort for 1772–4. Finally, the 1803 and 1813–15 returns did not specify the number of workhouses, only the number of paupers relieved indoors in each parish; as workhouses were often shared, the total number of parishes *using* workhouses in the returns is not the same as the total number actually *possessing* houses.

Imperfect though they be, the returns provide a rough notion of numerical dimensions found in no other contemporary source.[13]

There is little else in the parliamentary papers after 1776 relating to workhouses before the evidence for the 1834 report; that evidence is a bonanza, particularly the two volumes of Reports of Assistant Commissioners, the five of Answers to Rural Queries, and the two of Answers to Town Queries, but the basis of selecting the over 1,500 parishes and places investigated or queried from the some 15,000 available entities is not stated.[14]

In addition to pamphlets and parliamentary papers, there are magistrates' and overseers' handbooks, particularly the many-editioned Richard Burn.[15] But poor law authorities needed and received far more help in interpreting the complex laws governing settlement of paupers in their proper parish than the few statutes that might make their workhouse subject for action in the courts. Consequently, information on workhouses in these sources is not impressive. Another source, the general value of which is evidenced by its use in almost every study of the pre-1834 poor law, is Sir Frederic Eden's three-volume *The State of the Poor* (London, 1797). Unlike his contemporaries, Eden did not merely assemble enough fact to give verisimilitude to his opinion. In his two-volume parochial survey, he touched on every English county excepting Huntingdon, presenting evidence to sustain various opinions. Admittedly, the survey was unbalanced in favour of northern England; in Cumberland alone, seventeen parishes were examined, while Sussex received only four examinations of parishes. Yet the evidence for the 1834 report, while far more extensive, of course, appears to be only scarcely less haphazard.

The primary sources are parish records, semi-interred in parishes or, more accessibly, county record offices; and quarter sessions records, found in the latter depositories. The bulk and location of this material discourage synthesizers,[16] while local historians hardly feel competent to generalize on the basis of a parish or county. The present study has drawn upon all the above forms of evidence, from pamphlets to overseers' accounts, although the local records are taken primarily, but not exclusively, from Devon.[17]

'Working houses' received statutory sanction in 1597, but only as privately endowed institutions. However, there was nothing in this statute or the great consolidating statute of 1601 to prevent a parish from establishing a workhouse wherein the poor would be provided with work.[18] It was the difficulties in meeting initial expenses, the small size of most parishes and the lack of success of many early experiments that hindered development of workhouses until the late seventeenth century, except as an occasional expedient adopted primarily in towns.[19] Interest in workhouses gained in the late seventeenth century, partly because increasing destitution consequent upon the economic dislocation resulting from the long wars with France caused increased interest in palliatives. The success of some experiments, often initiated under local Acts of Parliament, provoked emulation. Statutory assistance without need of a special Act of Parliament came with the General Workhouse Act of 1722, which made it easier for parishes to raise funds for establishing houses, to join together for economy and to use the workhouse to check burgeoning outdoor relief through a 'test'—the poor who refused to enter 'shall not be entitled to ask or receive collection or relief . . .'.[20] Under this statute, as well as under many local statutes, workhouses were established throughout England in the eighteenth century. Proselytization came by successful example; if one enterprising parish in a region established a house that reduced poor rates and relief applicants, neighbouring parishes followed suit either by building a house of their own or making arrangements with the parish possessing the house for use of its facility.[21] Both urban and rural parishes adopted workhouses, either building a new structure or, more commonly, renovating an old. Gilbert's act of 1782 (22 George III c. 83) providing for the optional union of parishes for poor law purposes, may have contributed to still further expansion of this mode of relief, an expansion that may have reached maximum extent around the turn of the century.[22]

The insoluble problem of terms must be raised. The original meaning of 'workhouse' implied a house where work was performed. It came in time to apply also to a house where the inmates were fed and housed under a regimen. By 1834, C. P. Villiers, an assistant poor law commissioner, did not believe work was essential to the definition:

> A workhouse is known by having a master or a matron, a regular dietary, and the inmates being subject to some control.[23]

In fact, the term was used increasingly loosely in the eighteenth and early nineteenth centuries so that it came to imply virtually any residence in which the poor were housed. Other names, such as 'poorhouse', were often used interchangeably with 'workhouse' by the late eighteenth century. When 'workhouse' appears in local records it merely means in most instances that the parish had at one time made an attempt to work the inmates. When the term is used in parliamentary returns, it means any residential relief respondents thought fit to mention. This utter confusion in terms frustrates analysis; in consequence, contemporaries and later historians have invented definitions in order to categorize indoor relief. Evasion of the problem is tempting, for the purposes of a house were often as ephemeral as the annual rotation of parish officers. The Webbs, while discussing a number of abstract functions the workhouse was intended to serve, discount the importance of the name used as any indication of the character of the institution, but perhaps that is to go too far. Names may indicate, to some degree, attitudes; that 'workhouse' won the struggle for precedence in the parlance of the eighteenth and early nineteenth centuries suggests the compelling attraction of the concept that the poor should work.[24] What is meant by the term in this essay is what was generally meant by contemporaries by the late eighteenth century, residential relief that involved more than simply the supply by the parish of a cottage.

The 1776 returns provide the first national accounting of workhouses. No English county, excepting Monmouth, was without some and even tiny Rutland claimed four. There were almost 2,000 houses in England and Wales, with Wales furnishing only nineteen of the total. The given capacity of all these institutions was almost 90,000, ranging in size from two to 500 inmates, with the typical house having a capacity of twenty to fifty inmates.[25] But houses under local acts were excluded and most of the largest English workhouses were under such acts, about two thirds of these being located in East Anglia and the environs of London, with the remainder scattered in cities such as Bristol and Liverpool.

These houses had more than their fair share of influence in formulating impressions of workhouse relief. Clearly, there were differences between the house in the Devon moorland parish of Chagford, with a capacity of twenty inmates, and the Duke's Palace Workhouse in Norwich, which actually held over a thousand inmates between 1772 and 1774, yet the former type of house far exceeded the latter both in number of houses and, in the aggregate, capacity.[26]

More comprehensive returns of the scope and cost of poverty were undertaken in the wake of the severe dearth of 1799–1800. On the surface it would appear that the number of houses had almost doubled: 3,765 parishes or places maintained all or part of their poor in workhouses in 1803 compared with 1,970 houses listed in 1776. However, the 1803 returns include 764 parishes or places maintaining the poor under local Acts of Parliament. In addition, an unknown number of parishes maintained poor parishioners in the workhouses of *other* parishes, and so are listed in the 1803 returns even though they did not possess houses of their own.[27] Probably the most critical unknown is the degree to which a looser interpretation was placed on 'workhouse' at the later date. In both surveys, small and large houses appear, but did more overseers in 1803 think fit to record the parish poorhouse than at the earlier date? Probably they did in so far as 1776 was closer in time to the actual use of workhouses in employing the poor. By the turn of the century, the fond wish survived, but the failures in employing inmates may well have contributed, in general, to a looser construction of the term.[28]

One parallel between the 1776 and 1803 returns is that the capacity given in the earlier returns is very close to the enrolment in the later returns, with almost twice the number of parishes included in 1803. While this reflects workhouse sharing in 1803, it also suggests that the Webbs' charge of overcrowding in workhouses needs qualification. Overcrowding was certainly critical in some workhouses, but it was not in others. The growing popularity of outdoor relief may not have been because workhouses could no longer cope with the number of poor relief applicants, but because workhouses were not expected to cope with the type of poverty occasioning more extensive outdoor relief.[29]

In addition to numbers of inmates, the 1803 returns contain the costs of workhouse relief. Using the national average, it was about four times more expensive relieving a pauper in a workhouse as opposed to giving him outdoor relief. However, outdoor relief was often given on casual and supplementary bases while workhouse relief was usually reserved for the most necessitous cases. Therefore, this disparity in cost is not surprising, nor does it provide reason for believing workhouses were a financial failure, although it may have served to reinforce that belief in contemporaries viewing the returns.[30]

The final set of parliamentary returns suggest that there was no significant change either in number of inmates or costs between 1803 and 1813–15: both had increased, but perhaps only roughly proportionate to population and price increases. The evidence of the 1834 report gives no reason to suspect either much growth or decline from the level achieved earlier in the century.

The 1803 returns suggest that the counties spending most on workhouse relief also spent most on relief generally; although the parallel did not always hold on the parish level, it is broadly true that the workhouse was a supplement, not a substitute, to allowances and casual payments in money and kind, that the so-called Speenhamland counties were also, to some extent, the 'workhouse' counties.[31] The south-eastern counties of Norfolk, Suffolk, Sussex, Essex, Middlesex, Kent and Surrey (not all of which bear the mark of Speenhamland) in 1803 and 1813–15 held half of all workhouse inmates in England, while possessing, according to the 1801 and 1811 censuses, about one third of the total population. The majority of houses in the seven counties were small, the mean average being twenty-seven inmates, compared to a national mean of twenty-two inmates in 1803, and this is with the inclusion of the giant institutions of East Anglia and Middlesex. It is fair to add, however, that the mean average for Middlesex alone was eighty-three.

The impression made by the returns is that the typical workhouse was an institution of between twenty and fifty inmates, that they were widely dispersed in England, although more common in urban centres and south-eastern England than elsewhere, and that they provided relief for approximately one fifth of those on permanent relief.[32] The returns are easy to misinterpret;[33] one wishes the three inquiries had been conducted differently and with more relationship one with the other, yet they are too important to neglect entirely.[34]

'As Ann Peacock is troublesome to the Parish it is agreed that the Overseers of the Poor do remove her to Aisker Poorhouse as soon as convenient to be committed to the Masters care.'[35] This simple story was countlessly repeated in vestry meeting minutes and overseers' accounts of the time. The troublesomeness might be strictly a question of finances or it might be the pauper's character or the nature of his infirmities.[36] Overseers were also swayed by other considerations, the precise amalgam of motives for using a workhouse varying with time, place, officer and pauper, but the view of most overseers was, surely, fundamentally pragmatic: to relieve the poor in the least troublesome manner possible.

Whether a workhouse punished, reformed (educated the young and provided productive work for the able), deterred or merely comforted the poor, the key to success lay less in statutory provisions and workhouse rules than in individual leadership. That is why biography figures so importantly in many discussions of pre-1834 workhouses. How often a promising social experiment abruptly failed upon a change of workhouse governors or the withdrawal of one individual's influence within a parish! However, there was one service almost every workhouse provided that was fulfilled in times of ephemeral success and even in times of failure to achieve more ambitious aims, that is as a receptacle for what the pre-Victorians called the 'impotent' poor—children, the aged and every variety of the handicapped. The quality of relief was dependent, of course, on the aims, efficiency and resources of local administrators, but the convenience of providing undifferentiated institutional relief for the impotent, a term we shall now adopt, is the reason why workhouses survived in considerable numbers until the Poor Law Amendment Act of 1834, in spite of a long history of failure to achieve any other aim.[37]

The centrality of this purpose is exemplified by considering the types of inmates workhouses relieved. Indoor relief of the able-bodied was not common, at least from the late eighteenth century onward. It was expensive relative to the alternative of outdoor relief, it often led to disciplinary problems, and made little practical sense to the men administering the law. Of the 368 returns from Town Queries, gathered for the 1834 report, only two indicated a desire to relieve the able-bodied in workhouses,[38] the sort of figure that may partly explain the curious failure of the Poor Law Commissioners to abstract fully the evidence from the volumes of Rural and Town Queries.

Children were often relieved in workhouses. The horrors Jonas Hanway uncovered in the treatment of pauper children in London at mid-eighteenth century, both in and out of workhouses, were partly corrected later in the century,[39] but London was scarcely typical of child-relief in any case. Where a parish possessed a workhouse, it was common to relieve the orphan and the pauper's child there, but usually only after the child has reached a certain age; this 'birthday present' often fell at age six or age seven. But it was *also* common to find foster homes for homeless children, the custom in parishes without workhouses, and to allow the poor parents a family allowance for a child living at home, particularly in cases of large families. The compulsory assignment to workhouses of children whose parents were on parish pay was not unknown,[40] although it provoked horror and opposition from most local officials responding to Rural Queries. It must be said, however, of the period under discussion that children were in the poorest position to protect themselves in workhouses. They were subjected to the most work, in comparison with other categories of inmates, and the most discipline.[41] Their exit, if they lived, was often in the form of an unwelcome apprenticeship.[42] Women with dependent children, such as widows or the wives of soldiers, were sometimes relieved indoors. The aged and infirm were often so assisted. Few workhouses possessed separate facilities for treatment of the mentally retarded or the mentally ill, yet the workhouse was a common abode of such persons.[43] The workhouse, in short, relieved all those categories of poor that were sometimes difficult to provide for cheaply through outdoor relief.

The governorship of workhouses assumed three principal forms. In some houses, usually the smaller ones, authority was given to a pauper inmate or someone whose economic status might otherwise qualify him for relief.[44] A second common arrangement was

E

to employ a professional parish officer who would undertake, among other duties, management of the workhouse.[45] Only in large institutions was it feasible to hire a professional administrator capable of imposing a strict regimen. In most workhouses, successful governorship rested upon the ability to minimize workhouse expenses on the one hand and complaints of inmates to parish officers or magistrates on the other; how often the formula was achieved is questionable, but there was often at least some motivation for workhouse governors to combine efficiency with humanity.[46]

Another method of managing the workhouse or even all the parish poor was to contract or 'farm' the responsibility to an entrepreneur. This was frequently done in the eighteenth century,[47] but toward the end of the century it became rare, the result most likely of the economic crises at the turn of the century that made contracting too risky to attract businessmen.[48] There is, however, an indication of some revival of contracting in the evidence for the 1834 report.[49] It is not clear if contracting entirely deserves its unsavoury reputation. True, contractors were in the business for profit, at the expense of ratepayers or paupers or both. The contracts were usually based on payment by the parish of so many shillings a week per pauper inmate. Consequently, times of rapid inflation gave contractors particular incentive to grind their charges. Yet not all parishes gave free rein to contractors any more than to workhouse governors; both workhouse rules and workhouse contracts often established means for inmates to appeal to higher authority.[50] It still remains true that there were fewer rules and checks on contractors than workhouse governors; the latter were often bound by as many rules relating to their duties and conduct as were their pauper charges.[51]

Overseeing the work of governor or contractor were officers of local government. The Town and Rural Queries of the 1834 report provide a profile of sorts. As there was no apparent basis for selection of respondents, any more than for parishes, and as the answers apparently came from those who felt most responsible for responding, the positions of the respondents to the two sets of queries may suggest those positions that exercised greatest initiative in poor law matters on the local level.

Position	Rural queries	Town queries
Magistrates	11·7%	2·4%
Clergymen	12·9%	7·7%
Overseers	22·6%	22·6%
Assistant overseers	8·8%	11·2%
Vestry clerks	1·7%	22·2%
Churchwardens	7·8%	8·1%
Not given or other	34·5%	25·8%

One must not automatically assume the Town and Rural Queries were fully representative; it is possible the above percentages mislead for England and Wales as a whole. Even if the queries are assumed to be representative, the category in the final line denotes a large percentage of respondents who often gave nothing more than their name. One must make still another assumption to make this table highly significant; the respondents who did not declare their position would, if their position were known, be fairly equally distributed among the categories given above. I suspect that both assumptions are correct and that the positionless respondents came from all the above categories, perhaps most frequently being men who had previously served in an office that had given them experience with poor law administration. The presentation of this highly suspect profile has a point; it is to suggest that the role of the magistrate in poor law administration may have been less than sometimes supposed.[52] The men who did most of the work and made most of the decisions came, it is argued, from lower in the social order.

When power in the parish was exercised through an open vestry, relief could be munificent; if it rested in the hands of a few, relief dispensation or costs could be venal.[53] But the principal weakness in most parishes was inefficiency arising out of indifference. Here the local records are misleading, for those accounts that have survived were more likely to have been kept by efficient and conscientious officers than those accounts that are no more. The parish that allowed its grocer to use pages of the parish account book to wrap his parcels[54] is less likely to have exercised competence in parochial affairs than the parish whose accounts are now open for perusal of students in county record offices!

When parish officers were neglectful, as no doubt they often were, magistrates might step in to check workhouse abuses, but the magistracy was short in numbers[55] and long on duties. Magistrates interfered, particularly after statutes of 1790 and 1796 increased their power of so doing,[56] partly to improve in-house conditions and partly to order relief out of workhouses to paupers whom parish authorities wished to relieve indoors. The Poor Law Commissioners deemed the latter interference worthy of a wordy question in Rural and Town Queries:

> If an Appeal from the Vestry or Select Vestry shall continue, what do you think would be the Effect, immediate and ultimate, of restoring the Law as it stood before the Stat. 36 Geo. III. cap. 23, was passed, so that in any Parish having a Workhouse or Poorhouse, the Magistrates should not have the Power of ordering Relief to be given to Persons who should refuse to enter the Workhouse or Poorhouse ?[57]

Approximately one-third of the respondents to both sets of queries opposed this magisterial power, but almost a quarter of the respondents in Town Queries and a fifth from Rural Queries favoured magisterial interference. The plurality of respondents either fell foul of the Commissioners' syntax and answered irrelevantly or did not answer at all. What is most apparent in the answers—and perhaps implicitly in the number failing to answer—is that the question was clearly considered by most respondents to be academic; in many cases respondents were unaware magistrates *had* such power and even those who opposed magisterial power to order outdoor relief when the parish could offer a workhouse usually admitted magistrates did not, in fact, interfere. While it must be recalled that a number of respondents were magistrates and a still larger number may not have wished to return an answer reflecting unfavourably on the local bench, it is clear that the respondents were not nearly so hard on the magistracy as the Poor Law Commissioners were to be in their report.[58]

This may shed a kinder light on the relationship between magistrate and overseer than contemporary outcry might lead one to suspect, but it says nothing to the benefit of workhouse inmates. At least at the time of the gathering of evidence for the 1834 report it appears that magistrates seldom exercised their power to restrain parish officers from using the workhouse 'test'. This does not mean parish officers were *ipso facto* tyrannical; it merely indicates that the magisterial check on workhouse administration was sporadic and probably, on the whole, not very effective.

That work and workhouses were seldom married is a commonplace of pre-1834 poor law studies, and the 1803 returns appear to bear this out. The following is a sample from that source.

	Kent	Lancs	Norfolk	North-umberland	Oxford
Number of parishes/places making returns	409	652	691	513	284
Number purchasing materials to use in working inmates	167	71	144	9	31
Number that spent more than was earned in attempt	55	7	6	2	6
Number making net profit in excess of £50 per annum or more in the attempt	16	15	13	1	6

Almost £40,000 was spent that year in England and Wales in efforts to employ the workhouse poor, but only a little more than £70,000 was earned, 'small potatoes' when relief was costing over £4,000,000 a year, about a quarter of which was going to the workhouses. What can be said for this monumental failure?

1803 was at the end of a severe dearth. One might have expected that the inflated costs of relief resulting from that dearth would have given incentive for employing workhouse inmates, but the collapse of local craft industries and the putting-out system of cloth manufacture had an unfortunate effect, for it was spinning, carding, weaving, knitting, beating and winding various materials that were the principal workhouse employments. The workhouse, no less than the handloom weaver, was a casualty of industrialism.[59] In addition, the increasing exclusion of the able-bodied from workhouses in the late eighteenth century, which made capital sense, given the collapse of most workhouse employments, deprived the houses of those most physically able to turn a profit. Finally, we have no adequate indices of the work that *was* done in workhouses. The 1803 returns take no account of private arrangements for employing the poor that did not result in direct profit to the parish. Peculation and inadequate account keeping would erode recorded profits still further. Most important of all, there were hidden returns never accounted for at all, namely the mending and making that went on in workhouses for the benefit of inmates and the employment of inmates in the domestic economy of the workhouse and sometimes in social services, such as schooling, tending the sick and watching the dead, throughout the parish. Most teachers and 'social welfare workers' at that time, it is well to remember, *were* paupers, employed by their parish.

It is British policy today that work for the disabled is desirable even if often unprofitable.[60] The pre-1834 attempts to provide work and to sweeten it, as so often was done, with 'encouragement money', were not invariably unenlightened. To be sure, the management of workhouse schemes was often unimaginative and inefficient. Inmates were often less than ideal employees. No one could claim that the unreformed workhouse was a model of industry, but it was not a total failure. Nanny Barnes, a little girl born and raised in the West Alvington carehouse, knitted stocking after stocking for her fellow inmates in the 1780s. In terms of the profits recorded to the house she might as well have been skipping rope.[61]

What of other aspects of workhouse life? An old lady, living in 1910, had fond memories of the suet puddings served to the inmates of Holy Trinity Parish Workhouse in Cambridge in the early 1830s,[62] and it is not necessary to imagine she was remarkably eccentric in her culinary tastes or that her childhood workhouse was unusually solicitous of inmates' fare or even that her memory had mellowed. Of all aspects of the pre-1834 workhouse, the diet has received least criticism, although it inspired contemporary critical comment for being often more generous than that which independent labourers could afford.[63] Sanitary facilities and medical attention were less impressive, however. Vicar, overseer and vestry clerk of Harrow were in agreement on their own workhouse: 'We have no right to profess to give relief, and in fact to give typhus fever, cholera, vice and ruin to body and soul.'[64] Fevers of various sorts decimated workhouses regularly. Entries in accounts for soap, mouse-traps, mercury, whitewash, medicines, inoculations and doctor's contracts speak of efforts to have cleaner, healthier houses, but with the young and old so often in close proximity, mortality from communicable disease was high, particularly in the large urban workhouses. The most serious problem of in-house relief of the impotent may well have been this.[65] Other aspects of workhouse life are suggested in various records. Workhouse rules and vestry minutes, for example, often indicate that Sunday church attendance was required. This rule, where enforced, provided parishioners with a rough check of the inmates and probably insured inmates of many houses a weekly cleaning and a decent suit of clothes that they might otherwise not have had. Workhouse inventories, found in overseers' accounts and elsewhere, list furnishings, often giving the items by the room. This source tells something of living arrangements, but does not disprove or prove the contemporary criticism that there was an improper segregation of the sexes.[66] Workhouse enrolments sometimes appear in, or can be deduced from, workhouse accounts. Transient factors, such as weather (the winter months saw a swelling of enrolments), curable illness, the securing of an apprenticeship, as well as death, of course, influenced the often rapid turnover in impotent workhouse inmates.

The local records contain evidence to suggest that life within workhouses was not always as grim as one might suppose. Terminology can be taken over-seriously, but the common reference to inmates and governor as 'the family' in itself conveys a different outlook to that of 'inmate' or 'patient'. The care in some houses was lavish.[67] On occasion, inmates found the convenience of workhouse life so attractive that they rejected opportunities to leave even when they clearly no longer had need of the house.[68] Much has been written of the workhouse 'test' that compelled paupers to enter workhouses in order to receive relief, but there was a reverse workhouse 'test' that operated to keep paupers out, namely that parishes liked to have as low a relief bill as possible and workhouse relief was usually far more expensive for ratepayers than outdoor relief; paupers could sometimes make use of this in their requests for additional outdoor relief.[69] Even those houses that undertook to house and work the able-bodied could be pleasant, as C. P. Villiers, hardly a sanguine observer, discovered at Exeter.[70]

There was no golden age of the pre-1834 workhouse, only one long time of experimentation. The concept of workhouse relief was attractive in the eighteenth century, partly because it fitted so neatly with a compelling concern of reformers to enlarge the unit of poor law administration, but the failure of so many schemes, especially the ones involving parochial consolidations, to accomplish the purposes for which they were established made the concept increasingly less attractive as the century drew to a close. The increase in poverty during the French and Napoleonic wars led to expansion in outdoor relief, not because workhouses were full to overflowing in most instances, but because the workhouse appeared to be an inappropriate prescription for the transient results of corn dearths and war-inspired inflation. Outdoor allowances were more practical, geared to the need, to the size of the family and to prices, as with the legendary bread scale of the so-called Speenhamland system. While workhouses continued to function, confining themselves ever more exclusively to care of the impotent, some of the attention of reformers, particularly in the post-war years, was directed to the reform of outdoor relief. The result was that the workhouse, although still a target of critics, enjoyed a slight respite before becoming the panacea of the Poor Law Commissioners in the 1830s.[71]

Outdoor relief was 'the master evil of the present system', according to the Poor Law Commissioners,[72] but they were not sparing in their criticism of the unreformed workhouse, which they found to be inefficient in administration and lax in discipline. The very humanity found in many houses was target for criticism. The Commissioners' conclusion that *reformed* workhouses could reduce pauperism through a workhouse test for the able-bodied influenced their whole evaluation of the unreformed workhouse to far greater degree than the generous but ambiguous evidence published along with the 1834 report.[73] Indeed, perhaps the most striking quality of the report is the gap between the twenty-two recommendations the Commissioners made and the welter of conflicting facts and views upon which the recommendations were purportedly based. With specific reference to workhouses, the only point of general agreement between the report and evidence was the need for greater classification of inmates.[74]

For generations the hope of many reformers had been for a larger unit of poor law administration than the parish; that was recommendation number three in the report. Tabulations of the answers in Rural and Town Queries reveal that less than 16 per cent in the former, and about 25 per cent in the latter, queries favoured any kind of change, be it into smaller or larger units of administration—clearly no mandate for the poor law unions that were to come. It may be suggested that many respondents had a vested interest in the existing parochial structure—although it has often been claimed that overseers did not enjoy their annual stint in parish office, and many respondents were overseers—but the question asked in the queries was scarcely very threatening and gave no hint of compulsory unions to come:

Do you think it would be advisable to afford greater facilities than now exist, either for the Union or for the Subdivision of Parishes or Townships, for any purpose connected with the Management of Parochial Affairs ?[75]

From answers to this and to other queries, one might possibly arrive at the outrageous conclusion that the respondents, on the whole, may have been reasonably satisfied with the way things were *before* the 1834 act.[76]

Not all contemporary comment on the workhouse was harsh. Even Crabbe praised the administration of a large workhouse in one of his poems.[77] Most of the 137 workhouses in Eden's survey escaped criticism and those that did not often were commended but for one or two defects.[78] The 1834 report expatiates on the humanity of pre-1834 workhouse administration, for the whole thrust of their argument was, as one of their witnesses put it, that 'parish poor-houses as at present administered, have the effect of attracting paupers'.[79] This humanity has not escaped all later writers certainly,[80] but the pre-1834 workhouse is commonly thought to have been 'an administrative and social failure'.[81]

But was it ? The workhouse failed, small wonder, to end or reduce, as far as we know, the incidence of poverty. It failed—again, small wonder—to turn a financial profit, except in rare cases, from the work of inmates. The contrast between the ideals of founders and the reality of workhouse administration was often stark. Whatever the original ideal had been, 'the institution', as the Webbs put it, 'was perpetually crumbling back into the General Mixed Workhouse'.[82] Finally, one may presume, the roseate view of the Poor Law Commissioners to the contrary, that the workhouse failed to be a palatable form of relief for most of the poor confined therein. Those who preferred in-house relief, such as an inmate at Kidderminster who declined a wage of 30s a week to remain with his family in comfort in the workhouse,[83] may often have been victims of the sickness of institutionalization, a sickness so often found in mental and penal institutions today, in which the comfort and security of an institution are preferred to the challenge and uncertainty of freedom.

All this conceded, there remains a way in which the unreformed workhouse did not fail—as an institution for relieving precisely those victims of society or their own infirmities who are often at present, wisely or unwisely, institutionalized—the mentally and physically ill, the aged, the unmarried mother, the retarded, the physically handicapped and the orphaned.[84] One may criticize, as contemporaries of that era did, the lack of categorization of inmates in the 'General Mixed Workhouse' but there were limits to what could be done, imposed by the small size of most communities—England was still predominantly rural—the state of transport development—it was the pre-railway age—and the deficiency in contemporary knowledge of the best treatment for the aged, the ill, the handicapped and other disadvantaged persons. Certainly from the standpoint of paupers living at that time an institution near home must have seemed far preferable to a distant one, and a complex categorization of the poor would have resulted in the majority of paupers being placed in institutions far removed from their homes. Given all this, a local facility for the care of those who could not care for themselves made considerable sense. Misery was indeed resident in the pre-1834 workhouse, as it is in our twentieth century equivalents, but the unreformed workhouse, for all of its inadequacies, fulfilled a social need, and may have done so better than has hitherto been suspected.

Notes

1. This essay was assisted in part by a research grant from the College centre of the Finger Lakes.
2. S. & B. Webb, *The Parish and the County* (1906), p. 593. Twenty-one years later, the Webbs had not altered their opinion: 'The over-crowding, insanitation, filth and gross indecency of workhouse life during the whole of the eighteenth, and even for the first thirty or forty years of the nineteenth, century are simply indescribable', *English Poor Law History* (1927), vol. I, p. 248. See also Dorothy Marshall, *The English Poor in the Eighteenth Century* (1926), ch. IV.
3. Mark Blaug, 'The Myth of the Old Poor Law and the Making of the New', *Journal of Economic History*, XXIII (June 1963), p. 157.
4. The Webbs claimed that Crabbe gave a 'terrible description' of the Suffolk incorporated workhouses, *not* of the parish poorhouse, *English Poor Law History*, vol. I, p. 146. Crabbe, in fact, treated both, the former in *The Borough* (1810) and the latter in *The Village* (1783), but it was the description in *The Village* that caught the public imagination. See Crabbe's son's notes in *Poetical Works* (1834), vol. II, pp. 83–5.
5. C. D. Brereton, *An Inquiry into the Workhouse System* (1825?), pp. 123–4.
6. Royal Commission Report; 1834 (44), XXVII, p. 31.
7. The post-1834 union workhouses, sketchily reconsidered by David Roberts in 'How Cruel was the Victorian Poor Law?' *Historical Journal*, VI (1963), pp. 97–107, are also in need of further study.
8. Sydney Smith, *Edinburgh Review*, XXXIII (January 1820), pp. 91–2. As E. Gilboy put it: 'Practically every eighteenth century pamphleteer was trying to prove something; either that parish relief was bad or that it was good; that more workhouses were needed or less', *Wages in Eighteenth Century England* (1934), p. xxi.
9. A. W. Coats in 'Economic Thought and Poor Law Policy in the Eighteenth Century', *Economic History Review*, XIII (1960–61), pp. 39–51, and J. R. Poynter in *Society and Pauperism, English Ideas on Poor Relief, 1795–1834* (1969), make good use of this source.
10. Reports from Committes of House of Commons, IX, 299–539; *Abstract of the Answers and Returns* . . . Accts. & P., 1804 (175), XIII; *Abridgement of the Abstract of the Answers and Returns* . . . Accts. & P., 1818 (82), XIX, respectively.
11. Letter to Poole, 1803 (undated) in H. Sandford, *Thomas Poole and His Friends* (1888), vol. II, p. 110.
12. Letter to Poole, 1803 (23 July), *ibid.*, vol. II, p. 112; and 'Miscellaneous Observations' in 1813–15 *Returns*, p. xi.
13. The imperfections are made clear in 'Remarks upon the Answers returned', in the 1813–15 *Returns*, pp. ix–x. E. M. Hampson, in *The Treatment of Poverty in Cambridgeshire, 1597–1834* (1934), p. 99, finds the returns useful as corroboration of figures derived from parish records,

75

but more often than not there are no parish records available with which to make comparisons.

14. In addition to the parishes and places investigated by the Assistant Commissioners, there were 1,212 replies to Rural Queries and 368 to Town Queries. The number of places selected in each county bears no observable relationship to the proportionate cost of poverty or population or number of poor relieved. Compare, for example, with *Poor Laws*. Select Committee. (Lords); 1831 (227), VIII, 248.

15. *The Justice of the Peace and Parish Officer*, 5 vols. There were thirty editions between first compilation in 1755 and the last in 1869.

16. Poynter, in the previously mentioned work, for example, makes no reference to local records. It would be absurd to suggest that ideas on poor relief cannot be found sometimes explicitly stated in vestry meeting minutes and implicitly in overseers' accounts, to name only two sorts of records, but the bulk and location of this material provides justification for ignoring them. This is not intended as criticism of an excellent work, but as a comment on the convenient convention that local records are only really essential to local history.

17. My doctoral dissertation was concerned with poverty in Devon; in addition to some of the records of that county, I have very brief acquaintance with some material in the county record offices of Cambridge, Lincoln, The North Riding of Yorkshire, Cumberland, Westmorland, Lancashire, Shropshire and Wiltshire.

18. 39 Elizabeth c. 5, & 43 Elizabeth c. 2.

19. W. K. Jordan, *Philanthropy in England* (1959), p. 271, states that little charitable wealth was given for this purpose before 1660.

20. 9 George I c. 7.

21. This method of dissemination is suggested by distribution patterns observed in the 1776 *Returns*.

22. Lack of significant increases in the number of parishes using workhouses and the number of workhouse inmates between 1803 and 1813–15 are indicative of this.

23. Asst. Comm. Reps., XXIX, 1. However, some of the Assistant Commissioners distinguished 'workhouse' from 'poorhouse' on the basis of whether or not work was provided.

24. The Webbs found 'hospital', 'abiding house', 'poor house', 'workhouse', 'house of industry', 'house of maintenance', 'house of protection', and 'bettering house'; see *Poor Law History*, vol. I, p. 220. L.F.C. Pack states that 'workhouse', 'workshop' and 'shop' were used interchangeably in Winchester, in 'A Study of the Evolution of the Methods of Poor Relief in the Winchester Area, 1720–1845' (M.A. Thesis, Univ. of Southampton, 1968), pp. 199–200. In the Devon parish of West Alvington 'carehouse', 'poorhouse' and 'workhouse' were used by the same man in reference to the same house in the parish accounts, see Dev. Rec. Off., 818A/PO4. J. H. Clapham, in *The Early Railway Age* (1930), p. 356, claims 'workhouse' *meant* work in the 1776 *Returns*, yet the number of respondents who returned capacity figures as low as five

strongly suggests that many respondents made returns for nothing more than poor cottages.

25. The most frequent range was between twenty and thirty inmates. Houses with a capacity less than ten numbered 152: only 174 houses had capacities over a hundred. Less than half of the houses could hold more than forty inmates. The evidence in Town Queries, XXXV, Query 15, suggests that relatively few towns even in the 1830's had houses with enrolments over a hundred.

26. For houses under local acts in 1772–74, see the detailed returns in Reports from Committees of House of Commons, IX, 247–87

27. It is interesting that there are 13 per cent fewer houses in the actual tables in the 1803 Returns than appear in the county summaries: the totals in the summary for all of England and Wales were taken from the county summaries. It is possible the tables indicate number of houses while the summaries indicate number of parishes and places using houses. If this guess is correct and if houses under local acts are excluded, as was done in the 1776 Returns, then the increase in houses given in the returns between 1776 and 1803 was approximately 22 per cent.

28. The following comparison is suggestive.

Percentage of houses under ten inmates in Kent—Oxfordshire—Lancashire

1776 (capacity	7	4	2
1803 (enrolment)	38	8	64
1813–15 (enrolment)	33	16	33

Of course, capacity cannot be equated with enrolment, but even so it seems probable that more smaller houses were being included in the later returns. However, these counties may not be representative.

29. In Kent, Oxfordshire and Lancashire most houses that appear in the 1776 Returns and in the later returns did not have enrolments in 1803 or 1813–15 equalling their given capacity in 1776. This takes no account of building additions or new buildings, which, if known, would probably give further support to the conjecture that most workhouses were not overcrowded in the early nineteenth century. Again, these counties may not be representative.

30. Poynter, p. 190, believes the contemporary impact of the returns was slight. The obvious guess is that recovery from the 1799–1800 dearth led to a relative reduction of interest in the operation of the poor law.

31. Blaug, pp. 178–9, indicates that relief per head in 'Speenhamland' counties in 1803 was approximately one third higher than in 'non-Speenhamland' counties. While his division of counties is questionable in itself—see my 'Mythology of the Old Poor Law', Journal of Economic History, XXIX (June 1969), p. 295—it is of interest that the cost of workhouse relief was also approximately one third higher in Blaug's 'Speenhamland' counties.

32. This proportion is based on the exclusion of children, vagrants and occasional recipients. The percentage relieved in workhouses of those

receiving permanent relief was 21 in 1803 and 18 in 1813–15, as calculated from the 1803 *Returns*, p. 715, and the 1813–15 *Returns*, p. 629.

33. Poynter, p. 15, for example, states that 'by 1815 some 4,000 actual workhouses where there was a regular dietary, some control, and authority in the form of a master or matron' existed. This is to put far too much faith in the numbers provided in the 1813–15 *Returns*.

34. The 1803 *Returns* provide the most comprehensive survey of poverty under the pre-1834 poor law ever undertaken by Parliament. The Webbs, for all their research, make no direct use of this source, although they were aware that it existed; see *Poor Law History*, vol. I, p. 233.

35. 1788 (18 May), Scruton Vestry Minutes, North Riding (Yorks.) Rec. Off.

36. Stockland in Dorset would give six shillings a month outdoor relief in 1796 and more in cases of sickness or misfortune: the workhouse awaited those who needed regular monthly pay in excess of that sum. The 'test' in Hartland in Devon in 1809 was less humane—sixpence a week outdoor relief or the workhouse. Stockland and Hartland Overseers' Accounts, Dev. Rec. Off., 1215A/PO6 and unlisted, respectively. Sometimes a happy blending proved convenient: Joseph Bankes was given permission in 1799 to live without but take his dinner in the workhouse. Drayton Vestry Order Book, Shropshire Rec. Off., 121/65.

37. Even large institutions under local acts that were designed to include the able-boded often provided even more relief to the impotent. See the 1772–74 *Returns* in Reports from Committees of House of Commons, IX, pp. 252–87.

38. XXXV, queries 15–23. The two were Bristol and Kenwyn, Cornwall. The able-bodied were increasingly relieved outdoors in the late eighteenth century, a trend Thomas Gilbert's influence may have furthered. Eden found few houses providing relief to the able-bodied, as did the Assistant Commissioners a generation later. Indoor relief of the able-bodied was associated with the aim of making the workhouse a deterrent, the chief virtue of workhouses to contemporaries, according to Marshall, *op. cit.*, p. 150. But for those administering the law, deterrence of the able-bodied through the workhouse 'test' was an ideal only fitfully achieved, if at all, and achieved best in that uncommon place, the large institution under an efficient disciplinarian. This is not to question the distaste of the poor for workhouses, but to suggest also the distaste of local authorities for taking the trouble and added expense of incarcerating the poor, particularly the able-bodied, if outdoor relief were cheaper.

39. *Serious considerations on the salutary design of the act of Parliament for a regular, uniform register of the parish-poor* (1762), p. 10. For improvements made, see Reports from Committees of House of Commons, IX, pp. 541–2.

40. See Hartland Overseers' Accounts, 1801–10. Devon Rec. Off., unlisted.

41. Eden noted that most workhouse earnings came from children (*op. cit.*, vol. II, p. 537). The records seldom say enough. At Easter, 1801,

Mary Daley was kept from her four children who were then being worked by John Pattinson in the Wigton workhouse. Her appeal to Quarter Sessions was quashed. But why? Qtr. Sess. Rolls, Petitions, Q/11, Cumb. & Westmor. Joint Archives Committee.

42. Apprenticeships to local farmers or tradesmen were common; so too were apprenticeships to manufacturers. Sometimes the master was from another locality and it was this sort of apprenticeship that offered greatest opportunity for exploitation.

43. The Webbs believed the few private asylums existing before 1834 were probably better for pauper lunatics than incarceration in workhouses; see *Poor Law History*, vol. I, p. 301. However, relief in small institutions near home in the company of fellow societal victims of sound mind may well have constituted superior therapy to that of private asylums. The mentally retarded—'idiot' was the contemporary term—probably were treated more humanely in local workhouses than in many of the institutions that now receive them. For a picture of current inadequate institutionalization of the mentally retarded, see Pauline Morris, *Put Away* (1969).

44. According to Burn, *op. cit.*, vol. IV, pp. 548–9, a workhouse governor obtained a settlement if it was recognized that his position was a public annual office. The frequency of settlement cases hinging on this point suggests the frequency of near-pauper appointments.

45. George III c. 12 facilitated appointment of assistant overseers, but the existence of professional parish officers long antedated that act. A frequent combination office was overseer and workhouse governor.

46. Eden believed success in large houses depended primarily on 'a governor and matron who know how to blend firmness with humanity...'. It was not always easy to find such servants, particularly for the smaller houses. George Body, in 'The Administration of the Poor Law in Dorset, 1760–1834' (Ph.D. thesis, University of Southampton, 1964), p. 186, concludes that the workhouses in his county 'were seldom well run and most of them experienced frequent changes of management'.

47. Workhouse farming may have been usual in the larger houses in 1772–4, but it is not known whether most small workhouses were also farmed at that time; see Reports from Committees of House of Commons, IX, pp. 252–87.

48. The 1803 *Returns* state that only 293 out of 14,611 parishes and places responding farmed their poor, and there is no reason to suppose in this case that the returns are particularly inaccurate. Eden found it had been practised, was being practised or was about to be attempted in 40 of the 181 places in which the topic of farming arose. He also mentions instances of the troubles contractors were undergoing at the time of his survey; vol. II, p. 168; vol. III, pp. 808, 902–3. Some contracting survived on a 'Speenhamland' basis, the price per inmate being determined by fluctuations in prices. Examples are Wroughton, Wiltshire, in 1798 (Qtr. Sess. Rec., Corn Dearth, 1795–1801, Wilts. Rec. Off.) and Bassingbourne, Cambridgeshire, in 1809 (Bassingbourne Accounts,

Camb. Rec. Off., PII/12/2). This evidence creates a different impression to the extended treatment of contracting in the Webbs' *Poor Law History*, vol. I, pp. 277, 289–90, where workhouse contracting was assumed to have been ubiquitous from 1723 to 1834.

49. However, of those responding to Town Queries, well over half did not farm the poor; of those that did, many farmed only children, refractory poor, lunatics or some other special group. Farming apparently was common in London and Middlesex in the 1830s. To the extent that it took children to the country, it no doubt was an improvement over conditions in metropolitan workhouses; to the extent that it provided means for workhouse governors to rid themselves of their most un-disciplined inmates, it may have improved the tone of some workhouses as well as given scope for tyranny in others. Farming, although not farming of special categories of the poor, appears to have had a bad reputation by the 1830's. The Shoreditch workhouse governor referred to it as letting 'the bellies of all the Poor wholesale'. Farming sometimes meant oblivion, as in St Mary the Virgin, Aldermanbury, no check being made on treatment provided. This was not always the case: the quality of farming for the parish of St Stephen Walbrook was reported to be good, 'grounded upon personal observation' of churchwarden and over-seer.

50. Contracting was not always done blindly. Even in the comparatively harshly administered parish of Hartland, the contractor in 1805 was required to provide specific kinds and quantities of food, in addition to other enumerated services. Hartland Overseers' Accounts, Devon Rec. Off., unlisted.

51. Workhouse rules, as workhouse contracts, were no more than state-ments of intention, of course, and no doubt in some cases were patterned after a neighbouring institution or after a well-known house, with little thought to the precise applicability of every rule to the local circumstance. The considerable similarity among workhouse rules also resulted from legal restraints and the parallel purposes of institutions. Crude mono-tonous diets and long hours of work, which were often established in rules, probably in most instances represented no harsher regimen than that endured by the poor in general. However, restrictions on un-sanctioned travel away from the workhouse are the sort of rules that must have occasioned most discontent. For the hell a governor might be asked to live, see papers relating to the Tavistock Workhouse (mid-eighteenth century) in Bedford Muniments, Devon Rec. Off., L1258, among Vouchers 3/1. [I owe this reference to Mr R. L. Taverner.]

52. Elie Halévy, for example, believed magistrates had come to admini-ster the poor law themselves, 'whilst the overseers became reduced to the status of mere rate collectors', *England in 1815* (1961), pp. 378–9. Some respondents given in the above table held more than one office—magistrate and clergyman, overseer and churchwarden and even one case in Berkshire of magistrate and overseer. In these cases the respondent was placed in the first category to which he would belong in the above

table. *All* respondents were included, 1,470 to Rural Queries and 581 to Town Queries. As there were only 1,212 queries in the former and 368 in the latter, it is clear there were a number of cases in which two men responded in the same return. Most common examples of dual respondents were two overseers in Rural Queries and an overseer and vestry clerk in Town Queries; in consequence, the percentages for these positions in the table above in terms of *places* are slightly inflated. The positions given above were simplified: parish clerk is given as vestry clerk, permanent overseer as assistant overseer and so forth. Finally, in the last category the word 'other' stands for the few who indicated positions numerically insignificant in the queries—farmer, ratepayer, select vestryman, mayor, guardian and the like.

53. Venality may have existed in West Alvington in Devon in the late eighteenth century as there is a direct correlation between the men who approved the account books and the suppliers of food to the workhouse. Devon Rec. Off., 818A/PO2. The administration of this house under a professional parish officer appears to have been remarkably efficient and humane. Cooked books could be at the expense of ratepayers as well as inmates.

54. Eden, vol. III, pp. 806–7.

55. The 1811 Census, p. xxix, provides the 'Acting County Magistrates' for each county. English counties with more than one magistrate per 2,000 inhabitants were Berkshire, Buckingham, Essex, Hereford and Rutland. Twenty-five counties fell within the range of one magistrate for every 2,000 to 4,000 inhabitants. Counties with a proportion greater than that were Chester, Derby, Lancaster, Leicester, Lincoln, Middlesex, Northumberland, Stafford, Warwick, Worcester and the East and North Ridings of Yorkshire. Northern England, then, even in proportion to population, was less well served in 1811 than the southern counties.

56. 30 George III c. 49, gave magistrates greater powers of inspection, emergency powers in granting relief and facilitated the certification of complaints against overseers or workhouse governors at Quarter Sessions. 36 George III c. 23 gave magistrates power to order parishes to pay outdoor relief even when the workhouse was available, although within certain temporal restrictions. Magistrates already had this power in the few Gilbert Unions that had been established under 22 George III c. 83.

57. This question is number 48 Town Queries and number 45, 3rd issue, in Rural Queries.

58. See pp. 66–84 in the *Report*. There were some respondents who were most unhappy with magistrates, such as the respondents from York. Asst. Comm. Rep., XXVIII, pp. 872–3.

59. Few workhouses were successful in the early eighteenth century—financial success was always very rare—but there was more opportunity for some profitable employment. For occupations pursued in houses on the eve of industrialism, see W. Bailey, *A Treatise on the Better Employment and More Comfortable Support of the Poor in Workhouses* (1758) and Reports from Committees of House of Commons, IX, pp. 252–87. Of

the many occupations listed at that time only picking oakum, agricultural work, pin-making and some weaving were mentioned with any frequency in Town Queries in 1834.

60. Remploy Limited, assisted by the British government, employs the severely disabled. It has been operating for the past twenty-five years, averaging a loss of £500 per employee a year, according to *The Economist*, 17 January 1970, p. 61.

61. In-house accounts. Devon Rec. Off., 818A/PO2. 'In estimating the work of the old overseers,' C. R. Oldham wrote, 'too much attention has been directed to their misuse of the allowance, and too little to their constant efforts to put the poor to work, and so do their duty by the Elizabethan poor law,' in 'Oxfordshire Poor Law Papers', *Economic History Review*, V, 1 (1934), p. 97. The work done in workhouses also deserves kinder scrutiny than it has hitherto received.

62. The Rev. Dr Stokes, 'Cambridge Parish Workhouses', *Cambridge Antiquarian Society Proceedings*, XV (1910–11), p. 123.

63. Meat (beef, pork, mutton) appears to have been in weekly workhouse diets to an extent exceeding the diet most independent labourers could afford. According to N. Mitchelson, in *The Old Poor Law in East Yorkshire* (1953), pp. 14–15, green vegetables were in short supply. This deficiency was made up in many instances from workhouse gardens, while entries in overseers' accounts and established dietaries may often have indicated only food provided by purchase.

64. Town Queries, XXXVI, p. 101.

65. Eden found fevers raging in the workhouses of Manchester, Nottingham and North Shields at the time of his visits. His mention of child mortality in workhouses in Preston and Heckingham, Suffolk are also indication of the seriousness of this problem. A popular and widely practised panacea was whitewashing, one of the devices which The Society for Bettering the Condition of the Poor, in *Information for Overseers* (1799), attempted to propagate.

66. Information in Town Queries suggest that daytime segregation was not usual, but there is no question that separate sleeping quarters were standard, although a few houses did not separate married couples. A problem that escaped much contemporary attention was the conduciveness to homosexuality in having members of the same sex sharing beds. See XXXV, query 19, particularly the slightly suggestive return from Brighton, p. 228!

67. E. Melling, editor of *Kentish Sources*, IV 'The Poor' (1964), pp. 100–1, writes, to take an early eighteenth century example, of a case in Dartford workhouse. 'In April 1742 when Mrs String was ill she asked for fresh meat, so mutton broth and part of a loin of mutton was provided. She did not like either so more broth and mutton was given her cooked according to her own instructions but she was still not satisfied. A suggestion that she be given invalid food brought the answer that she did not like slops and the report ends with the statement that she seemed

hard to please.' The Assistant Commissioners almost a century later found numerous instances of lavish care.

68. An able-bodied resident in the Bishopsnympton workhouse in Devon in 1834 employed outside at full wages could not be prevailed upon to vacate without a court order. *Woolmer's Gazette* (12 April), p. 3, cl. 3.

69. This appears to have been the case in Lynn, Norfolk, according to Asst. Comm. Rep., XXVIII, p. 596.

70. Asst. Comm. Rep., XXIX, p. 3.

71. Poynter provides a useful discussion of the shifting emphases in poor law reform from 1795 to 1834.

72. Royal Comm. Rep., XXVII, p. 156.

73. D. Roberts, in *Victorian Origins of the British Welfare State* (1960), p. 41, states that the facts reported were 'selective'. There is some truth to this in the case of the Assistant Commissioners' Reports, due to the nature of the original instructions they received (XXVII, p. 249), but it is less true of the Rural and Town Queries. The selectivity lay not so much in the evidence itself as in the slanting of the questions local respondents were asked and the evidence upon which the Commissioners chose to rely.

74. Royal Comm. Rep., XXVII, p. 172. Query 23 in Town Queries, XXXV, enabled respondents to make recommendations with regard to workhouses, an opportunity that most forewent. Of those answering, the most frequent points were that workhouse authorities needed more power to punish refractory inmates, inmates needed to be given more work and there should be a clearer classification of inmates by sex, character and age.

75. Rural Queries, XXXIV, query 52; Town Queries, XXXV, query 14. The above percentages are based on the number of respondents, not the number of returns. In Rural Queries, 24 per cent favoured no change and 60 per cent either did not answer or expressed mixed feelings. In Town Queries, 40 per cent opposed change and 26 per cent had no answer or mixed feelings. Unions were most favoured in the Home Counties, particularly Essex.

76. Roberts believes parishes failed to 'stem the tide of pauperism' so that a central board of control, as was to be established with the Poor Law Amendment Act, had come to be a necessity (p. 39), but there is no clear evidence that pauperism *was* increasing in the early 1830s; indeed, parliamentary returns for twenty years preceding the 1834 Act indicate no radical increase in the cost of poverty in spite of increase in population. Of course the *cost* of poverty is a very crude barometer to the *extent* of poverty and many aspects, particularly retail price fluctuations, would have to be considered before one could accept or reject the claim of increasing pauperism. Nevertheless, it seems more correct to speak of a 'tide or reform' than a 'tide of pauperism' in this era.

77. Crabbe concedes comfortable and decent accommodations and even sympathetic administrators. The inmates 'have no evil in the place to

state, And dare not say it is the house they hate'. *The Borough*, Lettei XVIII, vol. III, p. 288.

78. The defects mentioned—and many of the houses were guilty of more than one—were: 12 houses awkwardly planned, usually because they had not been originally designed as workhouses; 11 without a stated dietary; 8 with inadequate ventilation; 7 lacking in cleanliness; 5 over-crowded; 5 infested with vermin; 4 improperly administered; and 1 had an improper classification of inmates. Criticism was scattered fairly evenly about the kingdom, with the workhouses of Bristol, Norwich, Nottingham, Oxford and Wolverhampton coming off most badly.

79. Royal Comm. Rep., XXVII, p. 30.

80. Melling, pp. xiv–xv, 78; F. G. Emmison, 'The Relief of the Poor at Eaton Socon, 1796–1834', *Bedfordshire Historical Record Society*, XV (1933), p. 30; Clapham, p. 358.

81. Poynter, p. 14.

82. *Poor Law History*, vol. I, p. 416.

83. Asst. Comm. Rep., XXIX, p. 3.

84. B. and D. Braginsky and K. Ring write of the American experience, but it can perhaps as easily apply to the British: 'What has changed is our system of classification; the social situation of the residents of our public institutions, such as mental hospitals, has remained remarkably constant. Our present-day "mental patients" are only the societal descendants of the nineteenth-century poor.' *Methods of Madness: The Mental Hospital as a Last Resort* (1969), p. 169.

4
Speenhamland in Berkshire

MARK NEUMAN

Certain moments in the history of England, of no great majesty
in their own right, have been lifted out of time to serve as titles
for complicated developments which might otherwise elude a
label. At best these titles are beacons, inviting historians to explore
the developments they signify and illuminate. Too often they are
totems; their significance is taken on faith alone. The word
'Speenhamland' may be such a totem, and it is my intention to
examine its long history and to suggest what the word might truly
mean, at least in respect to the county of its origin.[1]

The events which occurred on 6 May 1795, at the Pelican Inn
in Speenhamland[2] near Newbury, Berkshire, are well known.
Nevertheless, given the intentions of this paper, it may do to
review them once again, along with certain associated developments.

In 1794 England's harvest of wheat, the staple grain of nearly
everyone's diet in the midlands and south, was insufficient. This
insufficiency alone would have excited alarm (the crop was one-
fifth below the average of the 1790s) but circumstances soon
conspired to make matters bleaker than they might otherwise
have been. The winter of 1794–5 was terribly severe. A frost hit
the growing crop in December and lasted until March, when it
was clear that the coming harvest could not restore the already
short supply. Further, imports could not quickly close the gap;
the hard winter kept the Baltic frozen into the spring and consequently shipments from Poland and southern Prussia, where the
1794 crop had been plentiful, were delayed. For a time a Prussian
embargo on corn exports added to the general concern, although
this was later lifted. Beyond these particular developments was

85

the fact that England was at war with revolutionary France, whose naval vessels delighted in seizing supplies bound for English ports.[3] The presence of a revolutionary government across the Channel points to another matter troubling the minds of many Englishmen at this time; namely, the possibility that labouring people, faced with scarcities, high prices and discomfort, would be seduced by Jacobin doctrines and turn furiously on their betters. Countless loyal addresses and resolutions, charges to grand juries, and letters to newspaper editors attest to widespread concern on this account even before the short harvest of 1794, and indeed before the declaration of war.[4]

In Berkshire as elsewhere, present scarcities and the prospect of future ones meant high prices for wheat and bread. In September 1794 wheat had brought no more than 53s a quarter at Reading; by late March 1795 it was bringing 71s a quarter at Windsor and there was every indication the price would continue to rise.[5] It was in these circumstances that the county Easter Quarter Sessions, under the chairmanship of Charles Dundas, earnestly addressed itself to the threatened condition of the labouring poor.

In January 1795 the Epiphany Sessions had been content to urge that individual justices, clergymen and parish overseers pay special attention to the poor in these difficult times, and that private subscriptions be established to prevent normally independent persons from having to seek parish relief.[6] Now, in the worsening conditions of April, Charles Dundas and the Easter Sessions turned to the question of labourers' wages, and how these might be made sufficient when the price of wheat was perhaps 70s a quarter. Speaking to the county Grand Jury, Dundas described the present difficult situation of working people, and how even a modest increase in their wages, to bring them into line with the higher cost of bread, might free many persons from their dependence on the parish. To this end, observed the chairman, he was addressing the jurymen as those 'grave and discreet persons' whom, according to the statute 5 Elizabeth c. 4, the Sessions might

call unto them . . . to limit, rate, and appoint the wages as well of such . . . whose wages in times past have been by any law or statute rated and appointed, as also the wages of all other labourers, artificers, workmen, or apprentices of husbandry, which have not been rated.

Although the complicated matter of regulating wages in Berkshire could not be attended to at this already fully-booked Sessions, the court agreed that the justices would meet at the Pelican Inn, Speenhamland, on 6 May 'for the purpose of consulting together with such discreet persons as they shall think meet', and to establish rates of wages for day labourers.[7]

It was the justices' intention, then, to meet specifically to set wages pursuant to 5 Elizabeth c. 4. Why those who gathered at the Pelican Inn on that date rejected by a large majority a plan to rate wages, and instead adopted an elaborate bread scale for allowances *in aid of wages*, will never be entirely brought to light; no formal records of the meeting remain. However, some few facts respecting the Speenhamland discussions are known, and others can be inferred. According to Frederick Page of Newbury, who may have been one of the 'discreet persons' in attendance, those who spoke in favour of fixed wages rested their case upon a single argument.

> Some encouragement would have been held out to the labourer, as what he would have received, would have been payment for labour. He would have considered it as his right, and not as charity, and the spirit of independence, now almost extinct, would have been preserved and cherished.[8]

The chief opponent of fixed wages may have been the Reverend Edward Wilson, county magistrate, canon of Windsor and rector of Binfield parish.[9] In October 1795 Wilson published his *Observations on the Present State of the Poor and Measures Proposed for Its Improvement*, the substance of which he had put forward at the Speenhamland meeting. In this document, Wilson revealed himself to be a stern exponent of *laissez-faire*, quoting Adam Smith to the effect that 'Experience shews that the law can never properly regulate wages', and going on to observe that

> Labour, like everything else brought to market, has in all ages found its own level, without the interference of law, and cannot

87

fail of effecting the same purpose in all future times, with sufficient advantage to itself, and the least danger of interrupting the peace of society.[10]

It has been suggested that despite Wilson's affection for Smith's notions he may have been the original proponent of the bread scale which the justices ultimately adopted.[11] This is unlikely; although he appended to his treatise a table of relief for poor families, he used in his calculations borrowed figures which he had earlier sought to discredit, and his recommended levels of relief were below those fixed upon at Speenhamland. Accordingly, his proposed scale may have been a hurried attempt to soften the effects of the scheme his fellow justices had adopted in spite of his reservations. A remedy for distress Wilson did most enthusiastically advance was the foundation in every parish of a 'Provident Parochial Bank' under the direction of the parish officers, who were to encourage labourers' participation by the paying of interest.

In any case, the Speenhamland magistrates, after deciding against fixed wages and rejecting one proposed table of allowances in aid of wages, resolved upon a less generous scale which provided that when the gallon loaf of wheaten second bread cost one shilling

> every Poor and Industrious Man shall have for his own Support 3s weekly, either produced by his own or his Family's Labour, or an Allowance from the poor Rates, and for the Support of his Wife and every other of his Family, 1s 6d. When the Gallon Loaf shall cost 1s 4d then every Poor and industrious Man shall have 4s Weekly for his own, and 1s and 10d for the Support of every other of his Family. And so on in proportion as the price of Bread rises or falls.

It was calculated that every man would receive a sum equal to two gallon loaves per week, plus a shilling or so for other food purchases. The allowances to other persons varied somewhat with the price of bread; a man's dependents were each to receive one and a quarter to one and a half loaves, and a single woman one and a half to two. The magistrates unanimously resolved they would adhere to these calculations in their own divisions.[12]

The Speenhamland justices regarded the bread scale as their most important accomplishment,[13] but they put forward a

number of supplementary recommendations. They urged that
farmers and others throughout the county raise their labourers'
wages to offset the higher price of bread. They suggested that the
overseers of every parish set aside a few acres for the raising of
potatoes by industrious poor persons, who would be allowed to
keep one-third or one-quarter of the crop while the remainder
was sold to other needy poor at one shilling a bushel.[14] Overseers
were also urged to collect stocks of fuel in the summer, for sale at
a low price to the poor in wintertime. Although these measures
were framed as recommendations only, it was made clear to parish
officers that the magistrates' good will and cooperation depended
on their compliance. 'In those parishes which may adopt these
precautions; the magistrates will, in making allowance for relief,
and punishing persons stealing wood, take these circumstances
into consideration, and give them their due weight.' Offering a
carrot as well as a stick, the justices requested the county Agricultural Society to consider giving premiums to those overseers
who most carefully followed their recommendations.[15]

The core of the Speenhamland justices' accomplishments, the
scale of allowances in aid of wages, did not quickly attract the
fame it was later to possess. There was, after all, no particular
reason why it should have. In the first place, the giving of monetary
allowances to the able-bodied was hardly an innovation at
Speenhamland. It is a commonplace of poor law history that,
whatever the intentions of the Elizabethan statutes which remained
the basis of the poor law until 1834,[16] individual parishes had
given these allowances for many years, particularly to labourers
overburdened with children. The Webbs noted the existence of
this practice at Colchester even from the time of the great 1601
statute itself, and E. M. Hampson found evidence of it in
Cambridgeshire soon afterwards. The early and middle years of
the eighteenth century witnessed an extension of such out-relief,
and in the last quarter of the century, owing partly to the example
of Gilbert's Act, these allowances were further extended and
regularized.[17] In the second place, the Berkshire justices' decision
to promote a uniform, county-wide, scale of relief for the able-
bodied was not an unusual one in the troubled year 1795. Other

Quarter Sessions, confronted with shortages, high prices and the possibility of Jacobin-inspired tumults, adopted similar though sometimes less elaborate schemes, in some cases before the Speenhamland decision in May. Indeed, the magistrates of Dorset passed a resolution as early as November 1792 which encompassed within its broad perimeter the principle of the Speenhamland plan. In the still more distant past was a scale for supplementing wages fashioned by the justices in the neighbourhood of Whittlesford, Cambridgeshire; this in 1782.[18]

Given these developments it is not surprising that the early notice of the Speenhamland meeting which appeared in Arthur Young's *Annals of Agriculture* was quite brief; more attention was paid to the Suffolk justices' efforts at wage regulation.[19] The first detailed account seen outside Berkshire of the results of Speenhamland was the communication by Frederick Page to his friend Frederick Morton Eden, which appeared verbatim in the latter's *The State of the Poor*.[20] After this notice the Speenhamland meeting was hardly mentioned in the literature of poor relief for decades, even in the years after Waterloo when the practice of giving allowances to the able-bodied came under sustained attack from almost every shade of opinion. James Ebenezer Bicheno's reproduction of the Speenhamland bread scale (that 'curious and preposterous document') in his *Inquiry into the Nature of Benevolence* (1817) was an exceptional reference to a largely forgotten event; perhaps it related to Bicheno's being a native of Newbury, where the meeting may have had a local fame.[21] Even so, Page, also of that place, who had written Eden his opinion of the Speenhamland bread scale soon after its creation, made no mention of it in his *Principle of the English Poor Laws Illustrated and Defended* (1822) although his subject in the last section of the treatise was the necessity, when giving relief, of discriminating between the 'able-bodied man willing to work and unable to procure it, and the able-bodied man unwilling to work although able to procure it'. His omission of any reference to the 1795 decision is all the more striking because he cited the parish of Speen, with its tithing Speenhamland, as a recent successful example of such discrimination.[22] The word 'Speenhamland' does not appear in the 1824 report of the House of Commons Select Committee on Labourers' Wages, although the chief intention of the report was to condemn the practice of allowances to the able-bodied.[23]

The first important notice of the Speenhamland bread scale since that recorded in Eden's *State of the Poor* is to be found in the report of the Poor Law Inquiry Commissioners, printed in 1834. The Commissioners, determined to secure the abolition of out-relief in favour of the workhouse and 'less eligibility', traced the noxious practice of allowances in aid of wages back to 1795, and referred to Eden's account of the Berkshire proceedings. However, the Commissioners appear to have used Eden's account to point up the sorts of measures being adopted in various places at the end of the eighteenth century; they did not declare the Speenhamland bread scale to have been the specific origin, or even the epitome, of a widespread practice.[24] This was not true of Sir George Nicholls, the noted poor law administrator and reformer, and author of *A History of the English Poor Law* (1854). Like the Poor Law Inquiry Commissioners, Nicholls was a determined opponent of allowances for the able-bodied.[25] Unlike the Commissioners, however, Nicholls pointed to the Speenhamland meeting as the genesis of systematic allowances in aid of wages. He spoke of the Speenhamland bread scale as 'famous', observed that 'it was extensively adopted in other counties', and emphasized his concern for it by citing, not the version of the meeting which appeared in Eden's *State of the Poor*, but the even more detailed account published in the *Reading Mercury*.[26]

Ever since Nicholls first used the word Speenhamland as a synonym for systematic out-relief to the able-bodied, its suitability as a title, and symbol, for that practice has remained unchallenged, at least until very recently. Before the turn of the present century, when assessments of the industrial revolution were being formulated by Arnold Toynbee and William Cunningham, Speenhamland was put to service to describe a profoundly influential, indeed traumatic, event, after which the character of English social and economic life was never the same.[27] Some years later, when the Hammonds turned their acute and sympathetic minds to the deteriorating circumstances of English countrymen in the decades before the first Reform Bill, the Speenhamland meeting was made the central event of that tragic story—and so it remained for commentators of every historical persuasion, whether or not they recognized its antecedents and parallels.[28]

In his comments to Eden regarding the Speenhamland bread scale, Frederick Page complained of the 'fatal tendency of the system'. It offered relief beyond the real needs of the poor, was unequal in its effects on employers, and reduced the amount of work actually undertaken.[29] This early assault set the tone for generations of critics of Speenhamland, when the word had come to stand for systematic money allowances to the able-bodied. Nicholls, in great measure responsible for that connotation of Speenhamland, condemned the Berkshire resolution as 'contrary to the behest of Providence', an unnatural interference with the forces of an ideally free, unregulated, economy.[30] In his *Lectures on the Industrial Revolution in England*, Toynbee echoed earlier critics of allowances in general when remarking on the particular influence of Speenhamland; it seduced labourers into laziness and insolence, and indeed the entire character of English working people was corrupted by their having a right to relief without work.[31] The Hammonds, too, emphasized the effect of Speenhamland on the attitudes of labouring people, particularly after the end of the French wars when in many places agricultural prosperity gave way to depression. The Hammonds' powerful sympathies lay entirely with the rural poor, who they claimed were altogether demoralized by the wicked Speenhamland system. They lamented that owing to Speenhamland there was no reason for the working man to keep his pride or ambition; he was condemned to a barely adequate income whatever he did. In fact, observed the Hammonds, Speenhamland actively punished incentive and the property it might bring; a man with possessions would probably be refused parish relief and work. With no hopes for an independent livelihood, compelled to witness the deterioration of their own circumstances and very character, increasingly isolated from the corporate village world which for centuries had been the source of both their security and pleasure, the only recourse remaining to the rural poor was futile violence. The 'Captain Swing' riots of 1830 were the result.[32] J. H. Clapham, always the 'realistic' economist rather than the mourner, concluded that Speenhamland, by depressing the weekly money wage, augmented the post-war burden of poor relief and brought ruin to yeomen and small cottagers everywhere.[33] Karl Polanyi, in his individual version of the development of the modern market economy, pointed to Speenhamland as the single great cause of the labourer's enslavement between 1795 and the new poor law of 1834, years when only a genuine labour market and concomitant working class could have enabled that person to cope.[34]

Whatever, therefore, these authors' convictions may have been on other matters, on one particular they all agreed: Speenhamland was a bad business. The ingredients of this consensus were forcefully presented long ago by Lord Ernle in his still useful *English Farming Past and Present*. It would do, in the way of a summary of this point of view, to cite his opinions here.

It was Ernle's belief that even before 1814 and the end of the farming community's wartime prosperity, Speenhamland allowances had 'delayed the natural rise of wages, lowered earnings by making the needs of unmarried men the most important factor, and encouraged improvident marriages'. Afterwards, when Speenhamland became the chief mechanism of poor relief, its effects were more general and far worse. Ernle writes:

It enabled (the farmer) to reduce wages to the lowest possible point, because it made good the deficiency out of allowances from the rates. . . . It also provided him with an inexhaustible supply of cheap and temporary labour. Bound to defray the whole cost of maintaining the able-bodied poor, the parish gladly accepted any payment, however small, in part relief of their liability. It became almost impossible for a farmer to keep a man in permanent employment at reasonable wages. If he did, he was only saving the rates for neighbours, who put their hands into his pockets to pay their labour bills . . . Against the mass of subsidized labour, free labourers could not hope to compete. It was so cheap that men who tried to retain their independence were undersold. Those who had saved money or bought a cottage, could not be placed on the poor-book; they were obliged to strip themselves bare, and become paupers, before they could get employment . . . In the most practical fashion, labourers were taught the lessons that improvidence paid better than thrift; that their rewards did not depend on their own exertions; that sobriety and efficiency had no special value

93

above indolence and vice. All alike had the same right to be maintained at the ratepayer's cost. Prudence and self-restraint were penalized. The careful were unemployed, the careless supported by the parish; the more recklessly a man married and begot children, the greater his share of the comforts of life. The effect was seen in the rapid growth of population. Among unmarried women morality was discouraged, and unchastity subsidized. The more illegitimate children, the larger the allowance from the parish.

With all this 'it was evident that the fund from which the rates were provided must become exhausted. Rents were already disappearing . . . A drastic remedy was needed.' A drastic remedy was found; the stern new poor law of 1834.[35]

Recently Mark Blaug, in two stimulating articles, has challenged this traditional view of the character and significance of Speenhamland and the allowances it signifies.[36] Likening the condition of England at the turn of the nineteenth century to that of any present-day underdeveloped nation, he argues that at this time the English economy was characterized by both a high-wage industrial sector and a low-wage agricultural one, and that each existed independently of the other. In the agricultural, chiefly wheat-producing, areas of the south and east, wages were inadequate because of massive disguised unemployment, a condition unrelated to any effects of an allowance system. Here allowances subsidized institutionally inadequate wages, raising standards above the 'biological minimum' necessary for a working man to labour effectively. By way of allowances, then, the total labour output was increased, and not dramatically reduced as previous commentators claimed.

Attacking a widely-held notion, Blaug finds that nowhere and at no time were allowances so generous that they prompted people to 'breed recklessly', and so contribute to overpopulation and unemployment. Given the modest character of allowances, it also follows for Blaug that 'the scale at which outdoor relief was given does not suggest that it could have devitalized the working class by offering an attractive alternative to gainful employment',[37] and the remarkable increase in agricultural output after the turn of the nineteenth century is cited as additional support for this opinion.

Using Clapham's earlier calculations, Blaug determines that in 1824 there were eighteen 'Speenhamland counties' where wages were widely subsidized.[38] However, he finds that except for the cost per head, the patterns of relief in 'Speenhamland' and 'non-Speenhamland' counties did not differ significantly between 1802 and the new poor law. Accordingly he argues that there is nothing to suggest a snowballing of relief costs because of allowances to the able-bodied. He further claims there is no good reason to believe that the old poor law, with its allowance system, served to depress rents, or that it was responsible for the disappearance of the English yeomanry in the post-war years (the number of small owner-occupiers, says Blaug, declined sharply in the eighteenth century).

In the second of his two articles, 'The Poor Law Report Re-examined', Blaug offers additional evidence that allowances could hardly have been responsible for the disastrous consequences laid to them, and brings his analysis to bear even more directly on the meanings, real and imagined, of Speenhamland itself. After closely examining the Rural Queries circulated by the Poor Law Inquiry Commissioners in 1832,[39] he finds that the Speenhamland system, of tabular allowances from the single man onward, had by now been discarded almost everywhere in favour of allowances only to families with large numbers of children. It appears, maintains Blaug, that the Commissioners who drew up these questions were entirely aware they were confusing the two separate issues of supplements to earned wages (the Speenhamland plan) and family allowances. Yet they persisted in doing so because they calculated that the public would be more likely to accept the conclusions of their forthcoming report if it believed that new-fashioned wage subsidies, rather than the older and generally approved family allowances, were responsible for the apparent recent deterioration of the poor relief system. One result of this initial deception was the confusion of these two sorts of allowances by generations of poor law historians, who uncritically accepted the findings, and distortions, of the Poor Law Inquiry Commissioners.

When Frederick Page gave his impression of the Speenhamland meeting to Frederic Morton Eden, he included the observation that not only was the bread scale soon very notorious, but that

95

after the harvest of 1795 it was 'universally adopted'.[40] Once again this report anticipated many later assessments, which assumed that whatever other attributes Speenhamland allowances possessed, order, universality, and persistence were among them. By *order*, it is meant that wherever magistrates (with whom scales of allowances were chiefly associated) set allowances, their directions were uniformly and quickly implemented by the parish officers under their supervision. *Universality* is intended in two senses; first, that allowances were widely used geographically, and second, that they were used extensively within those parishes to which they pertained. *Persistence* refers to the retention of those allowances from their adoption in 1795 or soon after, straight across the years to, or nearly to, 1834 and the new poor law.

Of course these characteristics were implicit in many of the traditional, or even unusual, assessments of the character of Speenhamland. It will be recalled that Nicholls, in his condemnation of allowances to the able-bodied, stated that the Berkshire bread scale had been widely adopted in other counties. He also appears to have believed that these allowances persisted until the new poor law, except in some few places like the parishes of Bingham and Southwell where he and his fellow Nottinghamshire reformer, the Reverend Robert Lowe, had taken exceptional measures against the practice.[41] The Hammonds and the Webbs both wrote of the rapid extension of Speenhamland-like scales into every county in England and Wales, except perhaps Northumberland and Durham, and although these authors recognized that after the end of the French wars some localities markedly reduced the amounts of allowances, even so their focus was chiefly on decisions of county magistrates in favour of uniformly lesser scales. They further affirmed that, in spite of the efforts in various neighbourhoods, almost everywhere systems of allowances persisted with such vigour that their effects were not meliorated until the 1830s.[42]

Polanyi rested much of his argument on the universality and persistence of Speenhamland. For him, the system

very soon became the law of the land over most of the countryside, and later even in a number of manufacturing districts; actually it introduced no less a social and economic innovation than the 'right to live', and until abolished in 1834, it effectively prevented the establishment of a competitive labour market.[43]

Clapham used more sensitive instruments when assessing the extent and character of Speenhamland. While he announced at one point that the 'Speenhamland emergency policy . . . became, over so great a part of England, the standing policy for a whole generation', his analysis of the returns to the 1824 Select Committee on Labourers' Wages led him to restrict the impact of allowances in aid of wages chiefly to the south and east, and here he found many differences of degree. He further questioned whether the strictly formal and systematic bread scale was so general in the south as had been supposed, and he anticipated Mark Blaug by drawing an explicit distinction between allowances for all able-bodied persons and those for fathers of large families whose wages were manifestly insufficient. Still, as noted earlier, what Clapham generally terms the 'Speenhamland policy' was held responsible by him for a number of economic sins, most notably the depression of wages.[44]

Mark Blaug's opinion that allowances in aid of wages were an appropriate device 'for dealing with the problem of surplus labour in the lagging rural sector of a rapidly expanding but still under-developed economy'[45] is an original one. Yet when he comes to discuss the likely extent of systematic allowances to the able-bodied, he is less independent-minded. Although he recognizes that by 1824 in only eighteen counties did most parishes subsidize wages from the rates, and that by 1832, if not before, this practice pertained chiefly to overlarge families, he cannot entirely give up the notion that *at some time* allowances were a good deal more widespread, and more comprehensive in their local application. 'It is conceivable', writes Blaug, 'that the Returns of the Select Committee on Labourers' Wages correctly depict the situation in 1824, but that great changes had been made since 1795. Perhaps the allowance system was practised everywhere in 1800 or in 1815'. He reasons that the effect of sharp attacks on allowances to the able-bodied by the 1817 House of Commons and the 1818 House of Lords Select Committees on the Poor Laws, and by the 1824 Select Committee on Labourers' Wages, may have discouraged the practice.[46]

G

Blaug's version of the character and effect of allowances under the old poor law has won him many admirers. It has also gained him a stern critic; in a recent commentary, James Stephen Taylor sharply admonishes Blaug for the range and use of his evidence.[47] But wherever one stands in regard to Blaug's particular thesis, one must applaud him for challenging many enshrined assumptions pertaining to this portion of social welfare history, and for attracting the attention of other historians to a complicated chapter of England's past. Some of those historians, while provisionally accepting Blaug's opinions, suggest that a firm judgment must wait on further evidence—particularly on evidence from that most local of administrative districts, the parish, where the giving and withholding of allowances was a daily, concrete, business. J. D. Marshall, who has the highest regard for Blaug's work, laments that even Blaug relies—must rely—on official questionnaires for evidence of parochial use of allowances. 'We are sharply reminded', writes Marshall, 'that grass-roots research on the original parish documents will be the ultimate arbiter.' Even more recently, J. R. Poynter has pleaded for a long look at the 'ecology' of poor relief, to discover whether Speenhamland deserves its fame 'as a true and influential beginning of a new order of policy and practice, or even as a symbol and precursor of things to come'.[48]

The call for inquiries into the practical, parochial, operation of allowances in the Speenhamland years has not gone wholly unanswered, and many recent, post-Blaug, examinations of the matter have been both expert and fruitful, although few have yet been published. Taylor's exploration of poor law administration in Devon, George Body's of poverty and its relief in neighbouring Dorset, and N. D. Hopkins' inquiry into the operation of both the old and new poor laws in East Yorkshire (to 1850), contribute much to our understanding of the character of allowances in three of Blaug's 'Speenhamland' counties. Indeed the notion of those counties properly being Speenhamland precincts would seem a dangerous one in the wake of these scholars' findings.[49]

What of the county where the Speenhamland plan was conceived? Could we not hope to find in Berkshire evidence which, when placed alongside that collected from other places, would enlighten us at least a little respecting the character of English poor relief in this time? The answer to this question is visibly an affirmative one, and justification enough for the following remarks.

Given the Berkshire origin of the Speenhamland bread scale, it almost goes without saying that Berkshire was one of Clapham's and Blaug's 'Speenhamland' counties, where most parishes subsidized wages from the rates.[50] Yet the evidence of allowances in Berkshire collected by the 1824 Select Committee, to which Clapham and Blaug owe their Speenhamland label for the county, is extremely thin. Four of the seven returns refer to boroughs, with their own separate, extra-comital jurisdictions, and in any case the questions and answers are so framed that two of the three returns pertaining to the county itself are altogether confusing.[51] Certainly these insignificant returns do not reveal whether Berkshire was a 'Speenhamland' county according to those forementioned characteristics held to be conclusive by generations of poor law historians, namely order, universality and persistence. Did Berkshire parishes adopt the particular bread scale which the magistrates had enunciated? Did they adopt this or a quite similar measure soon after the Speenhamland meeting, and therefore obviously in response to the justices' proposition? If parishes seldom did one or the other of these things what case can be made for *order* across either space or time? Within the individual parishes were the justices' allowances, or something similar, given to every able-bodied person whose inadequate wages entitled him to them, or were the allowances offered to some and withheld from others? If the last is true, what case can be made for *universality*? Did the individual parishes make those allowances available continuously from the moment of their inception, or did they sometimes offer them and sometimes not, depending on the judgment of the parish officers for that year (and incidentally, independent of the magistrates' determinations)? What of *persistence* if the latter was the case? In brief, can we speak of a 'Speenhamland system' in the county where Speenhamland lies? Given the inadequacy of other evidence, even a provisional answer to this question will be found only in the records of Berkshire parishes themselves.

To understand the effect of the Speenhamland decision in

99

Berkshire it is necessary to know something of poor relief practices in the county before 1795. As elsewhere, Berkshire parish account and minute books confirm that since at least the 1770s it was common for parish officers to relieve unemployed able-bodied persons. It was also the case that relief was given to able-bodied persons in employment whose wages were inadequate for one reason or another, although the extent of this practice is uncertain. In November 1772, and for the next twenty years, Bradfield parish paid allowances to men in 'want of work', particularly in the jobless winter months.[52] From the winter of 1778 Brimpton paid sums to the seasonally unemployed, and occasionally to persons suffering 'lost work' at other times. In the early years of the following decade, similar payments began to be made by the parishes of Uffington, Hungerford and Warfield; in the first two places they continued into the 1790s. From 1787 the same practice was found at Drayton. An interesting entry in the vestry minutes of East Hendred for December 1786 refers to a combination of allowances in aid of wages and what comes to be referred to as the 'roundsman' system. Labourers not in regular employment were to be

> Billeted on the Occupiers of Land, etc. in a proper proportion and be paid Six pence a Day by their respective Masters and what more is thought necessary for their support to be Allowed and paid by the Overseers.

In March 1788 this same vestry resolved that every unemployed labourer with four children was to have a bushel of flour weekly.[53]

Thus it can be seen that by 1795 the practice of supporting the able-bodied with allowances from the parish was commonplace in Berkshire. The Speenhamland bread scale meant no innovation on that account. Historians have repeatedly observed that statutory reforms of the old poor law were often little more than legislative recognition of widespread local practices.[54] The same pattern may be seen in the relationship in Berkshire between parish and county; C. R. Fay is probably on the right track when he calls Speenhamland an attempt to systematize 'a practice which, because it was becoming widespread, needed to be conducted on some regular plan'.[55] In fact it is just possible that much of the inspiration for Speenhamland came ultimately from the practice of Uffington parish. Here, where allowances to the able-bodied were common, lived the Reverend George Watts, vicar and county magistrate. It was Watts who as early as the 1791 Mid-summer Quarter Sessions drew up a county-wide scale of relief for the able-bodied which, perhaps after local practice, he based on family size and a roughly estimated cost of living. His draft order, if in fact it was considered by the bench, was not adopted. However, Watts was also present at the Pelican Inn in May 1795, where he may have revived his earlier suggestion and helped refine it into the elaborate Speenhamland bread scale.[56]

Of course the issue at present is not the effect of parish practices on magistrates, but the opposite; the effect of the Speenhamland decision upon a routine of parish relief which, as I have just noted, already often encompassed the giving of money and other relief to unemployed, underpaid and overburdened labouring poor. How shall we gain some notion, then, of the effect of that decision?

To this end, I have selected sixteen parishes for investigation. Bradfield, Brimpton, Drayton, East Hendred, Uffington and Warfield, already noted in connection with pre-1795 allowances, are among this number. The remainder are: Aston Tirrold, Cheiveley, Cholsey, Pangbourne, Peasemore, Shinfield, Sulhamstead Bannister, Sunninghill, Thatcham and White Waltham. These places have been chosen largely because enough of their overseers' account books, vestry minutes and the like survive for us to gain some impression of how relief operated there after 1795. It is also the case that the parishes are geographically scattered, from Uffington in the Vale of the White Horse to Sunninghill on the edges of Surrey and Bagshot Heath. Accordingly, most variations within the economic geography of Berkshire are likely to be represented here.[57] Finally, although the sixteen parishes varied greatly in population size, the 1801 census stated that, in all but one, the chief occupation was agriculture. The exception was Pangbourne which, lying across the Reading to Oxford road at an important junction, had most employed persons engaged in some 'trade, manufacture, or handicraft'. But much of the population of Pangbourne was agricultural too, and this fact, along with what we know of the other parishes, might indicate that all these communities would be especially susceptible to Speenhamland allowances, which have been most often identified with agricultural populations.[58]

What enlightenment may be gained from these parishes respecting those qualities of order, universality and persistence so widely associated with Speenhamland? The best way of proceeding is to focus on the relatively plentiful evidence pertaining to an orderly (i.e. uniform and/or immediate) response to the magistrates' will, and note the less ample evidence regarding universality and persistence where it chances to surface.

Thus the first question to be asked is: How many of these parishes ever adopted the particular bread scale of allowances for the able-bodied which was promoted by the Speenhamland magistrates? The evidence is not sufficient for any final determination, because not all the sixteen parishes have complete runs of records for the forty years from 1795 to 1834, and when they do parts of their records are often imprecise. However, so far as the evidence does go, it may be asserted that *not one parish* of the sixteen can be said to have definitely adopted the Speenhamland scale at any time.

The overseers' account books from Aston Tirrold, complete from 1790 to 1836, fail to indicate the presence of a formal scale at any period, or even significant amounts of very 'casual' relief to able-bodied men or their families.[59] No evidence of a scale can be found among the White Waltham overseers' accounts (1811–36); there are only infrequent 'no work' entries of a pre-Speenhamland sort. Indeed, after the establishment of a stern select vestry here in 1822 even such occasional relief disappeared, or took the form of rare, discriminative, food allowances.[60] The records of Bradfield, East Hendred and Sunninghill indicate the presence of allowance systems there, but clearly these were in the form of family allowances to labourers overburdened with children and, as Blaug observes, they should not be confused with Speenhamland allowances in terms of origin or character. Too, evidence suggests these allowances were often of a temporary sort, in response to unusually severe seasons and high prices, or the prospect of rural violence. In early October 1800 the vestry of Bradfield, reacting to a scarcity and high prices exceeding even those of 1795–6,[61] determined that every poor family with one child or more should have its flour from the parish (or the money equivalent; this is unclear). This support of the poor ceased in the summer of 1801, when it was seen a plentiful harvest would soon end shortages. 1808 was another bad year, and again Bradfield assisted poor families. From 1813 to the end of our period, the parish appears to have had a permanent family allowance, at first the equivalent of a gallon loaf to every child beyond the second plus something more for the parents, but later beginning with the fourth child. The vestry of East Hendred in October 1797 resolved that families with more than three children were to have 1s per week (probably per child), or 1s 8d if the children went to school; the last was an inducement to education unusual for this time. The vestry minutes (1785–1884) do not indicate how long these allowances persisted, but in late November 1830 the vestry, by now select, determined that poor labourers with more than two children would receive the value of a gallon loaf for every child above this number. Almost certainly this measure was inspired by fears that the incendiarism and terror of the 'Captain Swing' riots, which had come to the county earlier that month, would trouble East Hendred if the labourers were not appeased. This allowance apparently persisted for some time; in 1832 the report from East Hendred to the Poor Law Inquiry Commissioners included notice of it. Sunninghill, too, instituted a family allowance under the threat of 'Swing'; 1s 6d weekly through the winter for every child beyond the fourth. There is only one notice of this allowance and perhaps it did not outlive the season.[62]

Although Blaug speaks of a general extension of family allowances at the expense of those in aid of wages during this period, at least one of the sixteen parishes moved the other way. In August 1811 the vestry of Cholsey resolved on an allowance of 2s for every labourer's child beyond the third, but in May 1817 it ordered that single able-bodied men were to have their wages made up to 4s 6d weekly, while a man and wife without children were entitled to 9s.[63]

Drayton and Thatcham parishes may fit Blaug's hypothesis better. From the autumn of 1812 the overseers of Drayton began to cite the price of the gallon loaf at the head of columns of weekly relief payments, and these payments, at least to 'regulars', varied according to that price. This indicates the presence of a formal bread scale, although the extent of its application is uncertain. In

103

any case it was apparently less generous than the Speenhamland allowances; perhaps at the rate of two gallon loaves for a single man, one and a half for a single woman and one for a child. If this bread scale was indeed in the fashion of allowances in aid of wages, by the time of 'Swing' it was only a family allowance, which became more bountiful in the wake of those disturbances. Within six months after the Speenhamland meeting, the Thatcham overseers' accounts (1791–1836) begin to include payments of 'bread money', frequently a synonym for allowances in aid of wages. These payments ceased after October 1796 but reappeared briefly during the 1799–1800 crisis.[64] From perhaps June 1820, and certainly from February 1822, Thatcham was (again?) making up wages from the rates, probably according to a bread scale. The parish select vestry ultimately took a dim view of this practice, and after 1828 allowances were limited to families with three or more children. In March 1830 the criterion of need was raised to four or more. It should be carefully noted in respect to some allowances at Thatcham that they could not have been universally applied. For instance, if the 'bread money' entries from October 1795 indicate the parish had adopted the Speenhamland table, only six male persons received this support during the first month in a parish of nearly two thousand inhabitants.[65]

In the case of two parishes, Chieveley and Peasemore, there is firm evidence of Speenhamland-like allowances, and while their amounts may have altered there is no notice that they changed their character. In neither parish, however, were those bread-scales of allowances in aid of wages identical with the Speenhamland table. The elaborate, undated (but evidently post-war) scale which survives among the papers of Chieveley parish promised less relief than Speenhamland for every combination of persons at every price of the gallon loaf, while the allowances resolved on by the vestry in May 1820 were usually less than, and never identical with, the Speenhamland rate. At Peasemore sometime in the first decade of the nineteenth century a 'New Make up Table' promised the equivalent of two, one and a half and one gallon loaves to every man, woman and child; this too did not agree with the justices' calculations[66].

It might seem at first glance that Uffington parish, like Chieveley and Peasemore, had a Speenhamland-like arrangement at some time between 1795 and 1834. However, a longer look suggests that the undated printed scale which is pasted in the Uffington overseers' account book for 1782–1805 antedates Speenhamland. The sums pertaining to labourers and their dependents are identical with those in an engrossed order by the Faringdon division magistrates. This order, in turn, closely resembles the draft order which the Reverend George Watts wrote up for the consideration of the Quarter Sessions in the summer of 1791. It may be that after the bench rejected Watts' proposal he succeeded in having a variation of it endorsed by his colleagues in the Faringdon division and urged upon the parishes there, including Uffington. If this was so, it probably happened before 1795. The Uffington account books, which include detailed entries of relief to that year, provide less information after that date.[67]

Evidence of relief practices in the remaining five of the sixteen parishes is spotty and inconclusive. A safe observation about these places is that sometime between 1795 and 1834 they probably gave allowances, based on the cost of bread, to able-bodied persons. 'Bread money' payments are recorded at one time or another in the accounts of Brimpton, Pangbourne, Shinfield, Sulhamstead Bannister and Warfield and, as already noted, these payments often signify such allowances. However, a striking fact about the 'bread money' entries is that they are so infrequent. Perhaps two or three persons who could possibly be able-bodied labourers might have received these sums weekly in a parish of many hundreds. As was sometimes true at Thatcham, the appearance in these places of (perhaps) systematic allowances does not have to mean they were universally applied.[68]

The second question to be asked in regard to the orderly nature of allowances is this: How many of our sixteen parishes appear to have adopted *some* bread scale of allowances in aid of wages soon after, and so presumably in response to, the magistrates' Speenhamland table? Relevant records survive from 1795 and the years immediately following for seven of those parishes; Aston Tirrold, Bradfield, Brimpton, Drayton, East Hendred, Warfield and Thatcham. In the case of East Hendred, the evidence is very incomplete; only the vestry minutes remain. Nonetheless, the minutes are quite detailed from 1785 onward, and they indicate the absence of a formal parish scale until the family allowance of October 1797 which has already been noted. Probably this measure owed less to the Speenhamland example than it did to the parish precedent of March 1788, which promised assistance to every unemployed poor labourer with four or more children. Of Aston Tirrold and Drayton, overseers' accounts reveal that although the cost of relief here rose significantly in the year after Speenhamland, this was largely due to higher weekly payments to regular impotent paupers, and higher and more frequent payments to semi-regulars among whom were only a handful of persons who might have been able-bodied labourers with or without families.[69] Furthermore, when payments to existing paupers were augmented in the year or so after Speenhamland, this occurred at different times for different individuals; sudden general increases which might suggest the parishes had embraced a system did not occur. The records of the two parishes reveal a reaction to the deepening crisis of these months along a broad front and in an irregular fashion; nothing more. The same may be said for Bradfield, where in July 1795 'out of work' payments were resumed after a three-year lapse, and where the parish perhaps bought flour to sell to the poor at or below cost.[70]

At Brimpton, Thatcham and Warfield, notices of 'bread money' might be seen as support for Frederick Page's contention that the justices' allowances were 'universally adopted' after the 1795 harvest. However, it has already been observed of these parishes that if those payments mean scales were present there, the scales were not likely to have been widely applied. 'Bread money' entries, even at the height of the crisis, are remarkably uncommon.[71]

Allow me to refer one more time to Page's opinions about the early career of Speenhamland. Page's conviction that the scale was soon universally applied must have been based on his experience in his own Newbury district, where the tithing of Speenhamland lies, and certainly one would imagine that if the justices' resolution was respected anywhere it would have been in the neighbourhood of its birth. However, the particulars Page cited regarding the local operation and effects of Speenhamland may point to another conclusion. The case of pauper 'W.E.', wrote Page, indicated how the Speenhamland scale worked to the employer's disadvantage in 'P' parish; the cost of W.E.'s allowance was unfairly distributed. Yet Page observed in passing that

106

W.E.'s case was not truly representative, because he was the only labourer in P parish who was being relieved strictly according to the Speenhamland table. Further, Page stated that in 1795 he was an overseer of his parish (P?), and that when he learned of the Speenhamland table he called five paupers to him, demanding they tell him 'their utmost desire' *vis-a-vis* relief. They told him, and in every case their figures were below those allowed by the justices. Page ignored the Speenhamland table and relieved the paupers according to their own estimates.[72]

A final matter relating to Speenhamland should be briefly mentioned. It will be recalled that besides settling on a bread scale, the Speenhamland justices urged overseers to set aside some acres on which the industrious poor might raise potatoes, and lay in stocks of fuel for poor parishioners to buy below cost in wintertime. The records from our parishes which cast light on the events of 1795 reveal that overseers in those places paid no attention to the recommendations; there is absolutely no evidence of ground being laid aside for potatoes, or of fuel being stocked, in the summer of that year. Further, the *Reading Mercury*, which had already encouraged local subscriptions for supplying the poor with potatoes and fuel, and had noted with approval parishes adopting these and similar schemes, made no mention of the justices' recommendations being acted upon in Berkshire parishes, as undoubtedly it would have liked to do.

What conclusions, or better, suggestions, may at last be drawn from this investigation of sixteen Berkshire parishes and, after a fashion, the neighbourhood of Newbury? Certainly it would appear that the qualities of order, universality and persistence associated with the word Speenhamland were seldom if ever associated with allowances to the able-bodied in those places. If the sixteen parishes were at all representative of Berkshire generally (and there is reason to believe they were), then it may be argued that in this county only a tenuous connection existed between the resolutions and recommendations of the magistracy and the practice of relief on the local, parish, level. It is probably true that at one time or another most Berkshire parishes adopted some sort of bread scale as a general guide for relieving their able-bodied poor. There is no reason to doubt the returns to the Poor Law Inquiry Commissioners' Rural Queries which indicate that in 1832 all but six of twenty-nine Berkshire parishes surveyed were giving allowances to certain classes of able-bodied poor.[73] But the point is this: The parishes gave this relief precisely as often, widely and generously as they chose. In doing so, the variations in practice within and between Berkshire parishes were enormous, and the sum of those variations may have been a procedure of allowance-giving to the able-bodied which was less influential, for good or evil, than many historians would imagine.

An objection might be raised here. Granting that the relationship between the Speenhamland justices and the parish officers was a distant one, was not the Speenhamland meeting in essence an adjourned Quarter Sessions, whose participants came from all parts of the county and therefore spoke forcefully to none? Could not there have been a much closer association between the overseers and those justices in their own neighbourhoods with whom they communicated frequently, and whose writs ran locally with greater vigour?

My provisional answer to these questions is that the response of the parishes to the directions of local, divisional, justices was no different than the response of many parishes to the Speenhamland justices' determinations, namely, very little if any. Unhappily no firm judgment can be made here; records pertaining to the operation of justices in petty and special local sessions during these years are sadly inadequate for Berkshire. Still, what evidence there is may provide part of an answer.

In two Petty Sessional divisions during these years, Berkshire magistrates promoted their own variations of the Speenhamland table. Sometime before 1807, when William Mavor reported on it in his survey of the county, the Faringdon division justices fashioned a table and sent copies of it around the parishes. This was in fact so nearly identical with the Speenhamland scale that it would be difficult to tell from the most specific overseers' accounts which one, if either, a parish was obeying.[74] The problem, however, does not arise. Uffington, the only one of our selected parishes belonging to this division, has no detailed accounts for the years after 1800. Nevertheless, evidence from Uffington does tell us something of the response of this parish to local magistrates' directions at a later time. Answering the Poor Law Inquiry Commissioners' Queries in 1832, the respondent from Uffington stated that his parish often subsidized wages in seasons of low pay and employment, particularly for labourers with three or more children. This, then, was a family allowance. He also observed that the local justices had authorized allowances in aid of wages to all labouring poor, irrespective of the size of their families.[75] Clearly, therefore, Uffington chose to go its own way in the matter of allowances. The same inclination may be seen at Speen parish in 1820. Here the newly-created select vestry paid more attention to the character and age of paupers applying for relief than it did to the bread scale, a Speenhamland variant, which the justices of the Newbury division had recently put forward.[76] The evidence from Uffington and Speen indicates that many Berkshire parishes may have pursued their own poor relief policies independent of the justices *in any capacity whatever*.

Two questions remain. First, was the parish officers' apparent disdain for the Speenhamland decision representative of a prevailing attitude to *all* directions and recommendations from the county justices, at least so far as poor relief was concerned? And if this was indeed the case, then what is the explanation for it? A positive answer to the first question has already been indicated in the paragraph directly above; a few more illustrations should confirm this view. A response to the second question is a more difficult affair. Many pieces must be fitted together, and no fully satisfactory answer can be ventured in a paper which, having gone on so far, must soon come to an end. Nevertheless, allow me to offer some thoughts and suggestions on the matter which may at least stimulate others to fashion an explanation for themselves.

Evidence of the parish officers' determination to go their own way irrespective of the magistrates' wishes is plentiful in Berkshire, particularly after 1815. However, even in the hard years at the turn of the nineteenth century when shortages, high prices and the enduring fear of domestic unrest on a French scale united all authorities in their desire to make the poor comfortable, this persistent disregard of the magistrates may be seen. Early in 1800, at their Epiphany Sessions, the justices recommended to parish overseers that they feed their paupers a substitute for bread in this season of scarcity; potatoes, pease soup, meat, herring and rice were suggested as alternatives. In March the magistrates went a step further and forbade overseers to allow more than a quarter loaf of bread per week to each pauper. Additional relief was to be in bread substitutes and the overseers were urged to collect stocks of them. However, account and minute books of seven Berkshire parishes reveal that only two of those places had undertaken to find substitutes for bread by the end of that year, and in these two cases the decisions in favour of substitutes came so long after the order (eight and ten months) it is unlikely that the parish officers by then had the justices' wishes in mind.[77] Continued disregard is seen in the parish officers' reactions to the magistrates' demand, early in 1801, that 41 George III c. 12 (for 'making better Provision for the Maintenance of the Poor and for diminishing the Consumption of Bread Corn') be implemented locally. Returns made by parishes to their divisional justices pursuant to the directions of the act indicate no prompt and universal adoption of the bread substitutes which the statute required. Indeed, from Faircross and Kintbury Eagle hundreds in the Newbury division, for which the returns are fairly complete, came word that less than one-third of the reporting parishes and places had fully complied with the justices' directions some two months after they were issued.[78]

In 1799–1801, as in 1795–6, the parish officers' unwillingness to take directions from the county bench was not owing to a callous attitude toward their pauper populations. Although the magistrates' continuing attentions to the poor involved impulses absent from the overseers' concern, all parties agreed in those crisis years that the wants of the poor should be attended to. The columns of the *Reading Mercury* with their many notices of parish-sponsored subscriptions and other charities are evidence of a widely shared solicitude. Unity among parish and county authorities on this issue did not survive the end of the French wars. By 1815 the possibility of a French-inspired popular uprising seemed remote. Even the most impoverished and potentially discontented people appeared convinced of Bonaparte's malevolence and England's virtue, and accordingly there was less fearful concern about those persons' feelings.[79] More important were the effects of certain economic developments. The high prices for grain which had persisted during most of the war years came to an end after 1813; a quarter of wheat which fetched 136s at Windsor early in that year brought 84s after the 1814 harvest and only 72s the following year.[80] The post-war depression was selective in its effects, and the prices of all commodities varied from year to year, but wheat-growers in particular, who had enjoyed the highest profits in the French wars, lamented for a generation their reduced margins and thrashed about in search of explanations and remedies for them. Among the causes complained of was the burden of the poor-rates; this in spite of the fact that the national cost of poor relief fell steadily after 1818, to rise again only in the last years of the next decade.[81] Among the remedies undertaken were measures directed to diminishing the cost and incidence of this relief. A cult of severity became the fashion. Its followers' opinions, based in part on an intense if somewhat twisted reading of Smith and Malthus, ranged from a desire to abolish statutory relief altogether to a longing for its selective use to elevate the character of what was imagined to be a universally pauperized working class.[82] Its effects were seen in some legislation, many select committees of both Houses, a bundle of parish devices and, finally, in the Poor Law Inquiry Commission and the new poor law of 1834.

This new rigorous attitude quickly made itself at home among great numbers of Berkshire ratepayers and the parish officers who represented their views. Some persons, like James Ebenezer Bicheno of Newbury, urged the eventual abolition of all statutory relief as the way to restore national virtue, and regarded without alarm the hardship and even death this act would engender: 'The sun does not shine without occasional harm, and the pains and sickness to which our frames are exposed, are not sent without benefit to us.'[83] More ratepayers and overseers, however, stopped short of championing total abolition now or later. Instead, they adopted in their parishes a variety of mechanisms intended to make relief a more discriminatory and less costly business. Some of these devices had a new legislative sanction. Select vestries and salaried assistant overseers were widely utilized in the county pursuant to the 1819 Sturges Bourne act, and the use of the 'labour rate' became common after 1832 and 2 and 3 Williams IV c. 96. These instruments were not new with the statutes; like various forms of the 'round', employment on public works, and 'spade husbandry', they could be seen in some Berkshire parishes long before Parliament ratified their use.[84] What *was* new to post-war relief was the hardening of parish attitudes which the more general adoption of these devices signified. If certain types of allowances to the able-bodied continued to operate locally until 1832, they had by this time been joined by expedients directed to quite different ends.[85]

To these developments many Berkshire magistrates turned, if not always a disapproving eye, at least a distrustful one. In the years directly after Waterloo, when the great mass of ratepayers hurried to embrace the principles of thrift and discrimination, some magistrates continued, in the letters column of the *Reading Mercury*, to give evidence of that concern for the poor's welfare which had characterized the bench since the year of Speenhamland and before.[86] Occasionally the values and preoccupations of parishioners and magistrates collided directly. In 1829 a quarrel erupted between John Walter II, master of Bear Wood and county justice, and Henry Russell, chairman of the Swallowfield select vestry. At issue were the lack of privileges, the strict regimen and the spare diet which Russell and his select vestry had imposed on paupers in their parish. Walter, in applying for an order from the Quarter Sessions amending the select vestry's resolutions, argued that they 'inflicted the severest suffering that human nature is capable of sustaining', and were contrary to the divine laws which entitled the poor to 'an adequate protection from starvation, and such support as nature requires'. The Sessions, in effect, upheld Walter's objections.[87]

A similar battle was joined in January 1830. Taking the poor's part, first in his address to the county bench and then in the pages of the *Reading Mercury*, was Charles Dundas, Quarter Sessions' chairman and the most senior and respected of Berkshire magistrates. Dundas, it will be remembered, had chaired the Speenhamland meeting some thirty-five years before. Now, supported by his friend William Budd, who as deputy clerk of the peace had written up the Speenhamland proceedings, and by fellow justice William Hallett, Dundas defended the right of poor labourers to adequate wages and sufficient parish allowances when they could not find work. He and his supporters urged employers and overseers to pay unmarried labourers at least 4s weekly in wages or parish pay. At the present price of bread, argued Dundas and his friends, this was a bare subsistence. They cited the virtues of the Speenhamland scale itself, noting that their proposal of 4s weekly (the amount would alter with the price of bread) was only a return to this, and could hardly be construed as extravagant. But 'extravagant' was precisely what their opponents, led by Job Lousley, sometime churchwarden and overseer of Hagbourne, called 4s weekly. Writing on behalf of small farmers and ordinary ratepayers, Lousley lamented 'high wages, and the consequent habits of extravagance and intemperance', denounced the proposed parish allowance for ignoring character, and roundly assaulted William Budd for clutching at vast legal fees (Budd was an attorney in Newbury) while shedding crocodile tears for the less fortunate.[88]

In November 1830 the mobs, machine-breaking and incendiarism associated with 'Captain Swing' came to Berkshire. Almost all the landed interest—landlords and farmers, justices and overseers—reacted at first with confusion and alarm. Nevertheless, instances of the justices' compassion for even riotous poor, and concern about their ill-usage by farmers and parish officers, can be found throughout the disturbances. It is true that some magistrates, like old Morris Ximenes and others in the eastern part of Berkshire, took a hard line against treating with unruly persons or raising wages. But the persistent concern of many justices for the welfare of the poor was widely evident,[89] and the magistrates' motives were not the same as those of the officers and vestries of parishes like East Hendred and Sunninghill. There in this troubled winter, as was so often the case thirty years before, parochial efforts to allay the labourers' discontent were inspired almost entirely by fear. On the other hand, although fear may have played a part in the justices' concern, I do not believe its was a decisive part.

It seems clear, then, that many Berkshire ratepayers, and the parish vestries and officers who included and represented them, were suspicious of the magistrates' involvement in poor relief throughout the entire forty years before 1834. Sometimes this suspicion prompted angry quarrels; at other times it made its presence known by a sullen noncompliance. A final question remains: What can explain this state of affairs?

The first part of an explanation lies in the fact that, as has been implied already, a fairly clear line may be drawn between parish officers and county magistrates in terms of their socio-economic character. Poor-rate assessments, despite the ambiguities which characterize them, reveal that overseers were almost always among the most substantial occupiers in the parish.[90] But if the overseers had considerable wealth and reputation in terms of their own parish, their importance was local. These small-to-middling tenant farmers and working owner-occupiers were seldom found, before or after their parish service, on the Commission of the Peace.[91] Conversely the figure who most typified a Berkshire justice in these years was the landed gentleman of at least one thousand acres or a thousand pounds per annum, and no more than five thousand of either, without a title but with leisure time, and with a country seat where he was content to remain most of the year. The Berkshire bench did have a scattering of titled persons but, appropriately for a county where few of them were resident, they were not dominant in either numbers or influence. There was more than a scattering of clergymen, and undoubtedly this was to the magistracy's advantage; the intelligence and activity of clerical justices generally, remarked upon by the Webbs, pertained to this caste in Berkshire.[92] But once again it was the modest squire and country gentleman, whose income came mostly from his rental and whose interests, like his person, stayed at home, to whom the county bench owed its character.[93]

What were some effects of this social and economic distance between overseers and magistrates? First and most obviously, because the poor-rates were normally levied on occupiers rather than owners, overseers, who like most of their neighbours were counted chiefly among the former, felt the cost of poor relief more quickly and deeply than did the *rentier* magistracy. Given the staggering rise in the cost of relief everywhere since 1750, it follows that overseers would have been less than enthusiastic about directions aimed at further accommodation of the poor, other things being equal.[94]

The second half of the eighteenth century, and particularly the period of the French wars to 1814, were prosperous times for landlords and tenants alike. Magistrates and overseers were less sharply at odds over poor relief than they might otherwise have been, because of the good fortune which came to every part of the landed interest. This was all the more true because for a time both parties shared a fear of revolution by the unpropertied. However even then, as the evidence of this paper suggests, the relationship of squire-magistrate with farmer-overseer was not a comfortable one. The sudden end of prosperity in 1814 brought new and worsened circumstances, especially in wheat-producing areas. Now small owners, who in the good times had borrowed heavily to buy and enclose land, improve and augment buildings and equipment, and otherwise enhance their positions, could not pay their debts. Many sold their land, to become tenant farmers or leave farming entirely. For tenant farmers themselves things were hardly better. Rents, inflated by enclosure costs and decades of agricultural prosperity, could not easily be met. In Berkshire as elsewhere farms were being thrown on their owners' hands, in spite of landlords' often reducing or temporarily remitting rental payments.[95] An outcome of all these postwar developments was a heightened cost-consciousness on the part of tenants and small owners; a new concern for appropriate and efficient farming and a deeper reluctance to support anything that did not relate to their own immediate well-being. The 'cult of severity' in respect to the poor was a feature of the state of mind these circumstances fathered.

While tenants and small owners suffered the full effects of postwar changes, landlords' agonies were less severe. With their greater resources landlords could weather a temporary misfortune like some unoccupied farms, and if they were compelled to reduce their rents to keep their tenants, the general fall in the price level meant reductions were only an appropriate adjustment and entailed no real loss.[96] Not surprisingly, the new sterner attitude to the poor's needs which flourished elsewhere found a less enthusiastic welcome among the more secure squire-magistrates; here it did not entirely replace other, and very different, opinions about the responsibility of society for its less fortunate members. It might be added that in the case of Berkshire many magistrates' unwillingness to embrace the fashionable ideas of Malthus, Bicheno and the rest was all the stronger owing to one peculiar fact. For perhaps forty years before his death in 1832, Charles Dundas, the most frequent chairman of the Quarter Sessions, dominated the proceedings of the bench almost totally; the extent of his *imperium* is pointed up by the futility of attempts to over-throw it.[97] In 1795 Dundas chaired the Speenhamland meeting, and certainly he was instrumental in the adoption of suggestions put forward there. In 1830 Dundas again urged living wages and allowances for working men; his opinion of their rightness had not altered in thirty-five years. Given the presence of this remarkable person, who so long as his vigour lasted spoke and acted as though the bench were his freehold, and whose ideas on the proper treatment of poverty seemed so clearly of another era, the persistent tension between magistrates and overseers in Berkshire is scarcely to be wondered at.

Joining all the particular developments and local peculiarities which drove apart gentry and farmers, justices and overseers, in this county, was a quality of life and spirit pertaining to those of magisterial rank which cannot be neglected in any assessment of the justices' relations with the rest of society. It was a quality at once pervasive and obscure; it submits easily to applause and censure but escapes accurate delineation. Words like 'code' and 'club', 'obligation' and 'convention' are too often used to indicate parts of it, but none of these terms, alone or all together, communicate its essence. Perhaps its essence will always elude us, and we must be content to name the attributes by which squires announced themselves to a watching world. Whether this is so or not, some of those attributes relate to the squire in his role as magistrate, and so command our attention here.

Until very recently a large part of the English countryside belonged to the occupant of the 'Big House'. If his political power had been dissipated by the last quarter of the nineteenth century, his power to make others accept his conventions as the right ones had not, and has not in some places to this day. His rule over society was achieved and evidenced by a rich collection of activities and events intended to convey to his neighbours (who were often willing accomplices in this business) precisely how his character and position differed from their own. The editor of this collection has written elsewhere of this society as a 'ceremonial' one, and the word is apt.[98] The squire's birth and death, clothes and language, attendance at church and on the bench, shooting and hunting, feasting and being waited on, even his notorious eccentricities, were largely ritualistic affairs serving to enhance

116

that basic distinction which set him off from lesser beings—the possession of leisure. The emotions of awe and dependence which those ceremonial displays inspired among witnesses were a part of the squire's warranty against the dissolution of the village world he dominated; against the overthrow of his small but comfortable kingdom.

The squire, privately and as a magistrate, exercised certain other ceremonial functions: the giving of charity and the ordering of statutory relief. The effects of philanthropy are easier to identify than the impulses responsible for them, but among those impulses is often found the desire to emphasize, by way of benefactions, how very great the vertical distance is between donor and recipient. So it was then. The squire, particularly when ordering relief in his public magisterial capacity, was reiterating, through a ceremony, the fact of his dominion. The pauper, who benefited most immediately from this ritual, joined in its celebration and found his squire's dominion good. Thus the magistrate was doubly blessed; his sovereignty was assented to, and its exercise brought him the warm sensation of being liked. This is not to suggest that all magistrates, consciously or otherwise, used relief solely as a device for confirming their own great statures. More selfless impulses were not lacking; there is a little bit of Allworthy in everyone. In the case of clerical justices (who also depended on the effects of ceremony for their high status), a Christian pre-occupation with their flocks' well-being was sometimes evident. Nevertheless, at least some of the justices' generosity on behalf of the poor stemmed from the fact that poor relief was an affirmation of the squire's (and parson's) hegemony. Evoking appropriate emotions, beneficence helped fasten society on a firm foundation.

When we examine the relationship of the magistrate with the rest of society in this time, and with the parish overseer in particular, we cannot overlook this enduring characteristic of his mind, and measures. Aware of it or not, the justices who gathered at Speenhamland in May 1795, and those others who took the poor's part in later years, were participating in observances intended to glorify the paternal and hierarchic society they so entirely ruled. Of course the parish officers to whom the magistrates directed their instructions and recommendations did not share their superiors' particular vision. Gaining nothing from their landlords' customary supremacy and the ritual which proclaimed it, and everything from an entirely practical management of affairs, they went their own way, treating individual problems, and paupers, as they appeared. In the hard post-war years the smallfarming overseers and ratepayers were even more forcefully impelled toward an entirely rational, market-mechanistic, view of themselves and their responsibilities. The distance between the two attitudes grew wider, now manifesting itself in open confrontations and mutual abuse, as well as in the overseers' traditional disregard.

Local figures with the power of Charles Dundas are no longer seen in England. But the opinions for which Dundas and his fellow magistrates fought ultimately prevailed over those of the Reverend Edward Wilson, Job Lousley and the rest; some small economic security is today an Englishman's birthright. And if country gentlemen like Dundas have become only a memory, it is sometimes a thankful and even loving memory. 'I hear people run the gentry down now but they were better than the farmers in a crisis', reminisced Gregory Gladwell, blacksmith and artist in iron of not-so-mythical Akenfield. 'Theirs was the only hand which fed us which we could see.'[99]

Notes

1. I gratefully acknowledge the support of the American Philosophical Society in the preparation of this paper.
2. A tithing of Speen parish.
3. France declared war on Great Britain on 1 February 1793. For a detailed review of the 1795–6 scarcity and of measures taken to alleviate it, see Walter M. Stern, 'The Bread Crisis in Britain, 1795–96', *Economica*, new series XXXI, 122 (May 1964), pp. 168–87.
4. The Hammonds oversimplify and exaggerate when they state that 'in 1795 there was a fear of revolution, and the upper classes threw the Speenhamland system over the villages as a wet blanket over sparks', [*The Village Labourer, 1760–1832* (1911), p. 232]. Still, a glance at developments in Berkshire indicates that this fear of revolution ran deep enough. In the summer of 1792 the 'freeholders of Berks' twice gathered at Reading to frame loyal addresses to the King and to thank him for his recent *Proclamation against Seditious Writings*. Other loyal addresses by the inhabitants of Reading, New Windsor and elsewhere followed in the fall and winter. In January 1793 the Earl of Radnor, chairman of the Berkshire Quarter Sessions, charged the county Grand Jury to be

especially attentive to the threat of alien doctrines and the agitation they might inspire. The Grand Jury responded with a patriotic declaration. B(erkshire) R(ecord) O(ffice), Q(uarter) S(essions) O(rder) B(ook), and Q(uarter) S(essions) R(oll) 236, Epiphany Sessions 1793. R(eading) M(ercury), 2 and 9 July 1792.

5. Thomas Tooke, A History of Prices, and of the State of the Circulation from 1793 to 1837, 2 vols. (1838), vol. II, p. 389. RM, 29 September 1794.

6. RM, 19 January 1795.

7. RM, 20 April 1795.

8. Frederic Morton Eden, The State of the Poor, 3 vols. (1797), vol. I, p. 578. Frederick Page (1769–1834), sometime parish overseer, (acting) county magistrate and Deputy Lord Lieutenant of Berkshire, was always interested in matters pertaining to poverty and its relief. Besides his commentary on the Speenhamland meeting which appeared in Eden (pp. 576–87), he wrote The Principle of the English Poor Laws Illustrated and Defended' (1822). Some of his opinions are also revealed in his answers to the Poor Law Inquiry Commissioners' Rural Queries in the Commissioners' Report, App. (B.1.), Parts I–V, Sess. 1834, vols. 30–4; 'Speen'.

9. From about 1766 to 1793 Wilson had been engaged by the Earl of Chatham as tutor for his two eldest sons. It was at the instance of his former pupil William Pitt the Younger that he was rewarded with the canonry of Windsor in 1784. Earl Stanhope, Life of the Rt. Hon. William Pitt, 3 vols. (1879), vol. I, pp. 3–6, 8, 144.

10. Wilson, p. 12, quoting Adam Smith, The Wealth of Nations, 2 vols., reprint (1902), vol. I, p. 18.

11. Karl Polanyi, The Great Transformation (1940), p. 290.

12. Since perhaps the first part of the eighteenth century, Berkshire had been divided into Petty Sessional divisions for the better transacting of magistrates' business between the general quarterly Sessions. At the turn of the nineteenth century there were eight such divisions; Abingdon, Faringdon, Forest (or Wokingham), Maidenhead, Newbury, Reading, Wallingford and Wantage. Sometimes the neighbourhood around Windsor was regarded as a separate division. BRO, QSOB, adjourned Epiphany Sessions 1801, and 1780–1834 passim. William Mavor, General View of the Agriculture of Berkshire (1809), pp. 5, 15.

Many historians have assumed the authors of the Speenhamland scale intended that the man receive money sufficient for three gallon loaves. However, William Budd, the county deputy clerk of the peace in 1795, stated years later that the specific intention of the Speenhamland justices was to guarantee the equivalent of two gallon loaves and a shilling or so for other food expenses, and that the magistrates used the pay of a private soldier as their standard. RM, 15 February 1830.

13. Only the bread scale resolution, and the recommendation that farmers raise wages, were entered in the Quarter Sessions Order Book.

14. The grain shortages after 1794 led to the widespread recommenda-

tion that potatoes be used as a partial remedy for threatened diets. *RM*, 29 December 1794 *ff.*; Mavor, *op. cit.*, pp. 224–7; Eden, *op. cit.*, vol. I, pp. 501–10.

15. This account of the Speenhamland meeting is drawn chiefly from *BRO*, QSOB 6 May 1795; *RM* 11 May 1795; Eden, *op. cit.*, vol. I, pp. 576–8.

16. 39 Elizabeth c. 3 (1597–8) and its re-enactment, with amendments, as 43 Elizabeth c. 2 (1601). These two acts empowered parish overseers to supply stocks of materials on which able-bodied poor might be set to work, and also to raise money 'for the necessary relief of the lame, impotent, old, blind, and such other among them being poor and not able to work'.

17. Sidney and Beatrice Webb, *English Poor Law History, Part I: The Old Poor Law* (1927), pp. 151, 170–2; E. M. Hampson, *The Treatment of Poverty in Cambridgeshire, 1597–1834* (1934), pp. 37, 189, 190, 270; A. W. Ashby, *One Hundred Years of Poor Law Administration in a Warwickshire Village* (1912), p. 150 ff.; J. H. Clapham, *An Economic History of Modern Britain: The Early Railway Age* (1930), p. 357; P. H. Goodman, 'Eighteenth Century Poor Law Administration in the Parish of Oswestry', *Transactions of the Shropshire Archaeological Society*, LVI, 3 (1960), p. 329; Dorothy Marshall, *The English Poor in the Eighteenth Century* (1926), pp. 23, 104–7.

The adoptive act 22 George III c. 82, known as Gilbert's Act after its sponsor Thomas Gilbert, ordered among other things that out-relief be given to able-bodied persons when employment could not be found for them (s. 32). Although relatively few parishes adopted the statute it is believed to have encouraged such relief generally.

18. The justices of Buckinghamshire and Oxfordshire determined on allowances for the able-bodied according to the present price of necessities at their 1795 Epiphany (January) Sessions. The Gloucestershire magistrates fashioned a sophisticated Speenhamland-like table at their Michaelmas Sessions that year. See Hammonds, *op. cit.*, pp. 163, 164; Webbs, *op. cit.*, pp. 177, 179 note 1. Information respecting the activities of the Dorset magistrates and parish officers may be found in George A. Body's exceptionally competent unpublished Ph.D. thesis, 'The Administration of the Poor Laws in Dorset, 1760–1834, with Special Reference to Agrarian Distress' (University of Southampton, 1964). For Cambridgeshire see E. M. Hampson, *Victoria County History: Cambridgeshire*, (1948), vol. II, p. 97.

19. Arthur Young, *Annals of Agriculture*, XXV, (1796), pp. 537, 607 ff. This account of early notices of Speenhamland is taken in part from J. R. Poynter's *Society and Pauperism; English Ideas on Poor Relief, 1795–1834* (1969), pp. 77–9.

20. Eden, *op. cit.*, vol. I, pp. 576–87.

21. *An Inquiry into the Nature of Benevolence, chiefly with a view to elucidate the Principles of the Poor Laws* (1817), pp. 106–7. James Ebenezer Bicheno was the son of a dissenting minister and school master in

Newbury, and he spent the first part of his life in that town. He later entered government service and eventually became Colonial Secretary in Van Dieman's Land, where he died in 1851.

22. Page, pp. 111–30, and Appendix, of the 2nd edition (1829).

23. Sess. 1824, vol. 6, pp. 403–8.

24. *Report from His Majesty's Commissioners for inquiring into the Administration and Practical Operation of the Poor Laws* (1834), pp. 120–6.

25. A recent assessment of Nicholls' opinions and influence is J. D. Marshall's 'The Nottinghamshire Reformers and their Contribution to the New Poor Law', *Economic History Review*, 2nd series XIII, 3 (April 1961), pp. 382–96.

26. *A History of the English Poor Law*, 2 vols. (1854), vol. II, pp. 137–9.

27. Arnold Toynbee, *Lectures on the Industrial Revolution in England* (1884), pp. 104, 105; William Cunningham, *The Growth of English Industry and Commerce*, 3 vols. (1907), vol. II, p. 650; vol. III, p. 718 ff.

28. Hammonds, *The Village Labourer, passim*, and *The Rise of Modern Industry* (1937), p. 94. Some of my remarks here are indebted to the bibliography of Speenhamland appended by Karl Polanyi to *The Great Transformation*, pp. 280–6.

29. Eden, vol. I, pp. 580–4.

30. Nicholls, *op. cit.*, vol. II, pp. 138, 139.

31. Toynbee, *op. cit.*, p. 105.

32. Hammonds, *The Village Labourer*, ch. X *et passim*.

33. Clapham, *op. cit.*, pp. 125–32.

34. Polanyi, *op. cit.*, chs. 7 and 8. 'The abolishment of Speenhamland was the true birthday of the modern working class' (p. 101).

35. Ernle, Lord *English Farming Past and Present* (1912), pp. 328–30.

36. 'The Myth of the Old Poor Law and the Making of the New', *Journal of Economic History*, XXIII, 2 (June 1963), pp. 151–84, and 'The Poor Law Report Re-examined', *ibid.*, XXIV, 2 (June 1964), pp. 229–45.

37. 'The Myth of the Old Poor Law and the Making of the New', p. 162.

38. Clapham and Blaug both depend on evidence presented by the 1824 House of Commons Select Committee on Labourers' Wages. See Clapham, *op. cit.*, pp. 123–5.

39. Sess. 1834, vols. 30–4, p. 10b ff.

40. Eden, vol. I, pp. 580, 581.

41. Nicholls, *op. cit.*, vol. II, pp. 138, 240–51.

42. Hammonds, *The Village Labourer*, pp. 165, 184, 185; *The Rise of Modern Industry*, p. 94; Webbs, *The Old Poor Law*, pp. 180–9. The Webbs owe much to the Hammonds here, and so do E. J. Hobsbawm and George Rudé in their recent *Captain Swing* (1969), when they claim that for forty years 'the "Speenhamland system" in one form or another, hung like a millstone round the necks of all rural classes in southern England' (p. 47).

43. Polanyi, *op. cit.*, p. 78.

44. Clapham, *op. cit.*, pp. 123–32.

45. 'The Myth of the Old Poor Law and the Making of the New', pp. 176, 177.

46. *ibid.*, p. 160, and 'The Poor Law Report Re-examined', p. 231. See Poynter, *op. cit.*, ch. VIII, for an assessment of these attempts at 'reform by committee'.

47. James Stephen Taylor, 'The Mythology of the Old Poor Law', *Journal of Economic History*, XXIX, 2 (June 1969), pp. 292–7.

48. J. D. Marshall, *The Old Poor Law, 1795–1834* (1968), pp. 20, 21; Poynter, *op. cit.*, pp. 47, 77, 329. Long ago Clapham, too, called for local investigations; see his preface to Hampson's *The Treatment of Poverty in Cambridgeshire, 1597–1834*, p. xix.

49. James Stephen Taylor, 'Poverty in Rural Devon, 1780–1840' (Stanford University Ph.D. thesis 1966), pp. 50, 105–8; Body, *op. cit.*, pp. 203–26; N. D. Hopkins, 'The Old and the New Poor Law in East Yorkshire, c. 1760–1850' (University of Leeds M.Phil. thesis 1968), pp. 34–42.

50. Clapham, *op. cit.*, p. 124; Blaug, 'The Myth of the Old Poor Law and the Making of the New', pp. 158, 159.

51. Sess. 1825, vol. 19, p. 364. The one clear return is from Cookham parish, where owing to the efforts of a select vestry every sort of allowance to the able-bodied had been done away with. See *The Evidence of the Rev. Thomas Whately, vicar of Cookham, Berks, before the Committee of the House of Lords on the State of the Poor in the years 1830, 1831* (1833).

52. *BRO*, Bradfield, Overseers' Accounts, D/P 22 12–1, 2 (1771–98). Here as elsewhere payments to ill persons and to those doing parish labour were entered separately in the accounts, so there can be no mistaking allowances to the able-bodied unemployed.

53. *BRO*, Brimpton, Overseers' Accounts, D/P 26 12–4 (1774–96); Uffington, Overseers' Accounts, D/P 134 12–3 (1782–1805); Hungerford, Overseers' Accounts, D/P 71 12–5 (1783–94); Warfield, Overseers' Accounts, D/P 144 12–3 (1784–93); Drayton, Overseers' Accounts, D/P 48 12–1 (1739–94); East Hendred, Vestry Minutes, D/P 66 8–1 (1785–1884), minutes for 19 December 1786 and 11 March 1788.

The essence of the 'roundsman' system was the assigning of unemployed poor to the employers of the parish, who would take each labourer for a certain length of time. How long the man was kept by an employer often depended on the latter's poor-rate assessment or rent. In Berkshire this device was sometimes referred to as work 'by the yard' or 'by the yardland'. See Webbs, *The Old Poor Law*, pp. 190–3, and *BRO*, Cholsey, Vestry Minutes, D/P 38 8–1 (1811–56), minutes for 7 March 1814.

54. For example, see Dorothy Marshall, 'The Old Poor Law, 1662–1795', *Economic History Review*, VIII, 1 (November 1937), pp. 38, 39.

55. *Great Britain from Adam Smith to the Present Day* (1928), p. 339.

56. On this matter see my 'Suggestion regarding the origins of the Speenhamland Plan', *English Historical Review*, LXXXIV, 331 (April 1969), pp. 317–22.

57. Mavor's *General View of the Agriculture of Berkshire* reviews in detail the physical and economic geography of Berkshire in the first decade of the nineteenth century.

58. By 1831 Sunninghill, although still partly rural, also had more persons in non-agricultural pursuits than in agriculture. Its location on the Reading–Staines road probably accounts for this. Except for Sunninghill all the parishes kept their socio-economic character of 1801 until the end of our period.

In 1801 Thatcham had the largest population of the sixteen parishes; 1,995 inhabitants. Sulhamstead Bannister had the smallest; 259. In 1801 the average population of the sixteen parishes was 647, and by 1831 it was 886. The median population was about the same. The 37 per cent population growth in those parishes during these thirty years was somewhat more than that for the county (33 per cent) but much less than that for England and Wales (57 per cent). *Comparative Account of the Population of Great Britain in 1801, 1811, 1821, 1831*, Sess. 1831, vol. 18, p. 24 ff. *Abstract of the Answers and Returns, Enumeration Abstract*, Vol. I, Sess. 1833, vol. 36, p. xlviii ff. Blaug discusses the possible association between parish size and levels of relief spending per head in an appendix to 'The Poor Law Report Re-examined', pp. 243–5. His tentative conclusion is a negative one.

59. Normally 'regular' and 'casual' accounts were listed separately by overseers. The first referred chiefly to payments to aged and infirm persons, widows, and children, who were regularly on relief. 'Casual' payments were to persons of all descriptions who were not regular recipients. I have examined both accounts in overseers' books in an attempt to find systematic allowances to the able-bodied.

60. The Webbs, in *The Parish and the County*, (1906), pp. 152–63, discuss the origin and generally severe character of post-1819 select vestries.

61. E. L. Jones, *Seasons and Prices* (1964), pp. 154–57: Annual Summary, 1799–1801.

62. *BRO*, Aston Tirrold, Overseers' Accounts, D/P 10 12–2 (1790–1835); White Waltham, Overseers' Accounts, D/P 142 12–1,2 (1811–36) and Select Vestry Minutes, D/P 142 8 (1822–38); Bradfield, Overseers' Accounts D/P 22 12–2,3,4,5 (1785–1825) and Vestry Minutes D/P 22 8 (1832–72), minutes for 2 September 1832; East Hendred, Vestry Minutes, D/P 66 8–1 (1785–1884), minutes for 27 October 1797 and 22 November 1830; Sunninghill, Vestry Minutes, D/P 126 8–5 (1817–34), minutes for 27 November 1830. Sess. 1834, vol. 31, pp. 11b, 15b.

63. If it was calculated, after 1817 the Cholsey scale for families with children would have been less generous than the Speenhamland scale. *BRO*, Cholsey, Vestry Minutes, D/P 38 8–1 (1811–56), minutes for 5 August 1811 and 27 May 1817.

64. Regarding the meaning of 'bread money', see Henry Russell's evidence in the Poor Law Inquiry Commissioners' *Report* (1834), pp. 27, 28, and *RM*, 10 January 1831: 'Substance of a Conversation between a Rector and his Parishioner'.

In the two periods of shortages Thatcham also distributed actual bread to the needy, or so the large 'Bread Bills' to apparent bakers would indicate.

65. *BRO*, Drayton, Overseers' Accounts, D/P 48 12–2,3 (1794–1836); Thatcham, Overseers' Accounts, D/P 130 12–2 through 10 (1791–1836) and Vestry Minutes, D/P 130 8–1 (1815–37), minutes for 28 June 1820, 18 February 1822 and 6 October 1828. Sess. 1834, vol. 31, pp. 14b, 24b.

The response of the parish officers of Thatcham to the Poor Law Inquiry Commissioners' Rural Queries might appear to mean that Speenhamland-like allowances persisted here. However, given the evidence of the parish accounts, I am inclined to believe Thatcham was providing family allowances in 1832.

66. *BRO*, Chieveley, Miscellaneous Papers, D/P 34 18–5 (1818–20), 'Speen Table', and Vestry Minutes, D/P 34 28–1 (1820–41), minutes for 31 May 1820; Peasemore, 'Money paid to Workmen on Account', D/P 92 18–2 (1799–1810).

67. *BRO*, Uffington, Overseers' Accounts, D/P 134 12–3,4,5 (1782–1825); Undated scale of the Faringdon division, D/EEl O3–5.

68. *BRO*, Brimpton, Overseers' Accounts, D/P 26 12–4 (1774–96); Pangbourne, Overseers' Accounts, D/P 91 12–2 (1820–35) and Vestry Minutes, D/P 91 8–1 (1822–35), minutes for 9 October 1834; Shinfield, Overseers' Accounts, D/P 110 12–2 (1833–45); Sulhamstead Bannister, Overseers' Accounts, D/P 125 12–2,3 (1795–1831); Warfield, Overseers' Accounts, D/P 144 12–4,5,6 (1793–1837).

69. *BRO*, Aston Tirrold, Overseers' Accounts, D/P 10 12–2 (1790–1836); Drayton, Overseers' Accounts, D/P 42 12–2 (1794–1821).

In the six months from October 1795, when relief costs at Drayton were most elevated, four males were among the twenty regular recipients, and eighteen males, some perhaps with families, received relief 'at times'. Drayton had 484 inhabitants in 1801.

70. *BRO*, Bradfield, Overseers' Accounts, D/P 22 12–2 (1795–8). Sales of flour and bread to the poor at a low price occurred in many parishes in 1795–6, and again in 1799–1801. Often a parish subscription was raised for the purpose. See the *Reading Mercury* for notice of these schemes.

71. *B.R.O.*, Brimpton, Overseers' Accounts, D/P 26 12–4 (1774–96); Thatcham, Overseers' Accounts, D/P 130 12–2 (1791–8); Warfield, Overseers' Accounts, D/P 144 12–4 (1793–1811).

Warfield is an interesting case. Here the first payment 'for Bread' was sometime between 22 March and 5 April 1795, that is, at least a month before Speenhamland. Does this mean that these sorts of payments in the following autumn were a continuation of pre-Speenhamland practice? I am inclined to think so, although because the adoption of Speenhamland was possible in the parish I am giving it the benefit of the doubt.

72. Eden, *op. cit.*, vol. I, pp. 580–2.

Presumably 'P' was not Newbury, an incorporated town where the resolution of the county justices would not apply. If it were Newbury, there would have been no reason for allowing even 'W.E.' the Speenhamland rate.

73. Chiefly in the way of family allowances. Sess. 1834, vols. 30–4, p. 10b ff.

74. *BRO*, undated scale of the Faringdon division, D/EEl O–2. Mavor, *op. cit.*, pp. 417, 418. Mavor's book was published in 1809; the material for it was collected in 1807.

Mavor mentioned the Wantage division as also having this scale. I have found no local reprints of the scale from that precinct as I have from the Faringdon division, and Mavor's phrasing suggests some confusion on this point. Accordingly I believe the scale Mavor reported on pertained to the Faringdon division only.

75. Sess. 1834, vol. 31, p. 25b.

76. Anon., *Comparative Statement of the Accounts of the Parish of Speen, Berks* (1820), *passim*.

77. *BRO*, QSOB, and QSR 264, Epiphany Sessions 1800. *RM*, 20 January and 17 March 1800. The parishes whose records were investigated are Binfield, Drayton, East Hendred, Little Coxwell, Shinfield, Sunninghill and Uffington. Binfield and Shinfield were the parishes which adopted bread substitutes in 1800. Binfield, Vestry Minutes D/P 18 8–1 (1800), minutes for 10 October 1800; Shinfield, Vestry Minutes, D/P 110 8–1 (1768–1824), minutes for 17 December 1800.

78. *BRO*, QSOB, adjourned Epiphany Sessions 1801.

79. The confidence of the landed classes in their labourers' good will was premature; the cry of 'bread or blood' was soon to be heard in the neighbourhood of Ely; A. J. Peacock, *Bread or Blood: The Agrarian Riots in East Anglia, 1816* (1965).

80. Tooke, *op. cit.*, vol. II, p. 389.

Observations in this paper regarding wartime and post-1815 agricultural developments are based on a number of recent studies, notably J. D. Chambers and G. E. Mingay, *The Agricultural Revolution, 1750–1880* (1966), pp. 122–33, and F. M. L. Thompson, *English Landed Society in the Nineteenth Century* (1963), pp. 212–37.

81. The total cost of poor relief in England and Wales in the year to March 1818 was £7,870,801. The next year it fell some £350,000, bottomed in 1823–24, and then rose slowly once more. It never again reached the 1817–18 figure before 1834. Sess. 1830–1, vol. 11, p. 207, and Sess. 1835, vol. 47, p. 451.

82. Poynter (p. 223 ff.) discusses the changing fashions in Poor Law thought and literature during the postwar years. He contends that the cause of total abolition had run its course by 1820, while the trend toward Poor Law amendment and reformation became ever stronger after that date.

83. Bicheno, *op. cit.*, p. 138 of the revised 1824 edition.

84. For detailed descriptions of how these mechanisms worked, and how widely they were employed in England after 1815, see the Webbs, *The*

Old Poor Law, p. 189 ff., and *The Parish and the County*, pp. 152–63. Information about the incidence of these devices in Berkshire is plentiful among parish records at the Berkshire Record Office. It will be remembered that East Hendred had a variation of the round in 1786.

85. Sess. 1834, vol. 31, pp. 10b–29b.

Of course the argument of this paper is contrary to the notion that among the postwar measures was a sudden, universal, lowering of allowance rates from the Speenhamland level. No doubt many Berkshire parishes did lower their levels of relief in those years, but as the evidence above suggests, the history of relief by allowances is too complicated to permit generalizations even here. On this matter see the Hammonds, *The Village Labourer*, pp. 184, 185, and the Webbs, *The Old Poor Law*, pp. 182, 183.

86. *RM*, 14 March 1814, 14 December 1818 and 10 January 1820.

87. John Walter, *Letter to the Electors of Berkshire, on the New System for the Management of the Poor, proposed by the Government* (1834), p. 44 ff.

John Walter, besides being a very active magistrate, sometime county sheriff, and MP Berkshire (1832–7), was publisher of *The Times*. His pamphlets, speeches in and out of Parliament, and his vehicle *The Times* reveal him to have been a firm defender of the poor's right to adequate relief, and of local autonomy in administering that relief. As one would expect, he and his newspaper were staunch opponents of the new poor law.

88. *RM*, 18 January–5 April 1830.

Lousley's letters indicate he was a man of forceful wit who relished a war of words. See a recent memorial by his descendant Job Edward Lousley, 'Job Lousley (1790–1855) of Blewbury and Hampstead Norris', *Berkshire Archaeological Journal*, 63 (1967–8), pp. 57–65.

89. Note the favourable report from Frederick Page, then acting justice and deputy lord lieutenant for Berkshire, on the behaviour of 'rioting' labourers, the attempts of the Reverend Fulwar Craven Fowle and other justices to persuade farmers to meet their labourers' demands, and the reluctance of Charles Dundas, following his exertions to apprehend rioters, to prosecute them so far as the law allowed. The opinions of these persons, along with those of Morris Ximenes and his colleagues in the 'Forest Association', may be traced in the collection of Home Office correspondence (H.O. 52/6; Berkshire) at the Public Record Office.

90. *BRO*, Overseers' Accounts and Vestry Minutes for Drayton, Earley liberty, East Hendred, Hungerford and Longworth.

The standard work relating to the poor rate and its many peculiarities is Edwin Cannan's *The History of Local Rates in England*, 2nd edition (1912).

91. Some few persons held both offices at one time or another in their lives. One of the Berkshire respondents to the Poor Law Inquiry Commissioners' Rural Queries of 1832 was then both a magistrate and parish

overseer (William Mount of Wasing). By 1830 Frederick Page was an acting magistrate; years before he had been an overseer. Sess. 1834, vols. 30–34;. Eden, *op. cit.*, vol. I, p. 575. *Public Record Office*, H.O. 52/6; Berkshire, Frederick Page to the Home Secretary, 22 November 1830.

92. *The Parish and the County*, pp. 350–60.

93. Mavor discussed the large numbers, and characteristics, of the resident gentry (chs. II and IV). Compare his observations with Thompson's (ch. V *et passim*). Thompson has much to say about the quality of life pertaining to the greater and lesser gentry, and farmers, in nineteenth-century England, and he also remarks on the great portion of Berkshire land in the gentry's possession.

The names of Berkshire magistrates can be obtained from the Quarter Sessions Order Books and Rolls, the 'Berkshire Magistrates' Roll', 1801–95 (*BRO*, Q/JL 1), and other documents. Compare the names here with those of the proprietors of the 155 'Principle Seats' in the county as recorded by Mavor, *op. cit.*, pp. 56–62.

94. In the years 1748–50 the annual cost of poor relief in England and Wales was about £700,000. By 1775–6 it had risen to £1·5 million, and in 1802–3 it was over £4 million. In Berkshire the increase was equally notable, from £16,000 yearly in 1748–50 to £82,000 in 1802–3. Sess. 1830–1, vol. 11, p. 205.

95. Regarding conditions in Berkshire, see the evidence of the Reverend Dr Durell in *The Agricultural State of the Kingdom in February, March and April 1816*, by the Board of Agriculture (1816), p. 28.

96. Thompson, *op. cit.*, pp. 235–7. Thompson notes that some effects of the post-war depression did eventually serve to alter the landlord's position, but these were neither quickly nor cruelly felt.

97. See the letter from Thomas Goodlake, JP, to the Home Secretary, grumbling about Dundas's management of the bench (18 January 1830). *Public Record Office*, H.O. 52/6; Berkshire.

Charles Dundas was a newcomer to Berkshire. Descended from an aristocratic and well-landed Scottish family, he married Anne Whitley, heiress to Barton Court in Berkshire and Wiltshire. In 1785, after coming to occupy his Berkshire property, he became a county magistrate, and for the remainder of his life he devoted much of his energy to county affairs. He sat in the House of Commons for over fifty years but never cut a figure there. Shortly before his death in the summer of 1832 he was elevated to the peerage as Baron Amesbury. *BRO*, QSOB, Midsummer Sessions 1785 ff; Sir Lewis Namier and John Brooke, *The House of Commons, 1754–1790*, 3 vols. (1964), vol. II, p. 354; *Dictionary of National Biography*.

98. E. W. Martin, *The Shearers and the Shorn: A Study of Life in a Devon Community* (1965). The discussion which follows owes some of its character not only to Martin, but to the inescapable Polanyi.

99. Ronald Blythe, *Akenfield: Portrait of an English Village* (1969), p. 112.

5
Public Assistance in the United States
Colonial Times to 1860

BLANCHE D. COLL

The dominance of England in the American Atlantic seaboard colonies in the seventeenth century and its gain of territory westward by victory over France in the eighteenth resulted in a general extension of English laws and customs from the Old World to the New. Means adopted for care of the indigent were no exception. English poor law was copied. English investigations of the poor law and of economic and social conditions were publicized and studied. Indeed from colonial times until early in the twentieth century, the United States looked to England and freely borrowed from her many attitudes toward the impoverished as well as methods for their care.

Contrary to popular belief, the United States—even in colonial times—had not only significant numbers of poor persons but also its share of persons dependent on public assistance or voluntary charity. Paradoxical as it may seem, neither Americans nor foreign visitors exaggerated when they noted the general prosperity of the New World and the absence of a pauper class said to exist in the Old. However, the fact that at one time and another a good many Americans in the seventeenth and eighteenth, as well as the nineteenth century, found themselves in needy circumstances is not as incredible as it might seem, given the economic and social conditions under which the American colonies were founded.

It is a truism, of course, that the land destined to become the United States of America contained great potential wealth and

128

untold opportunity. But it is often forgotten that converting potential into reality was arduous and time-consuming work. Almost to a man the colonists were of moderate means if not actually poor when they arrived in this country. Moreover, many of them were paupers, vagrants, or convicts shipped out by the English government as indentured servants.

During the colonial period not only was farming the principal occupation, but as Stuart Bruchey points out, much of this was subsistence farming rather than production of cash crops. By the eighteenth century, a handful of cities—Boston, Massachusetts; Newport, Rhode Island; New York; Philadelphia, Pennsylvania; and Charleston, South Carolina—dotted the Atlantic coast. Economic dependency in colonial times was by no means confined to these centres of population, although the burden of poor relief was felt more acutely there. Marcus Jernegan's study of poor relief in Virgina shows that cases cared for by poor law officials[1] included the old, the sick, widows and orphans, as well as the more troublesome cases associated with desertion and illegitimacy, which were quite common, particularly among indentured servants.

Except in New England, where indenture was rare, indentured servants, whether bound or having served out their term, were the group most likely either to become dependent or to produce dependent children. The French and Indian wars drove impoverished refugees from the frontier to the coastal cities. Often a decline in trade made it impossible to absorb such persons in the local economy. The wars also created widows and fatherless children. Storms and disastrous fires occasioned other emergency needs. In addition, the arrival of a small but steady stream of poor immigrants presaged the flood of immigration of the nineteenth and early twentieth centuries. Undoubtedly, the frontier served as a safety valve to some extent, but the historian of Baltimore's eighteenth-century almshouse noted that 'the back lands which would offer a general resource to a surplus population, if it existed, tempt the young and hale, but not the halt and aged who remain on our hands'.[2]

It was to take more than a century for the United States to become an urbanized industrial society. Yet the course was set early in the nineteenth century with the establishment of a few

I

infant manufacturies, the construction of canals, and the building of a few railroad systems. Historians and economists are still investigating the movement of the American economy during the period before 1860 to pinpoint the nature and extent of economic growth. Certainly, however, from the 1820s on, these years were marked by large-scale construction projects, particularly in transportation; an increase in manufacturing; and flourishing foreign and domestic trade.[3]

During the first half of the nineteenth century, the present geographical boundaries of the continental United States were fixed by treaty, purchase, and conquest. Population growth was a marvel to all. The first census counted 3·9 million persons. By 1850 native births and immigration (mainly from the English-speaking countries and Germany) combined to make the population reach 23·2 million. The following ten years saw a net gain of more than 8 million persons; consequently, in 1860 the population stood at 31·5 million. Although remaining predominantly rural (700 thousand urban–8·9 million rural in 1820; 1·8 million urban–15·2 million rural in 1840; 6·2 million urban–25·2 million rural in 1860) this situation was beginning to reverse itself.[4] The period was notable also for a marked increase in the number and size of cities.

Between 1830 and 1860, the United States was in one of its recurrent periods of social reform. From public education to women's rights to temperance, leading Americans determined to purify and perfect their society. This period also saw the beginnings of the trade union movement. The most urgent problem, the abolition of slavery, did not become apparent to most persons until the 1850s, but then it absorbed the energy of nearly all reformers.

Public provision for aid to the poor established by colonial and state law was modelled on the English Elizabethan statute of 1601. Adoption of the Elizabethan poor law and of the English Law of Settlement and Removal of 1662 by colonial legislatures and by the new states is a matter of prime importance in the history of American provision for the indigent. It is, perhaps, not so extraordinary that these means were adopted as it is that many of the attitudes that inspired the legislation and much of the policy employed in its administration persist to the present. Although many changes in public assistance programmes and legislation have been made over the years, such changes have not been commensurate with fundamental shifts in the economic and social structure of life in the United States.

In adopting the English poor laws, colonial Americans established, first of all, a presumed right to assistance for the needy person. The word 'presumed' is used advisedly, because these laws did not approach poor relief from the point of view of the applicant but, rather, imposed upon secular administrators a public duty to provide for the indigent. Thus, a classic judicial decision held that an indigent man had no case when he sued the overseers of the poor for relief in civil court but rather that the town might might bring suit for criminal negligence against the overseers in the performance of their obligations. Nevertheless, the 'right' to public assistance has always been acknowledged to be more unconditional than that which might be bestowed through voluntary benevolence. The United States has an unbroken tradition of public responsibility for the care of the destitute.

The United States also has a tradition of requiring the establishment of legal residence in a particular geographic locality as a prerequisite for aid.[5] The base of settlement has been deemed the town, the municipality, or, in the south and west, the county. Residence requirements have been defended on the ground that to qualify for assistance a person in need should have contributed by labour or taxes to the exact place giving him his relief. Conditions for establishing residence have varied. Most early laws included property qualifications as well as a prescribed length of stay in a particular locality, a far from surprising requirement in view of the fact that the right to vote was also limited in these ways. Thus, the 1836 law of Pennsylvania provided that a $10 leaseholder residing in a specific place for one year might attain settlement entitling him to relief when in need. The more liberal New York law of 1827 merely required a year's residence in a particular locality within the state, thus waiving property requirements.

To further protect their communities from having to support persons without means, early laws also provided for 'warning off' newcomers—that is, town officials were authorized to urge those who seemed likely to become public charges to move on and to caution them against expecting relief if they failed to follow this advice. Although apparently seldom resorted to, this extreme legal limitation illustrates the great anxiety local communities felt about keeping the poor tax at a minimum.

Much more commonly invoked than 'warning off' was the practice of 'passing on' the indigent back in the direction of his place of legal settlement. Such persons were escorted by the constable of one town on to the next, until they arrived at their place of legal residence which would presumably accept responsibility for their care. Almost 1,800 persons, half of them women and children, were removed from one part of New York State to another in the year 1822 because of this policy.

Through the years a great deal of time and money has been spent litigating the question of which locality was responsible for the care of given dependents. In 1822, New York State spent $13,500 for court appeals, a sum that, it was estimated, would have provided institutional care for 450 persons for a year.[6] Total funds spent on litigation, plus fees to constables and other officials for removals, amounted to nearly one ninth of the total relief moneys in the state that year. In the first decade of the nineteenth century, a small town in New Hampshire spent $1,197 for relief, and for lawsuits, $517.

The poor laws commonly required that the economic resources of certain relatives be tapped to support their dependent kinfolk. Colonial poor laws specified these relatives as the parents, grandparents, or children. By 1836 all states on the Atlantic seaboard except New York and the southern states had added grandchildren to the list. Stiupulations were later expanded in many states beyond the consanguinal to the collateral line to make brothers and sisters liable.

However, litigation to enforce relatives' responsibility has never reached the higher courts to the same extent as suits about settlement laws. Poor persons usually have poor relatives. The general practice of the courts (except in the case of parents' responsibility for the support of children) has been to assign a small contribution and then to let the matter be forgotten if the court order was evaded.

If settlement had been established and relatives could not support an applicant for assistance, there remained the question of what categories of persons would be deemed eligible for public assistance. The original poor laws, following the English model, made a distinction between those able and those unable to work. The latter were identified as the 'lame, impotent, old, blinde, and such other among them being poore, and not able to work'.[7] Persons clearly unable to support themselves were to be helped. Josiah Quincy, a conservative politican, aristocrat, and Anglophile, and onetime mayor of Boston, wrote that if only those totally incapable of caring for themselves were applicants for public assistance, 'there would be little difficulty, either as to the principle, or as to the mode of extending relief'.[8]

Differences of opinion about the principle and the mode of relief did, however, arise early in the nineteenth century and debate continued for many years over such differences. During the early nineteenth century, as a result of the Napoleonic wars, the United States experienced a severe economic depression from 1815 to 1821. This depression, together with a modest increase in population, caused relief expenditures to rise. At the same time Americans became keenly interested in England's investigations of its own poor laws.

The immediate results of these circumstances were some inquiries—both public and private—and numerous recommendations for handling public relief. One such an inquiry was made in 1824 by the Secretary of State of New York, John V. N. Yates, whose principles were democratic and his political party, Jefferson-Republican.[9] The report he produced discussed the four major means being used to care for the needy: the contract system, auction of the poor, the almshouse, and relief in the home. Under the contract system, all dependent persons were placed under the care of a townsman or farmer and his wife who offered to care for them for a lump sum, fixed as low as possible. The second system, which became increasingly subject to adverse comment, was to auction off the poor to the couple who agreed to take care of them for the smallest amount. Actually it was an auction in reverse: instead of the prize (the destitute man, woman, or child) going to the highest bidder, the unfortunate person was sold to the lowest. Placement in an almshouse was the third important means of caring for the indigent. The fourth, relief to the needy in their homes, was usually referred to as 'outdoor relief', that is, relief outside the almshouse.

By the third decade of the eighteenth century all the leading seaport towns, except Newport, had almshouses, but almshouses were by no means the exclusive method of caring for the indigent. Yates, a century later, found about 30 almshouses in New York State housing not more than 2,000 persons (9 per cent) out of a total relief load of 22,111 persons. Thus the majority of the 6,896 persons whom Yates judged permanent paupers were not in almshouses, but were receiving outdoor relief.

For the New Yorker, Yates, and a number of others who expressed themselves on the subject, the ideal move was to make the almshouse the sole resort of both permanent and temporary paupers. Wrote Quincy:

> That of all modes of providing for the poor, the most wasteful, the most injurious to their morals and destructive to their industrious habits is that of supply in their own families. That the most economical mode is that of Alms Houses; having the character of Work Houses, or Houses of Industry, in which work is provided for every degree of ability in the pauper; and thus the able poor made to provide, partially, at least for their own support; and also to the support, or at least the comfort of the impotent poor.[10]

If county almshouses were established throughout the state, Yates estimated that New York could reduce expenditures by about half, for a yearly saving of approximately $250,000. So very persuasive were the arguments of men like Quincy and Yates and the seeming logic contained in the English poor law report of 1834 that, by 1860, few localities of any size lacked almshouses.

The assumed superiority of the almshouse over other means of caring for the poor was extolled on many points. Almshouses would deter those seeking relief, for the idle and dissolute, as soon as they learned that work would be required 'in the house', would just as soon seek employment on the outside. Those who did enter the almshouse would find their morals improved: lazy persons would become industrious; the intemperate become teetotallers; and the 'vicious' become virtuous.

Whatever their shortcomings, almshouses were humanitarian as compared with the irresponsible, cruel systems of auctioning the poor or contracting for their care with persons who were often on the edge of dependency themselves. Not infrequently, in the larger cities, at least, affluent citizens pointed to the almshouse with pride as the place their community's generosity had provided for its unfortunate citizens.

In the Atlantic seaboard cities in particular, almshouses were in large part free hospitals, admitting many newly-arrived immigrants. The tide of immigrants to the United States rose steadily—from only 129,000 in the 1820s, to 540,000 in the following decade, to more than 1·5 million in the 1840s, to a pre-Civil War peak of more than 1·75 million in the 1850s. Altogether about 6 million immigrants crossed to the 'land of opportunity' between 1820 and 1860—roughly half of them from Great Britain and Ireland, about 2 million from Germany, and about 50,000 from the Scandinavian countries. Many of the immigrants arrived ill from overcrowded and insanitary shipboard conditions or, soon after arrival, became ill or suffered accidents while building the canals and railroads. Most of them left the almshouse and found work as soon as they were restored to health. They were the kind of people we would term 'medically indigent' today.

Touched, perhaps, by the intense sufferings of the refugees from Ireland in 1847 and 1848, the Trustees for the Poor of Baltimore expressed sympathy toward the immigrant and complimented the charitable sprit of the community:

> The tide of emigration to America has—as was reasonably to be expected—brought with it much poverty as well as disease, and as a consequence has tended to increase the inmates of charitable public institutions. It is, however, a pleasant reflection to the philanthropist that the poor emigrant, borne down by privation and disease, may find on the shores of God's favoured land a charitable roof under which he may recover his wonted physical energy.[11]

A few years later, the Trustees expressed their 'astonishment' that the incidence of pauperism was as small as it was among recent arrivals when it is evident that the most of the emigrants . . . are poor—many cannot speak our language, very many experience a difficulty in obtaining employment upon their arrival, whilst others are rendered for a season incapable of labor by debility consequent upon the crowded condition of emigrant passenger ships. The increase of foreign admissions cannot be attributed in any degree to dissolute habits; on the contrary they are in the main of temperate habits and but seldom remain long in the Institution.[12]

Immigrants, with few exceptions, started work as unskilled labourers and were paid very low wages—at 1967 prices the equivalent of about $20 a week in the 1840s and about $25 in the 1850s. A large brewery in New York, in 1840, paid its labourers at the rate of 62·5 cents a day; women cotton-weavers in Massachusetts were paid at about the same rate.[13] When illness or unemployment struck, the immigrant rarely had savings to fall back on. Nevertheless, there was a great outcry about foreign paupers. Although the number of paupers sent to America at the expense of foreign governments was neligible, recent immigrants made up a large proportion of persons entering the almshouse.

Periodically, almost until the beginning of the twentieth century, the United States was ravaged by deadly plagues—yellow fever, cholera, typhoid, to name the most virulent—caused by filth, impure water, and other insanitary conditions. The plagues struck with most force in the cities, and here sickness and death claimed first—and in greatest numbers—the poor. The almshouse, as the poor man's hospital, often provided the only resource for caring for the stricken. Thus, in 1834 a student at the University of Maryland Medical School wrote enthusiastically to his uncle about his assignment to the Baltimore Almshouse:

My present situation offers great advantages to the medical student . . . I shall probably see almost every variety of disease which the climate and season present, having many under my own charge with the advice of the attending physician and the other resident students who are intelligent and well-informed young men. The subjects, though paupers, are not, as I had supposed, generally old and helpless, for we have them of all ages from birth upwards, and many are stout able-bodied men and women who come to this place where they can get good fare and medical attention for little or nothing. The house is now crowded with the sick.[14]

Some of the great public hospitals in the United States today—New York's Bellevue; Brooklyn, New York's Kings County Hospital; Philadelphia's General Hospital; and Baltimore City Hospitals—were originally almshouses. In the large Atlantic seaboard cities, at least, medical care in almshouses was apt to be excellent. For example, the physician at Baltimore's almshouse from 1789 to 1798 was an eminent physician and researcher, the first to discover that an organism could cause infectious disease. Another physician at the Baltimore almshouse, William Power, had studied under the great French physician, Pierre Louis. Power introduced scientific medicine when he took up residence at the almshouse in 1840 and continued his modernization of diagnosis and treatment during his eleven years as attending physician. Under Power's supervision, careful medical histories were taken, percussion and auscultation included in physical examinations, progress reports made and post mortem examinations undertaken.

Exacting work from persons in almshouses turned out to be virtually impossible, mainly because of the type of indigence present. Yet advocates of almshouse industry always assumed that the almshouse had a large group of able-bodied inmates. The actual situation was quite different. The classification of persons in Philadelphia's Blockley almshouse in 1848 shows this clearly and typically (Table 1). Only 192 men and women (about 12 per cent of the total) were capable of working.

There was, however, some seasonal variation in working capacity. More able-bodied unemployed persons were sheltered in the almshouse in winter than in summer. During the winter, unskilled labourers employed in shipbuilding or in other outdoor construction work were laid off, and some of these workers were forced into the almshouse. But the winter was the very time that almshouses, usually set up as farms, were least able to provide work. On the contrary, during the summer most almshouse superintendents had to hire farm labour from the general population.

For all their proliferation, almshouses did not have universal support; in fact, at times there was public revulsion against them.

TABLE I

Classification of Persons
Blockley Almshouse, Philadelphia
1848

Children	III
Hospital and lunatic	718
Old men's infirmary and incurable section	188
Male working wards	79
Mechanics wards	42
Old women's asylum and incurable	256
Women's working ward	71
Nursery with women	21
Nursery with children	23
Total white persons	1509

Source: Benjamin J. Klebaner, *Public Poor Relief in America, 1790–1860*, p. 211. There were also 79 Negroes in the almshouse, including three women and ten children. The statistics do not show how many Negro adults were capable of working.

Among the arguments presented by the out-and-out opponents of almshouses was that the idea of deterrence was overdone because a sense of shame would keep the deserving from entering the house, but the 'vicious and idle' would not hesitate. Others thought it cruel, especially in rural areas where persons were accustomed to solitude, to uproot them and force them into congregate living. Furthermore, some saw the almshouse system as relatively costly and believed that dependent persons could instead be placed with friends or relatives for a smaller sum—a mere portion of the cost of providing for their entire support in an institution—or they could be given some relief in their own home to supplement low wages.

One such instance of revulsion against almshouses occurred in New York, in 1830 the most populous state in the Union with almost 2 million persons. There by 1832, the exhortations of Yates and Governor Enos T. Thropp, a Jacksonian-Democrat,[15] led to the establishment of county almshouses in 51 of the 55 counties. But opposition developed when conditions of gross overcrowding and improper treatment in county almshouses were revealed. Information about such conditions was publicized in 1838 in a committee report of the State Assembly, then dominated by the conservative Whig Party—which was doubtless not adverse to making an issue over neglect of the poor by the Democrats, the very party which claimed to be more interested than the Whigs in the well-being of the poor.

The first section of this report described shocking conditions at the Genesee County almshouse. Because of its faulty buildings, this almshouse would have offered poor shelter even had it not been overcrowded. As it was, one small room held five beds occupied by 12 women and children—and this was not the most unwholesome of the sleeping compartments. Insane and feeble-minded persons were lodged with normal persons. The sick were mingled with the well.

With the Democrats back in power in 1856, another investigation of 55 poorhouses, exclusive of New York City and King's County, revealed conditions that were equally bad if not worse than those of 1838 and the Committee's report strongly condemned them:

> The poor houses throughout the State may be generally described as badly constructed, ill-arranged, ill-warmed, and ill-ventilated. The rooms are crowded with inmates. . . . In some cases, as many as forty-five inmates occupy a single dormitory, with low ceilings, and sleeping boxes arranged in three tiers one above another. Good health is incompatible with such arrangements. . . .
> The want of suitable hospital accommodations is severely felt in most of the poor houses . . .
> A great evil of the poor houses is idleness. Its effects are most visible in the winter season, when the houses are crowded, when there is little out door work to be done, and when the inmates are in the most vigorous state to do full work. In all the large counties at least, work houses should be established . . . and suitable legal power should be given to the proper officers to consign able-bodied paupers to the work house instead of the poor house proper.
> Such workhouses would tend to diminish pauperism; at all events to diminish the burthen of it.[16]

The report concluded with a vivid picture of conditions in New York's rural almshouses and pointed the finger of shame at an indifferent public:

> It is much to be regretted that our citizens manifest so little interest in the condition even of those in their immediate neighbourhood. Individuals who take great interest in human suffering whenever it is brought to their notice, never visit them, and are entirely uninformed, that in a county house almost at their own doors, may be found the lunatic suffering for years in a dark and suffocating cell, in summer, and almost freezing in the winter,—where a score of children are poorly fed, poorly clothed, and quite untaught,—where the poor idiot is half starved and beaten with rods because he is too dull to do his master's bidding,—where the aged mother is lying in perhaps her last sickness, unattended by a physician, and with no one to minister to her wants,—where the lunatic, and that lunatic, too, a *woman*, is made to feel the lash in the hands of a brutal under-keeper—yet these are all to be found—*they all exist in our State*. And the Committee are quite convinced that to this apparent indifference on the part of the citizens, may be attributed in a great degree, the miserable state to which these houses have fallen; and they would urge upon the benevolent in all parts of the State to look into their condition, and thus assist to make them comfortable abodes for the indigent and the unfortunate.[17]

The English Poor Law reform of 1834, which signalled an apparent shift from the Elizabethan poor law, had great impact on Americans of the mid-nineteenth century concerned about economic dependency. Many erroneously believed that the English, by passing the Poor Law Amendment Act, had done away with all outdoor relief. One of the intentions in providing almshouses in the United States was the proscription of relief to the poor in their homes. Nevertheless, as in England, outdoor relief remained common.

The nature and extent of outdoor relief varied from place to place and from time to time. Although no detailed study of public assistance in the middle west and western states has been made, their poor laws followed and sometimes copied verbatim the wording used by the older settlements in the east. In the newer states, too, almshouses appeared, and in all likelihood public officials and citizens weighed the arguments for and against indoor and outdoor relief, as in the older Atlantic communities. Thus, in 1832, although the law of Massachusetts was permissive as to the type of aid given, in 38 towns and cities, including Boston, almshouse care was favoured. At this time 4,535 persons were in almshouses and 398 persons and 1,666 families received outdoor relief.[18]

In contrast, during the years 1830–60, figures for New York State show that temporary outdoor relief accounted for 34 to 50 per cent of all expenditures for relief, except in New York City, where the percentage was generally less. Maryland authorized its counties to dispense only from 10 to 20 'pensions'—regular continuing relief payments. All other dependants on public aid were sent to the almshouse.

The Virginia House of Delegates suggested in 1830 that the county poor farm system be generally adopted, but not to the exclusion of other forms of relief. Of the contrary, the House directed that the Overseers of the Poor should have authority to give outside aid 'under particular circumstances' as 'humanity itself might require in numberless instances'.[19] South Carolina law-makers specified that, even in localities having almshouses, poor law administrators might find it best to have recipients stay with relatives or friends 'according to their peculiar circumstances, and in their sound discretion'.[20]

Such views were common among the southern states, doubtless because the Calvinistic principle of 'work hard, don't idle' was less pressing in the Anglican religion, the dominant religion in the south, and because the southern landed gentry had developed a strong sense of *noblesse oblige*. This was in contrast, of course, to New England and New York, where Calvinism underlay many attitudes toward the poor.

Most seaboard cities attempted to discourage all relief outside almshouses, but, with the exception of Baltimore, they were unable to prevail against it. Some idea of the size of outlays for outdoor relief in five seaboard cities from 1830 to 1860 is shown in Table 2. The data on Charleston are for rations (including food, clothing, and fuel) instead of dollars, and the sharp rise in the number of rations distributed between 1850 and 1860 was apparently caused

TABLE 2

Population of and Outdoor Relief Expenditures for Selected Cities,
1830–60

Year	New York	Philadelphia	Baltimore	Boston	Charleston
	(Population in thousands)				
1830	203	80	81	61	30
1840	313	94	102	93	29
1850	516	121	169	137	43
1860	814	566	212	178	41
	(Outdoor relief expenditures in thousands of dollars)				
1830	$16	$47	$1·8	$14	100*
1840	28	33	1·3	12	70*
1850	76	35	1·3	30	90*
1860	89	—	1·0	69	340*

* Number of rations.

Source: U.S. Bureau of the Census, *1960 Census of Population*, State
Volumes, Table 5; Klebaner, *Public Poor Relief*, pp. 329–30.

by annexation of suburban areas. In Philadelphia and Baltimore,
expenditures for outdoor relief reflected local policies rather than
population growth. In Boston expenditures more than doubled
between 1850 and 1860. Over that decade the progression of New
York City was erratic and reached outlays of $109,000 in 1857 and
$140,000 in 1858—the rise presumably reflecting in part the
consequences of the Panic of 1857.

During the 1820s, Philadelphia officials blamed the continuation of outdoor relief on inadequate facilities. Although Philadelphia's pensions were so small they provided only a minimum
subsistence, such payments over the ten years that ended in May
1824 totalled $621,000, about a third more than the $470,000
aggregate outlay for almshouse care.

Expressing the dominant official view of northern seaboard
cities, the Guardians of the Poor of Philadelphia deplored outdoor
relief as

calculated in an especial manner to blunt and ultimately
destroy that noble pride of Independence, the birthright of
every American Citizen on which the very pillars of our
Republic, have their basis—as its consequences are to create a

dependence on the bounty of others, rather than excite the laudable ambition of creating resources of our own, it cuts the sinews of Industry and of consequence promotes idleness and not infrequently crimes, its having become common has made it fashionable.[21]

These arguments prevailed for a time. In 1828 the Pennsylvania Legislature authorized construction of the large Blockley almshouse. After completion outdoor relief was to be restricted to persons needing only temporary help. Blockley, like many public institutions, was under construction for a long time. In May 1835 the Guardians of the Poor announced that as of 1 July, when Blockley was scheduled to be finished, nothing but temporary aid —no further pensions—would be allowed. But four years later, the Pennsylvania State Legislature gave in to public pressure against such a rule. Outdoor relief for six months, renewable for another six months, was again permitted under the supervision of agents employed by the Board of Guardians of the Poor who investigated applicants for relief and visited their homes.

In 1857 Philadelphia officials did a complete about-face. The mayor expressed his preference for outdoor relief. To send large numbers of persons to the almshouse would, he claimed, reduce the self-reliance of persons in temporary need. That same year the president of the Board of Guardians of the Poor concluded that outdoor relief was more humane and less expensive than institution care.

The Boston Overseers of the Poor, despite the pleas of Mayor Josiah Quincy and others who favoured almshouse care, zealously guarded their right of discretion about the means of relief. Pensions, temporary grants, and emergency distributions of fuel and cash in the winter were all used to aid the needy. Boston's expenditures for outdoor relief totalled less than for almshouse care, probably because outdoor grants were less expensive. During the years 1825–60, the average amount of money spent on relief outside the almshouse varied from one-fourth to one-third of the total expenditures for relief. And during the late 1850s, the proportion spent on outdoor relief rose as high as two-fifths.

In New York City, as in Philadelphia, the Commissioners of the Poor favoured the opening of more almshouse facilities to cut down on the number of pensioners. Between 1825 and 1835 the city spent about the same amount yearly as Boston in outdoor relief. As it had a much larger population than Boston, New York obviously followed a less liberal policy. But after the mid-1830s, New York spent more in keeping with its size. Yet in 1846, the city had only about 1,500 regular recipients of relief in their homes. For the depression year 1848, relief outside the almshouse rose to $95,000 distributed to 44,572 persons—nearly one-tenth of the city's population.

Of all the eastern seaboard cities, Baltimore was the most stringent in granting outdoor relief. During the 1820s, this city, then the third largest in the United States, was spending only about $2,500 a year on pensions, while Boston, with a smaller population, spent about $12,000. Baltimore even decreased its expenditures; by 1830 the city spent only $1,800 on pensions. As Table 2 shows, the amount spent by Baltimore for outdoor relief continued to go down during the next 30 years, although the population almost trebled.

By the end of the 1850s, an apparent tendency to favour outdoor relief was apparent in New York, as well as in Philadelphia. Thus, the New York State Senate Committee concluded its 1857 report with the following revolutionary proposal:

A still more efficient and economical auxiliary in supporting the poor, and in the prevention of absolute pauperism, consists, in the opinion of the committee, in the proper and systematic distribution of *outdoor* relief. Worthy indigent persons should, if possible, be kept from the degradation of the poor house, by reasonable supplies of provisions, bedding, and other absolute necessaries, at their own homes. Half the sum requisite for their maintenance in the poor house would often save them from destitution, and enable them to work in their vicinity, sufficiently to earn the remainder of their support during the inclement season when indigence suffers the most, and when it is most likely to be forced into the common receptacles of pauperism, whence it rarely emerges without a loss of self-respect and a sense of degradation.[22]

Outdoor relief might be temporary or it might be regular in the form of a pension. It cannot be said with certainty that New York

City's categories of pensioners were typical, but probably they did represent a general application of this form of aid. The categories were widows with young children, aged and infirm persons whose relatives were able to provide shelter but no other subsistence, and sick or otherwise incapacitated bread-winners and their dependents. Another common form of outdoor aid was the regular provision of a very small pension, given with the understanding that it be supplemented in one way or another, either by the recipient's own labour, assistance from relatives or friends, or voluntary charity.

Additional voluntary charity came by way of the annual winter collection for the relief of the poor. Mayors and city councils would regularly issue a call at the onset of winter for contributions to a poor fund. Often such funds became quite large.

But charitable grants, whether public or voluntary, whether given in the form of a pension or to meet a temporary emergency, were invariably at the subsistence level. In large cities payment was likely to be in money. But in rural areas, where most people lived at this time, grants were often given in the form of fuel, clothing, or food.

The idea behind niggardly grants and relief in kind rather than cash was akin to the supposed deterrent effect of the almshouse. Men were assumed to be goaded to work only by fear of want; to give an adequate relief allowance would supposedly discourage industry.

During the years 1800–60, the United States suffered two major economic depressions: in 1815–21 and in 1837–43. In addition, several shortlived financial panics occurred, including the panics of 1847 and 1857.

During such economic upheavals, normal channels for relief of distress, both public and voluntary, were strained to the breaking point. Able-bodied unemployed workmen—too proud to ask for charity—inevitably clamoured for work. They formed citizen committees and marched to the mayor's office demanding hearings. Crowds gathered at hastily called outdoor meetings. Fighting and other violence occurred. Looting was common. In New York City in 1837, for instance, a mob attacked two flour warehouses

K

and carried away hundreds of barrels of flour. Such outbreaks occurred during each economic crisis during the nineteenth century in all large cities.

Classical *laissez-faire* economics held that interference with normal market operations (supply and demand) would threaten if not overturn the economic system. But political considerations, tempered with humanitarian feelings, called for the provision of public work for the 'honest' unemployed. Sometimes such work was made available, but never on a scale large enough to take care of all of those suddenly thrown out of employment.

Other kinds of emergency measures were more common. Soup kitchens sprang up everywhere. Newspapers conducted campaigns to raise money, to collect used clothing, to create a bread fund. The winter collection call was intensified and sometimes repeated. However, drives for funds tended to be less successful in periods of depression or financial panic because almost everyone from the affluent down to the steady workman felt the economic squeeze.

Despite low wages, the ups and downs of the business cycle, and other debilitating facts of life by which the nineteenth century poor were victimized, 'pauperism'—as dependence on public assistance in whatever form and however temporary was commonly called—was almost universally deemed a result of moral defect. Such moral failures were expounded not only in public reports, but also by certain voluntary agencies. Thus, in 1818 the newly-founded (Quaker) New York Society for the Prevention of Pauperism listed the following causes of dependency: ignorance; idleness; intemperance (the foremost); want of economy; imprudent and hasty marriages; lotteries; pawnbrokers; houses of ill fame; and the numerous charitable institutions. Its members thought that relief-giving itself, either public or voluntary, had a particularly harmful effect upon the poor:

> Is not the partial and temporary good which they accomplish, how acute soever the miseries they relieve, and whatever the number they may rescue from sufferings or death, more than counter-balanced, by the evils that flow from the expectations they necessarily excite; by the relaxation of industry, which such a display of benevolence tends to produce; by that reliance

upon charitable aid, in case of unfavourable times, which must unavoidably tend to diminish, in the minds of the labouring classes, that wholesome anxiety to provide for the wants of a distant day, which alone can save them from a state of absolute dependence, and from becoming a burden to the community?[23]

However, this society did not remain altogether blind to the effects of economic conditions. Impressed by the hardships caused by the current economic depression, the society included 'want of employment' as a cause of pauperism in its report for 1821.

If intemperance were the 'cause of causes' as many emphasized after making informal estimates and various 'statistical' counts in almshouses, it was no wonder. Americans consumed large quantities of hard liquor. It was even common to pay wages partly in alcohol.

The rich seemed unable to understand why the poor could not save for a rainy day. To the prosperous, the indigent seemed improvident and extravagant. They could not understand why young men married before they could afford it, only, when hard times struck, to desert their families. Even while conceding that times were hard in 1820–1, the New York Society for the Prevention of Pauperism insisted that this was an unusual occurrence. Workmen who were temperate, frugal, and willing to work would not suffer or become paupers for want of employment. Although the demand for labour in the new nation was usually so high as to render this statement plausible, the society overlooked certain aspects which made for temporary unemployment. The lowest paid workers—unskilled labourers in shipbuilding and general construction work, for example—were usually unemployed during the winter.

According to calculations made in 1833 by Matthew Carey, a Philadelphia pamphleteer and economist, the wages of a canal construction worker were too low to support a family, even if employment were steady throughout the year. Carey found, by using the most economical budget for a family of four, that a deficit of about $30 (1967 prices, $103) a year would exist between wages and minimum needs. He declared that the earnings of women shirtmakers were even less adequate to subsistence. Some trades were over-supplied with workers. Carey concluded with a vigorous defence of relief, both public and voluntary:

> It follows, of course, that the poor rates, the aid of benevolent societies, &c., far from producing the pernicious effects ascribed to them are imperiously necessary, and that without them, numbers would . . . actually perish of want, or would have recourse to mendicity; and medicants impose a far heavier tax on a community than the same number of paupers supported by poor rates.[24]

All who commented on the subject of dependency made some bow in the direction of the 'deserving' or 'worthy' poor—those overtaken by misfortune, sickness, or other adversity, those physically unable to work, widows, and the helpless aged. The fact is that these groups accounted for most of the dependents. Yet those who cavilled at the poor laws and at voluntary charities inevitably wrote as if those thus handicapped made up a small minority and that most paupers were able-bodied. Carey, to show such conclusions false, listed the ages of those in receipt of outdoor relief in Philadelphia in the early 1830s. Of 549 persons out of an 80,500 total population, 390 were over 60 years of age (6 were over 100), 50 of these persons were blind, and 406 were widows.

Taking an opposite view from Carey, many argued in the vein of the English poor law 'reformers'. Although careful to allow for 'extreme cases', the logic of their argument led them to recommend the abolition of all public assistance, as well as a great diminution of voluntary charity. They held that the poor laws infringed on property rights because the industrious were being taxed to support the idle. The 'wage fund' theory—the supposed existence of a certain fixed sum to be spent on wages—was invoked. According to this theory, money to support the pauper was wages withheld from some industrious worker. The entire capital of the community having been decreased by the poor rates, a general lowering of wages resulted. This being the case, all poor laws should be scrapped, leaving but a few needy persons to be helped by voluntary charity.

Opponents of public assistance saw great danger in recipients regarding relief as a 'right', rather than as a gift for which they should feel gratitude. Furthermore, only voluntary charity had the desirable characteristics of precariousness and uncertainty. Voluntary charity, according to the New York Association for Improving the Condition of the Poor, 'bridges over the terrible gulf of pauperism, which sweeps downward with such tremendous force, that few who are down therein, are afterwards recovered'.[25]

Those defending public assistance argued that the very precariousness of voluntary charity counted against it as the sole recourse for the needy. Furthermore, the community at large had a responsibility to its dependent citizens. Public charity was equitable; the needy, having contributed to the community's economy in the past, had a right to expect assistance in time of trouble. With an anti-rent war going on in New York State from 1839 to 1846, with Baltimore capturing and recapturing the title of Mob Town from frequent looting and burning and general 'shooting off', and with staid Boston reeling from the Irish 'invasion', it was no wonder that some also favoured the poor laws because of their stabilizing effect on society.

When proponents of voluntary charity spoke, they often had in mind the benevolence of churches or other groups operating on a small scale. In the 1840s, however, each of a number of major cities followed New York's lead in establishing a comprehensive relief-giving agency, an Association for Improving the Condition of the Poor (AICP). Like the Societies for the Prevention of Pauperism, the AICPs were founded in the wake of an economic depression and were a middle-class, Protestant movement. To describe the philosophy and methods of the New York agency is to describe all of them.

The visitors to the poor—all volunteers and all men—were admonished to learn the causes that had brought the needy person to destitution. They were told:

You will become an important instrument of good to your suffering fellow-creatures when you aid them to attain this good from resources within themselves. To effect this, show them the true origin of their sufferings, when these sufferings are the result of improvidence, extravagance, idleness, intemperance, or other moral causes which are within their own control; and endeavor . . . to awaken their self-respect, to direct their exertions, and to strengthen their capacities for self-support . . .

149

Avoid all appearance of harshness, and every manifestation of an obtrusive and censorous spirit. Study to carry into your work a mind as discriminating and judicious as it is kindly disposed.[26]

The visitor was instructed to vary methods according to the cause that had brought the poor to indigence. The first group were those who had arrived at this deplorable state through 'unavoidable causes'. Provided the visitor met 'with industry, frugality, and self-respect, and a preference for self-denial to dependence upon alms' on the part of such persons, he was to guard against his charities becoming a means of 'undermining one right principle, or of enfeebling one well-directed impulse'. Alms were not to be considered the chief means of encouragement for such persons. Rather, 'sympathizing counsel which re-enkindles hope, and that expression of respect for character' were to be employed. Often, it was averred, this way of approaching the deserving poor would 'save them from pauperism'.[27]

A more stringent method was called for when the visitor was dealing with persons in the second category—those who had become destitute through their 'own improvidence and vices'. The association admonished the volunteer in the following words:

> The evils of improvidence can never be diminished, except by removing the cause; and this can only be done by elevating the moral character of the poor, and by teaching them to depend upon themselves . . . Let it be your endevaour . . . to instruct them; to encourage deposits in savings banks for rent, fuel and winter supplies. . . . The rule is, *that the willingly dependent upon alms should not live so comfortably with them as the humblest independent labourer without them.*[28]

Like the leaders of the Societies for the Prevention of Pauperism, leaders of the AICP movement asserted that intemperance was the most common cause of pauperism. They counselled the visitor as a general rule to withhold alms from the drunkard, but, if the family were in dire need, to grant aid, but not 'beyond the demands of urgent necessity'. The visitor should try to save the drunkard, but in any case should never abandon his interest in the children's welfare.

In regard to the third class of dependents—those able but unwilling to work and professional beggars—the Scriptural rule 'If any will not work, neither should he eat' was to be strictly applied. This meant, in fact, let the incorrigible be cared for out of public funds, for the AICP could not as a society founded on Christian principles countenance literal starvation.

Although moral preachments formed the cornerstone of the AICP's philosophy, these societies also engaged in some social reforms. The New York AICP recognized quickly that until the filth and overcrowding of the slums were cleared up, nothing much could be done to overcome alcoholism, promiscuity, and neglect of children. The association therefore became active in housing reform, first trying to interest capital investment, and, when that failed, building a model tenement itself. The AICP was also instrumental in the passage of a law requiring the arrest and detention of vagrant children. It established a juvenile asylum and campaigned long and hard for a pure milk law. As one of the first agencies to collect statistics of the survey type, the AICP's work served as a forerunner of the social research usually associated with the early twentieth century.

The New York AICP was a success when measured by its own strict standards of eligibility for outdoor relief. Its expenditures for relief can be roughly measured and compared with those made from public funds. Between 1845 and 1857, annual receipts and expenditures of the voluntary agency averaged $30,000. To be sure, administrative costs had to be paid out of this amount, but as the visitors were volunteers, such expenses were minimal. The number of families receiving assistance from the agency during those dozen years averaged 6,500. However, public expenditures for outdoor relief by the City of New York over this same period averaged $85,650—almost three times as much as those of the AICP.[29]

During this entire period and, indeed, until the administration of President Franklin D. Roosevelt during the Great Depression of the 1930s, public assistance continued to be handled through township, county, or state governments. In the 1850s, however, the federal government came close to breaking with this tradition. In 1854, a bill inspired by Dorothea Dix, the great friend of the mentally ill and an agitator for their humane care, which would have provided federal land grants to states to help pay for mental hospitals passed both Houses of Congress only to be vetoed by President Franklin Pierce. Had this bill been enacted, it is quite conceivable that similar legislation would have assisted the states in caring for other afflicted or needy groups. Pierce, a follower of Andrew Jackson and an opponent of federal aid to states, wrote:

> Can it be controverted that the great mass of the business of Government that involved... the relief of the needy, or otherwise unfortunate members of society, did, in practice, remain with the States; that none of these objects of local concern are, by the Constitution, expressly or impliedly prohibited to the States, and that none of them are, by any express language of the Constitution, transferred to the United States? Can it be claimed that any of these functions of local administration and legislation are vested the Federal Government by any implication? . . .

> In my judgment you cannot, by tributes to humanity, make any adequate compensation for the wrong you would inflict by removing the sources of power and political action from those who are to be thereby affected. . . .

> If the several States, many of which have already laid the foundation of munificent establishments of local beneficence, and nearly all of which are proceeding to establish them, shall be led to suppose, as they will be, should this bill become a law, that Congress is to make provision for such objects, the fountains of charity will be dried up at home, and the several States, instead of bestowing their own means on the social wants of their own people, may themselves, through the strong temptation, which appeals to States as to individuals, become humble suppliants for the bounty of the Federal Government reversing their true relation to this Union.[30]

Although the rise of the almshouse as the preferred method of caring for the destitute was characteristic of this period, several aspects tend to mitigate this generalization. For one, almshouses cared for the medically indigent, persons whom we would not call paupers today, though they were called so by nineteenth-century statisticians. Other kinds of needy persons who are today housed in large numbers in institutions—the mentally ill, the mentally retarded, homeless children—constituted large segments of the people in nineteenth century almshouse.

Administrators complained about the sending of loose women and men from skid row to mingle with the 'worthy' indigent. The aged and infirm—many of whom we institutionalize today—aroused sympathy from all but the few who claimed that the indigent aged should have saved for their old age or misfortune.

Recurring references to the able-bodied in nineteenth-century publications—references that read as if the able-bodied accounted for most persons in almshouses when, in fact, the opposite was true for at least nine months of the year—tend to cloud the issue even further.

The English poor law, as well as the official and unofficial surveys and reports which led to its reform in 1834, provided the philosophical base for an reinforced such rules of eligibility as residence requirements and relatives' responsibility. These rules, originally laid down by the Tudor monarchs for a rural population at a time when it seemed desirable to curb mobility, gained strength from American feelings of localism and pervasive efforts to keep expenditures at a minimum. The taxpayer apparently did not realize that often more was spent in litigation than was saved by withholding relief.

During this period, the almshouse was extolled as the best means of caring for the destitute, even though some were at pains to condemn it. Numbers of benevolent citizens were proud that their communities were presumably taking such good care of their dependants. Given the circumstances of the people the almshouses served and the fact that urban almshouses were largely free hospitals extending good medical care, these nineteenth century communities *were* making admirable provision for their 'worthy' and even their 'unworthy' poor.

The term 'pauper' and the stigma it carried was certainly misapplied to the medically indigent. Keeping in mind the dread of disease and contagion common to the populace of this period and emphasizing the fact that the almshouse was the poor man's hospital, and that they were *teaching* hospitals, one might wonder whether the poor did not in fact pay for their care and/or cure. This is not to suggest that the sick were looked on as guinea pigs, any more than are patients in teaching hospitals today; all the community, all the citizenry benefited from what was learned about medicine and surgery in city almshouses.

However, in rural areas, the almshouse was likely to be bad, and often scandalously bad. Often it was nothing more than some poor farmer and his wife trying to manage some pitiful old sick people and cast-off children in a run-down house. Often no physician was in attendance. Even where housing, staff, and medical care were somewhat better, as would appear to have been the case in the more prosperous townships and counties, almshouses were apt to be overcrowded and their facilities rapidly deteriorating—conditions that demoralized the staff and the dependants.

The idea persisted that the worthy poor—the widows, the children, the sick, the aged—could be separated from the unworthy poor—the drunkards, the idlers, the thriftless, and the shiftless. But one is struck by the generally good intentions, the charitable spirit, the expression of community responsibility evident in the writings of politicians, of almshouse trustees, of physicians—in short, those who came in direct contact with the poor.

The idea that almshouses should completely supplant all other forms of public aid, although often advanced, was almost always rejected. Public officials recognized that outdoor relief was often more suitable than referral to the almshouse. The result was a significant amount of public outdoor relief, as well as voluntary aid, to maintain indigent persons in their own homes.

Many of those commenting on economic dependency made a sharp distinction between widows and orphans, the aged and infirm, and able-bodied men and women. It is, perhaps, difficult to understand why the critics of public assistance assumed that most dependants were able-bodied shirkers in the face of statistical and social evidence to the contrary. The fact is that the able-bodied accounted for a small minority of public assistance recipients.

It is risky, however, to take the polemics at their face value. When misfortune struck the workingman during the various economic depressions and financial panics that occurred during this period, the more affluent citizens quickly responded to appeals for aid. Whether their response was prompted by a feeling of charity or by instinctive fear of rioting and looting cannot be determined. Probably both emotions were operating.

Two facts remain to be emphasized: public outdoor relief, either in kind or by money payment, usually won out over the hues and cries levelled against it; poor relief under public administration always did.

Notes

1. Until after the American Revolution, these officials were vestrymen of the Anglican Church. They followed an administrative pattern much like that of the Roman Catholic Church in the high Middle Ages; money for charity was collected by tithe. Marcus Wilson Jernegan, 'The Development of Poor Relief in Colonial Virginia', *Social Service Review* (March 1929).

2. [Thomas W. Griffith], 'Alms & Workhouse', MS. (*c.* 1819), p. 1, in Maryland Historical Society.

3. For an exposition of the work of historians and economists on this subject, see Stuart Bruchey, *The Roots of American Economic Growth, 1607–1861*, ch. IV.

4. Bureau of the Census/Social Science Research Council, *Historical Statistics of the United States*, Table A 1–3; Table A 195–209.

5. Residency as a factor in determining eligibility for public assistance was declared unconstitutional by the Supreme Court on 21 April 1969, in *Shapiro v. Thompson*.

6. The amounts claimed to have been spent on relieving the indigent seem to be out of line. In 1850, according to Alexander Clarence Flick, *History of the State of New York*, vol. VI, p. 355, New York State spent $11.64 for each pauper on almshouse care. Figures given by John V. N. Yates suggest that in 1822, New York State was spending $30 for each pauper on almshouse care. Probably the apparent discrepancy is due to Yates' inclusion of administrative costs.

7. 'An act for the relief of the poore', in Ralph E. Pumphrey and Muriel W. Pumphrey, *Heritage of American Social Work: Readings in Its Philosophical and Institutional Development*, p. 16.

8. Massachusetts, General Court, Committee on Pauper Laws, Report of Committee to Whom was Referred the Consideration of the Pauper Laws of the Commonwealth (Josiah Quincy, Chairman) (1821) in Pumphrey and Pumphrey, *Heritage of American Social Work*, p. 63.

9. The present Democratic Party in the United States was called the Republican Party during the early nineteenth century.

11. Trustees for the Poor of Baltimore City and County, *Reports* (1848), p. 165.

12. *ibid.* (1853), p. 297.

13. Derived from *Historical Statistics of the United States*, Table D 589–617; Carroll D. Wright, 'The Course of Wages in the United States Since 1840', *Bulletin de L'Institut International de Statistique* (1895), p. 115.

14. Letter from James L. Cabell to Joseph C. Cabell, 13 December 1834. (In University of Virginia Library.)

15. A follower of Andrew Jackson, President of the United States from 1829–37. It was during Jackson's first campaign for the Presidency that his party was called the Democratic Party.

16. Report of Select Senate Committee to Visit Charitable and Penal Institutions, 1857 (*New York Senate Document No. 8* of 1857) in Sophonisba P. Breckinridge, *Public Welfare Administration in the United States: Select Documents*, pp. 150–1, 152

17. *ibid.*, pp. 156–7.

18. These figures and others that follow are from Benjamin J. Klebaner, *Public Poor Relief in America, 1790–1860*, ch. III.

19. Virginia House of Delegates, *Journal*, 1830–1, Appendix, Doc. No. 9, p. 8, quoted in Klebaner, p. 302.

20. South Carolina, Statutes-at-Large, VI, 242, Act of 16 December 1824, quoted in Klebaner, pp. 314–15.

21. Philadelphia Guardians of the Poor XVI, 4 April 1827, quoted in Klebaner, p. 322.

22. Report of Select Committee to Visit Charitable and Penal Institutions, 1857, quoted in Breckinridge, *op. cit.*, pp. 152–3.

23. Society for the Prevention of Pauperism in the City of New York, *First Annual Report of the Managers* (New York, 1818), p. 25, quoted in David M. Schneider, *The History of Public Welfare in New York State, 1609–1866*, p. 213.

24. Matthew Carey, *Appeal to the Wealthy of the Land . . . on the . . . Situation and Prospects of Those Whose Sole Dependence for Subsistence is the Labour of Their Hands* (Philadelphia), stereotyped by L. Johnson, (1833), quoted in Pumphrey and Pumphrey, *Heritage of American Social Work*, p. 87.

25. New York Association for Improving the Condition of the Poor, *Sixteenth Annual Report* (1859), p. 24.

26. New York Association for Improving the Condition of the Poor, *First Annual Report* (1845), Visitor's Manual, pp. 26–7.

27. *ibid.*, p. 27.

28. *ibid.*, pp. 27–8.

29. Roy Lubove, 'The New York Association for Improving the Condition of the Poor: The Formative Years', *New York Historical Society Quarterly* (July 1959), p. 311.

30. President Franklin Pierce's veto of the bill resulting from Miss Dix's efforts, *Congressional Globe* (33rd, Congress, 1st Session). 3 May 1854,

pp. 1061–3, in Pumphrey and Pumphrey, *Heritage of American Social Work*, pp. 133–4.

Bibliography

Edith Abbott, *Public Assistance: American Principles and Policies*, Vol. I (1940).

Sophonisba P. Breckinridge, *Public Welfare Administration in the United States: Select Documents* (1938).

Carl Bridenbaugh, *Cities in the Wilderness, 1625–1742* (1955).

Robert H. Bremner, 'The Big Flat: History of a New York Tenement House', *American Historical Review* (October 1958), pp. 54–62.

Robert H. Bremner, *From the Depths: The Discovery of Poverty in the United States* (1956).

Stuart Bruchey, *The Roots of American Economic Growth, 1607–1861: An Essay in Social Causation* (1965).

James M. Bugbee, 'Boston Under the Mayors, 1822–80', in Justin Winsor (ed.), *Memorial History of Boston*, vol. III (1881).

Douglas Carroll, *History of the Baltimore City Hospitals*—reprinted from the *Mayland State Medical Journal* (1966).

Bernard L. Diamond, 'The Children of Leviathan: Psychoanalytic Speculations Concerning Welfare Law and Punitive Sanctions', *California Law Review* (May 1966), pp. 357–69. (Entire issue: 'Symposium: Law of the Poor'.)

Leah Feder, *Unemployment Relief in Periods of Depression* (1936).

Alexander Clarence Flick, *History of the State of New York*, vol. VI (1933–7).

Oscar Handlin, *Boston's Immigrants* (1941).

Oscar Handlin, *The Uprooted: The Epic Story of the Great Migrations that Made the American People* (1951).

Benjamin J. Klebaner, 'Public Poor Relief in America, 1790–1860', unpublished Ph.D. dissertation 1952, Columbia University.

John Allen Krout, *The Origins of Prohibition* (1967).

Roy Lubove, 'The New York Association for Improving the Condition of the Poor: The Formative Years', *New York Historical Society Quarterly* (July 1959).

New York Association for Improving the Condition of the Poor, *Annual Reports*, 1843–59. (In Library of Congress.)

Ralph E. Pumphrey, 'Compassion and Protection: Dual Motivations in Social Welfare', *Social Science Revieww* (March 1959), pp. 21–9.

Ralph E. Pumphrey and Muriel W. Pumphrey, *The Heritage of American Social Work: Readings in Its Philosophical and Institutional Development* (1961).

David M. Schneider, *The History of Public Welfare in New York State, 1609–1866* (1938).

Richard Harrison Shryock, *The Development of Modern Medicine* (1947).

Leo F. Solt, 'Puritanism, Capitalism, Democracy, and the New Science', *American Historical Review* (October 1967).

Trustees for the Poor of Baltimore City and County, *Reports*, 1829/30–1859. (In Baltimore City Hall Library.)

U.S. Bureau of the Census, *1960 Census of Population*, State Volumes, Table 5.

U.S. Bureau of the Census/Social Science Research Council, *Historical Statistics of the United States, Colonial Times to 1957* (1960).

U.S. Congress, 'Aldrich Report', *Reports of Committees of the Senate of the United States, 1892–93* (52nd Congress, 2nd session), No. 1394, Pt. I.

6
The American Historian and
Social Welfare
From the Civil War to World War II

MILTON D. SPEIZMAN

There is something anomalous about using 1865 as the dividing line for a discussion about historians' attitudes toward social welfare. Was not the war itself fought over such an issue? True, it was the welfare of one group that lay outside the pale of American society. That is, if the term 'social welfare' is used broadly. But historians today, no less than those of the past, have regarded black history as set apart in its own category—when they have paid attention to it at all. In our own time, historians of both races have accentuated this practice in their pell-mell race to get to the publisher first with what is at last, after 300 years, a recognized—and a selling—subject.

Little will, therefore, be said in these pages about that large minority which was and remains more in need of the instruments of social welfare than any other. Unless they were writing about Reconstruction or 'Redemption' or, possibly, the Niagara Movement or Marcus Garvey (rather unlikely, but occasionally to be mentioned) historians wrote, and their readers expected to read, white history. The interest of most white scholars in the history of Negro Americans came with the Civil Rights Movement of the 1950s and 1960s; in other words, concern about black history has reflected public interest—it did not precede or instruct it.

It is thus, indeed, with the general subject of social welfare. Until the Great Depression of the 1930s most historians' attitudes toward this topic can be divined far more by inference than by direct expression. We can, indeed, learn a great deal by such inference and it may be that a definitive study awaits the use of such tools as content analysis and quantification. Some day a scholar, skilled in the use of such techniques and at the same time a lover of history, will undertake this task. Pending the appearance of such a prodigy we must rely on the more traditional forms of literary and historical analysis.

But let us be fair to our historians. Slavery and afterward the Civil War, the greatest, or at least bloodiest, failures of the American Dream, so absorbed them that other aspects of human welfare—including the fate of the former slaves—were largely ignored.

This neglect of the freedmen should not be ascribed to the historians alone. What has just been said about the practitioners of the craft was equally true of other Americans, including the most fearless abolitionist of them all, William Lloyd Garrison, who shed four decades of devotion to the cause of Negro emancipation when the Thirteenth Amendment became law.

The post-war generation of historians was as intrigued as its successors have been by the question of why this nation, conceived in the highest ideals yet enunciated and delivered by the wisest political obstetrics ever practiced, had come so close to dissolution. The ablest of them, John Bach McMaster, 'the first historian of the people',[1] thought he could explain just that: the United States had moved, from its founding, with little deviation, toward the achievement of that perfect society envisioned by the Founding Fathers. In that light, the anti-slavery crusade and the Civil War itself could be seen as necessary, if unhappy, steps toward that accomplishment.

McMaster could thus admit that the condition of many Americans had been far from desirable in the early years of the Republic and that, indeed, much yet remained to be done, but the Nation was on its uninterrupted march toward its destiny of being the light toward which all peoples yearned. In the famous Introduction to his eight-volume *History*, he proclaimed that 'the subject of my narrative is the history of the people of the United States'. Although he would, of necessity, have much to say about political, diplomatic, and military events, 'the history of the people shall be the chief theme',[2] a theme, it will have been observed, which had already been that of the Englishman, John Richard Green. McMaster, it will have been observed, was in more ways than one a child of his time.

He proposed to describe 'the growth of the humane spirit which abolished punishment for debt, which reformed the discipline of prisons and of jails, and which has, in our own time, destroyed slavery and lessened the miseries of dumb brutes'. 'Nor', he went on, significantly it would appear for our subject, 'shall it be less my aim to . . . tell how, under the benign influence of liberty and peace, there sprang up, in the course of a single century, a prosperity unparalleled in the annals of human affairs; how, from a state of great poverty and feebleness, our country grew rapidly to one of opulence and power.'[3]

McMaster's interest in 'the lower classes' had, however, its limits, as shall be duly noted. As one searches through his volumes, one does indeed discover a concern shared by few of his contemporaries with the plight of the needy. He complained that information about the condition of the poor in the years immediately after independence had been achieved was sparse; 'there can, however, be no doubt that a wonderful amelioration has taken place since that day' in their situation. 'Their houses were meaner, their food was coarser, their clothing was of commoner stuff, their wages were, despite the depreciation that has gone on in the value of money lower by one half than at present.' Their wages, the historian admitted, were pitifully low—although there were those like John Jay who thought them 'very extravagant'. On such a pittance it was only by the strictest economy that a mechanic kept his children from starvation and himself from jail. But in that free land there was hope; even the serving girl, 'before bestowing herself in marriage on the footman or the gardener, laid away in her stocking enough guineas and joes to buy a few chairs, a table, and a bed'.[4]

His greatest sympathy went to those persons, nearly always of the working classes, who fell afoul of the law and were incarcerated in the unspeakable prisons of that age. Especially did his heart go out to those imprisoned for debt; to McMaster the greatest improvement in the lot of 'the poorest class' had been, not better wages, food, or clothing but the abolition of that practice. His language was graphic:

No crime known to the law brought so many to the jails and prisons as the crime of debt, and the class most likely to get into debt was the most defenceless and dependent, the great body of servants, of artisans, and of laborers, those, in short, who depended on their daily wages for their daily bread. One hundred years ago the laborer who fell from a scaffold or lay sick of a fever was sure to be seized by the sheriff the moment he recovered, and be carried to jail for the bill of a few dollars which had been rung up during his illness at the hucksters or the tavern.

The revolutionary generation was an incredibly cruel one by the standards of a later generation. At the same time as they 'put up a just cry of horror at the brutal treatment of their captive countrymen in the prison ships and hulks' of the British, 'the face of the land was dotted with prisons where deeds of cruelty were done, in comparison with which the foulest acts committed in the hulks sink to a contemptible insignificance'.

To a generation which has beheld great reforms in the statutes of criminal law and in the discipline of prisons and jails; to a generation . . . which has expended fabulous sums in the erection of reformatories, asylums and penitentiaries, houses of correction, houses of refuge, and houses of detention, all over the land; which has furnished every State prison with a library, with a hospital, with workshops, and with schools, the brutal scenes on which our ancestors looked with indifference seem scarcely a reality. Yet it is well to recall them, for we cannot but turn from the contemplation of so much misery and so much suffering with a deep sense of thankfulness that our lot has fallen in a pitiful age, in an age when more compassion is felt for a galled horse or a dog run over at a street-crossing than our great-grandfathers felt for a woman beaten for cursing or a man imprisoned for debt.[5]

In a series of lectures delivered exactly twenty years after the publication of these lines, at Western Reserve University, McMaster returned to this theme and offered an explanation. Again he described the terrible cruelty of the Revolutionary age, the nature of punishment. A pauper, he said, who received any public aid (as well as his wife and children) was required to 'wear on the sleeve of the outer garment in plain view a large P of red or blue cloth, and the first letter of the place to which he belonged'.[6]

Such penalties and the contemporary inequities in political rights were contrasted with the sublime declarations of the Founding Fathers. To McMaster, however, there was no inconsistency and in his proffered solution to what would certainly appear to this generation as a paradox, he revealed his philosophy of American history: the Fathers realized very well that injustices and inequities existed but they believed that to have 'recklessly removed from the statute books every law, to have ruthlessly broken down every custom or usage at variance with the new principles they had announced, would have been acts of disorganization of the worst kind'.[7] They were neither disorganizers nor anarchists, but statesmen who were simply waiting for the best opportunity to rectify those wrongs and to extend the rights of man. That they had shown consummate wisdom in this procedure was evidenced in the reflection 'that while our countrymen have been making such astonishing progress in all that administers to the comforts and conveniences of life, they have at the same time grown charitable and humane'.[8]

In his *History*, McMaster described on occasion the 'socialist', usually 'immigrant', agitation which sought to stir up workingmen during the periodic panics which beset the nation. He reported sympathetically proposals to provide relief during the Panics of 1854 and 1857. Typical was the New York Association for the Relief of Destitute Serving Girls which charged, in 1854, that 20,000 girls were unemployed, for so hard were the times that thousands of householders had been forced to do without servants. Benefit performances of many varieties were given for their aid and efforts were made to find work for them in the small towns where they would be paid a dollar 'or even fourteen shillings, which was a dollar and three quarters, a week'.

The crisis of 1857 caused even greater distress and led to new demands by German socialists who asked for such 'radical' measures as 'a judicious tariff, a sound currency, and no small bank bills', as well as public works and maximum food prices. Even New York's mayor, Fernando Wood declared that 'truly may it be said that in New York those who produce everything . . .

labor without income while surrounded by thousands living in affluence and splendor and who have income without labor'. Demonstrations, called by German and Irish labourers, asked the mayor to reinforce his words and threatened violence. The threat passed, however; troops were withdrawn; and, McMaster tells us, 'it was noted, as a sign that suffering was not so bad as represented, that the theaters supported by mechanics were well attended'. He continued:

> The worst was now over. At the Norris Locomotive Works [in Philadelphia] the hands resolved that there was no need for any sober, deserving workman to come to absolute want, warned their fellow workmen not to be led astray by designing men, and named a committee to receive applications for aid from any deserving man who had ever been employed at the Locomotive Works. Relief Associations were active in all the wards and a few more attempts to excite the unemployed came to naught.[9]

Thus ended the great Panic of 1857 and with it McMaster's reputed sympathy for the poor in his *History*. The historian agreed with the prevailing view that the best help which the poor could receive would be that which came from their fellows. (One may be reminded of the 'Share-a-Job' plans of the Great Depression of the 1930s or J. P. Morgan's 'Block Plan' during the same period in which the banker suggested that the residents of each block take care of the destitute on that block.)

But McMaster continued to be troubled by the evidences of poverty, cruelty, and slavery in his country's past and he returned to this theme in his Western Reserve lectures two decades later. Using as his final text the Dorr War in Rhode Island in the early 1840s, McMaster exulted in the eventual triumph of democracy in the little New England state. The final victory of freedom, however, came during the following half century. 'It is enough to know that the rights of the black man, the rights of children, the rights of women, the rights of workingmen have received in the last fifty years a recognition never before given them.' The abolition of slavery, the reduction in the hours of labour, the achievement of women's rights and free education

have produced an amount of human happiness which it is not

possible to rightly estimate. It is enough to know that the principles laid down by our forefathers have not been repudiated. . . . Never did our government so nearly derive its just powers from the consent of the governed, and never did the governed so fully recognize as self-evident truths the three inalienable rights of man.[10]

If we have dwelt overlong on John Bach McMaster it is because he was quite unique in expressing as much interest as he did in matters of social welfare. Richard Hofstadter has recently reminded us that most historians of the years between the Civil War and the Progressive period were conservatives. 'What is striking about the literature of this era', he has written, 'with a terrible Civil War behind it and the hideous problems of industrialism looming larger and larger ahead is the narrow range of the historians' social sympathies.'[11] To discover scholarly debate on the causes and treatment of poverty, slums, public health, and other issues which may be loosely labelled 'social welfare' it would be necessary to turn to history's daughter disciplines of economics, sociology, and political science. Such is not the present purpose.

It may, however, be instructive to pause briefly at the work of a man who, usually classified as a historian, was the most popular exponent of that Spencerian philosophy which dominated so much of American thought during the last third of the nineteenth century, particularly of the theoreticians of scientific philanthropy whose views were paramount in the enormously influential charity organization movement. John Fiske took little part in the arguments about poverty and charity, but in his effort to reconcile evolution with religion he proved to his own satisfaction—and undoubtedly that of his admirers—that the acquisition by mankind of altruistic impulses was the result of evolution. He carefully traced the long process by which primitive men 'began crudely shaping their conduct with reference to a standard outside of self'. This they accomplished through endless eons and without awareness of how their altruistic natures were developed.

The moral law grew up in the world not because anybody asked for it, but because it was needed for the world's work. If it is not a product of the cosmic process, it would be hard to find anything that could be so called.[12]

What then was the origin of unselfishness, surely a vital ingredient of any sound welfare programme? 'Of all kinds of altruism the mother's was no doubt the earliest; it was the derivative source from which all other kinds were by slow degree developed.'[13] God, Spencer, and Mother were to Fiske the new Trinity which explained and determined human behaviour.

On one subject related to the present topic, Fiske took a stand not shared by all social Darwinists: he strongly supported plans to limit immigration from the poorer lands, the underdeveloped countries of his day. He strenuously defended his position in a reply to a letter taking him to task for accepting the presidency of the Immigration Restriction League. He rejected the 'theory of the equal right of all human beings to the use of the earth'.

> A community of people . . . have a perfect right to build a wall around [themselves] . . . and exclude such people as they do not wish to have among them. It will be generally admitted, I think, that our government has a right to refuse to admit shiploads of criminals. . . . It appears to me that the same principle applies to shiploads of paupers.

Immigration had been good for the United States, Fiske contended, until the Civil War. In those earlier years, immigration had been a real test of determination and ability; consequently, superior types of persons had come to the American shores. Since the end of the war that situation had changed. It had become too easy for poverty-stricken peasants to go there and half of those who did were from Italy, Hungary, and Russia.

> As General [Francis Amasa] Walker forcibly reminds us—'they are beaten men from beaten races; representing the worst failures in the struggle for existence. Centuries are against them, as centuries were on the side of those who formerly came to us. They have none of the ideas and aptitudes which fit men to take up readily and easily the problem of self-care and self-government'. You appear to assume that we are bound to invite the poor and oppressed from all parts of the world to come to this country without any regard to the effect that may be wrought upon us. It appears to me that charity begins at home and that self-defence is the first law to be obeyed in the matter.

To say that we are under any obligation, either moral or Christian, to bring them to this country at the risk of inflicting serious damage upon ourselves and imperiling the great political and social problems which we were trying to solve, seems to me simply preposterous.[14]

To Fiske much of the struggle for existence had been decided long before, together with the obligations of philanthropy, upon the banks of the Oder and the heights of the Alps.

The last third of the nineteenth century was a crucial one for the development of American social welfare institutions and the foundations of what was to become social work. The charity organization and social settlement movements were imported from England and flourished even more vigorously in the New World than in the land of their birth. A solid beginning in the efforts to establish standards for the institutions which cared for the needy, the sick, and the abandoned was made in the State Boards of Charities. As the United States became an urban nation, widespread poverty became endemic as well as increasingly cyclical with the greater frequency of financial panics. Great movements of discontent ranging from backers of paper currency to labour union organizers to reformers like Henry George and to anarchists like Alexander Berkman and Emma Goldman. But little was said about these developments by the historians of the time or even by those who came after the turn of the century. The Civil War, its causes, and its immediate *political* consequences continued to preoccupy Clio's servants.

The youthful Woodrow Wilson, for example, writing in the early 1890s, conceived of American history revolving around the climactic struggle between north and south. He did, however, show the glimmering of an awareness that his country was no longer the bastion of the self-supporting farmer or artisan when he wrote about the changes in American economic life in the 1830s. He described the changes brought about by the rise of the railroads, the beginnings of industrialization, the concentration of workers in factories instead of in small shops, and the great increase in the wealth of the new captains of industry, 'so that dangerous contrasts both of fortune and opportunity should presently be created between capitalist and employee'. He went on:

> The nation, hitherto singularly uniform in its conditions of life, exhibiting almost everywhere equal opportunities of success, few large fortunes, and an easy livelihood for all who were industrious, was now about to witness sudden enormous accumulations of wealth, to perceive sharp contrasts between poverty and abundance, an ominous breaking up of economic levels.

Although the total wealth of the country was to increase vastly, 'individual opportunity was to become unequal, society was to exchange its simple for a complex structure, fruitful of new problems of life, full of new capacities for disorder and disease'. Indeed, out of the economic crisis of that decade, Wilson wrote, disorder did arise which 'spoke of a general social ferment'.[15]

Wilson, then, did show some awareness of the changes in American life and the resulting increase in poverty as well as wealth. His editor, Albert Bushnell Hart, for many years a dominant figure in American historical writing, was even more typical of his generation. He dedicated his own contribution to the famous *American Nation* series, which he also edited— *National Ideals Historically Traced*—to 'Theodore Roosevelt, Practicer of American Ideals'. This might seem hopeful but Hart had little interest in either the emergency of poverty or in efforts to eliminate it. He very evidently regarded his country as Man's single greatest achievement; the notion that need might be a permanent condition in that near-paradise and therefore worthy of close attention would not have occurred to him.

In his 'Author's Preface', Hart summarized the accomplishments of the twenty-five historians who had preceded him in the series as 'making a link in a chain which stretches from beginning to end of national existence'. Each contributor

> has consciously or unconsciously learned from Charles Darwin, who is the great historical master of our age in that he has taught us how, in the world of mind as in the material universe, there is steady progression from one condition to another; for human institutions also follow a law of natural selection, by the survival of those which are best adapted to their surroundings.

Indeed, the United States reflected this 'scientific law', and if the editor and his authors had done their task well, they had demonstrated that the nation was 'a steady and measurable growth, still enlarging, still to put forth new branches for the world's advantage'.[16] With such a social Darwinist viewpoint, Hart could scarcely be expected to waste his efforts on history's failures.

In only one regard did Hart object to the attitude that material success was the sole criterion for virtue, and here may be seen his affinity with Theodore Roosevelt. The American intellectual who had received any acclaim was remarkably fortunate, he wrote, 'because in most of the concerns of America the dominant person is the man of business' who rules politics, education, and even the pulpit from which he expected 'oblivion for his faults'. Many of the nation's difficulties were due, he thought, to this dominance of the businessman, who was often quite unsuited to the leadership seized or thrust upon him.[17]

Times and ideas were changing, however, and when, during the next decade, Frederic Austin Ogg prepared the next volume in the Hart series, the author was aware, not only of the reform tide of the first seventeen years of the century, but of the fact that changing conditions change men's minds. Ogg devoted considerable attention to the problems of children, describing in some detail the efforts by reformers in the various states on and the national scene to establish statutory restriction of the labour of children, the work of the National Child Labour Committee, and the creation in 1912 of the Children's Bureau. The Keating-Owen Child Labour law, enacted in 1916, had not, at the time of writing, been invalidated by the United States Supreme Court, and Ogg regarded its overwhelming passage as more than a mere augury of progress. He noted that the same Woodrow Wilson who had a few years earlier scorned Senator Albert J. Beveridge's mild child labour bill as 'obviously absurd', now, as President, 'was willing to use the spur' on behalf of a much stronger law. Thus, said Ogg, had the decade of reform between Beveridge's proposal and the new law changed a nation's way of thinking.[18]

Economic historians of the period and even socialist historians gave little attention to social welfare as such, the former because they were interested in other things, the latter because they regarded philanthropy and public welfare as ameliorative devices designed to divert the working class from its true and inevitably to-be-achieved goals. A. M. Simons, editor of *The International Socialist Review*, perhaps the best of American socialist historians of the turn of the century, typically had nothing to say about the subject other than to credit the primitive labour movement of the 1820s and 1830s with chief responsibility for such reforms as the abolition of imprisonment for debt and the establishment of the public school system.[19]

John R. Commons, probably the most distinguished American labour historian—and even labour economist—of all time, was deeply concerned about social welfare and social work. As a graduate student at Johns Hopkins University he had been assigned by Richard T. Ely to the Charity Organization Society of Baltimore as a case-worker. In this role he had learned how to combine compassion with reality by applying political pressure in order to secure a pension for a poverty-stricken tubercular Civil War veteran. Later he was to become a periodic resident at Hull House and president of the Wisconsin Conference of Social Work.[20]

His experiences in Baltimore and elsewhere had convinced Commons that only through law could justice, economic as well as political and juridical, be secured for all citizens. Law was needed, he pointed out, to regulate business and industry for its own good; without law, the economy would be in chaos. The sovereign power must use coercion for two reasons: first, because 'private self-interest is too powerful, or too ignorant, or too immoral' to serve the common good unless forced to do so; and, second, because society's common needs—roads, defence, justice—could only be provided by compulsion. The chief purpose of law, however, was to 'create and define legal rights', among them the personal rights of life, liberty, employment, and marriage. Slavery (and he was here referring to that institution in antiquity) had been an advance over the earlier custom of killing enemies and undesirables and a recognition of the value of human life, and the slaves had enjoyed considerable security and freedom from economic anxiety.

To replace this kind of security in an age when slavery had disappeared, 'the right to life has found a new recognition, the public poor-relief', of both the indoor and outdoor varieties. This new kind of guarantee to life had arisen because of the appearance of certain new conditions:

1. The freedom of the labourer.
2. His inability to engage in productive labour, or lack of employment.
3. Fear on the part of the ruling classes of popular uprisings, as in the English poor laws at the time of the French Revolution.
4. Ethical ideas regarding the sacredness of life.
5. Great accumulations of wealth, making possible generous provision for the dependent.

Thus, according to Commons, law and government gave recognition to the right to life of the labourer who had nothing but his skill and strength to offer; he was 'guaranteed a share of the social income equal, at least, to his minimum of subsistence. This is the fundamental and absolute right in its influence upon the distribution'.

As an economist Commons was especially concerned with the effects of economic depressions and employer arbitrariness upon workingmen. He proposed courts of arbitration which would prevent discharge for any reason other than inefficiency or dishonesty and would adjudicate wages, hours of labour, and conditions of work. Government labour bureaux and public works would offer relief from unavoidable private unemployment.

In a Malthusian mood, Commons denounced one right, 'the unrestricted right to marriage' of the poorer classes. Early marriages and too large families were leading to a degeneration of the race and were the chief reasons for the poverty of immigrants in the slums of the great cities.[21] He further suggested isolation in self-supporting but guarded colonies of 'degenerates', among whom he included the insane, the feeble-minded, the blind, prostitutes, prisoners, almshouse paupers and at least 20 per cent of the outdoor paupers. Then, with the 'ground cleared of the true degenerates', society could proceed to remedy the basic problems besetting it, by remaking itself and the individuals who comprised it. He would enact laws removing the benefits accruing to owners of congested tenements, ending low wages and long hours, abolishing saloons and periodic unemployment, and helping to elevate human personality instead of abasing it.

We hear much of scientific charity. There is also a scientific justice. The aim of the former is to educate true character and self-reliance. The aim of the latter is to open the opportunities for the free expression of character. Education and justice are the methods of social selection. By their cooperation is shaped the moral environment where alone can survive that natural yet supernatural product, human personality.[22]

It was Commons' hope that the wise application of scientific methods would help to create a society based upon Christian ethics. He saw no conflict between the new knowledge and the morality he had learned at the knee of his Presbyterian mother.

It may be argued that to include Commons in this discussion is pointless. He did not belong in the mainstream of the historical guild; much of his fame is in a field somewhat removed from it. Yet he was, in the words of his greatest disciple, 'the creator of American labour history' and in that work, as well as in economics proper, his influence upon American historiography has been impressive.

When we return to the undiluted historians who were, as late as the 1920s, turning out multi-volume histories of the United States we find little enough interest in social welfare history to warrant much of a pause. We should stop briefly at one of the last and ablest of them, Edward Channing who completed his six-volume series, carrying the story of this country only through the Civil War, in 1925. He exhibited little of the attention to the poor that McMaster had displayed, even in his limited fashion. Like the earlier historian, Channing tarried over the Panic of 1857 where he too found the chief motivation for unrest not so much in the distress caused by unemployment as in the agitation of the 'many German immigrants engaged in mechanical employments' who were 'particularly susceptible to the influence of radical agitators'. For a number of weeks this foreign element demonstrated in the streets, 'carrying banners with inflammatory inscriptions and adopting resolutions demanding work and the despoiling of the rich'. Recovery fortunately soon put an end to this agitation, although it was delayed in Pennsylvania, presumably because of the troublemakers, and consequently the Democrats were crushed in the elections of 1858.[23] Thus Channing's bow to welfare history.

A younger contemporary of Channing, Carl Russell Fish, developed, in the course of his career, an interest in social welfare which presumably was not merely induced by the editors of his later work. For he had little enough to say about the subject in *The Development of American Nationality* which he published in 1913, other than to remark that 'poor relief', like education and road-making in the south, was in 1783 usually the responsibility of the planter.[24] On the Panic of 1893, one which some later historians were to describe as the worst in history, Fish wrote mainly of the manful struggles of President Cleveland against a situation largely created by Republican economic and fiscal policies. Only brief mention was made of unemployment and of such labour unrest as was manifested at Homestead and Pullman. These latter were caused by 'the new labor organizations' which 'had for some years been resorting to strikes, which often endangered and occasionally broke the public peace'.[25]

One would expect that in a book bearing the title of *The Rise of the Common Man* the author would devote considerable attention to those of the commonalty who might, from time to time, have been in need of succour. And a careful reading of the book (Volume VI of the notable *History of American Life* series so ably edited by the elder Arthur M. Schlesinger and Dixon Ryan Fox) did provide a few worthwhile pages. In his discussion of the reform impulse of the Jacksonian period, which he likened to the 'progressive' label of a later age, Fish exhibited considerable admiration for Dorothea Dix who, coming relatively late in life to the cause of reform, devoted herself to combating 'the indifference of the public to the treatment of prisoners and of paupers, and particularly the unthinking inhumanity toward the insane'. Her career, Fish alleged, was devoted not so much to the origination of ideas but to the advocacy of reforms most of which had long been urged by Quakers and European philanthropists.

Little change was affected during the years between 1830 and 1850 in the care of 'the ordinary poor' whose condition depended largely on local action. Generally, less pauperism existed in America than elsewhere, although Irish immigration did bring problems of poverty to these shores. 'Stories were told of poor old Irishwomen in Philadelphia, who in their letters home chiefly recommended the United States because of its palatial almshouses'. Paupers were generally better treated because, in the main, the 'poor farms' were usually better than the English 'workhouse'. Unfortunately, most poor farms were operated by contractors 'who were seldom philanthropists'. The only real improvement came in the separation of the insane poor to special institutions. 'In fact, the treatment of the insane, in this separation and the beginning of the differentiation of the curable from the incurable, showed more general improvement than that of either prisoners or paupers.'[26]

That it was the editors' interest perhaps more than that originally held by some of the individual authors in this famous series may be adduced by the later volumes and, in at least one case, the editors' foreword. The authors selected may also have reflected the editors' own interests and it is useful to look through several volumes as the nation approached and entered the Great Depression.

Allen Nevins, who wrote the eighth volume, *The Emergence of Modern America, 1865–1878*, it can be assumed, needed no urging to discuss, even to a limited extent, the social problems of the age he was describing. The struggle against slavery had absorbed most of the reforming energies which could now, after the passage of the Thirteenth Amendment, be loosed upon the problems of 'the poor, the defective and the defenceless'. 'The nation', he wrote, 'awoke after the war to find conditions existing in its largest cities which till then it had fondly thought confined to Manchester, Paris, and Naples'.

The late 1860s, accordingly, saw the first important efforts directed against slums and for public health measures. Drives for prison reform and for prevention of cruelty to animals—and children—were renewed. During the next decade, many organizations of enormous importance for that time and the future were founded, among them the Women's Christian Temperance Union, the Prohibition Party as a political instrument, the National Association for Woman Suffrage, and the State Charities Aid Association in New York.[27]

Relief for the poor, Nevins wrote, was completely disorganized, but despite the terrible need revealed by his study, he agreed with the traditional view that an enormous amount of public aid was provided but carelessly—and dangerously. He cited the 'successful' Brooklyn experiment of 1878 during which the discontinuance of public relief led to no increased demand 'upon public or private agencies, and no unusual suffering appeared'.[28] A quick glance at Charles Loring Brace's efforts to educate the young and prevent their turning to crime was followed by a lengthier discussion of R. L. Dugdale's 'epochal work on *The Jukes*' and the need 'for some check upon the multiplication of the diseased and vicious'.[29]

Nevins was more realistic than McMaster and Fish about the reputed improvement of prisons, mental hospitals, and the like. Despite the endeavours of Dorothea Dix and others, the treatment of the insane was incredibly bad in the late 1860s. That of pauper children was at least as bad. Some slight improvement appeared in a few states after the establishment of state boards of charities, beginning with Massachusetts in 1863, but nothing truly important in this direction resulted. Particularly moving to Nevins was the work of Henry Bergh on behalf of animals, efforts which eventually led to the foundation of the New York Society for the Prevention of Cruelty to Children.[30]

Nevins was, in fact, apologetic for the rather limited welfare programmes and activities of the age by commenting that his own time—and it must be recalled that he was writing in 1927—'will seem, to the view of posterity, very nearly as ragged and inadequate. Special needs always outrun social provision to meet them'. Prophetic words, indeed! He further pointed out that, despite the numbers of great fortunes being created during the 1860s and 1870s, very few wealthy philanthropists appeared, so few indeed that the American visits of the expatriate George Peabody from his London residence always 'evoked a fervent welcome'.[31] It may well be worth reflecting on the contribution to American culture of public relations man Ivy Lee who persuaded the first Rockefeller to become a philanthropist, thereby creating a fashion.

Much different is the next volume in the *History of American Life* series. Appearing somewhat out of order, in 1936, Ida Tarbell's contribution, which covered the period of the depression of the 1890s, might have been expected to reflect the decade of its origin. This would appear to have been the anticipation of the editors who must surely have written their foreword before the delivery of the completed manuscript.

Not the least value of the book is the mirror it holds up to the troubled present. No reader can fail to feel the contemporaneity of many of the problems with which this earlier generation struggled. The maldistribution of wealth, the paradox of poverty amidst plenty, the fluctuations of the business cycle, the tug of war between capital and labor, the unequal position of the farmer in the national economy, the danger to a democratic society of vast economic power vested in irresponsible hands— such were the deeper issues that vexed the eighties and nineties. In their efforts at solution, in their failures as well as their successes, wise men of our own day may find signposts for the future.[32]

The declaration becomes less convincing when one reads the book, for in her discussion of the Panic of 1893, that period most like the one described by the editors, Miss Tarbell showed little interest in its effects upon the people themselves, preferring to discuss one bank's or one industrial firm's difficulties after another. On the Pullman and Homestead strikes she managed to display amazing objectivity. As for popular reaction to need, she cited almost exclusively the 'armies' of Coxey, Kelly, and others.[33]

Her final words on the crisis of the 'nineties are startling: the depression 'had not paralysed the productive energies of the nation, however much it had temporarily weakened them. If four million men were thrown out of work, twenty million had work'![34] Finally, she said, American industry and finance emerged stronger than ever from that trial.

With the work of Schlesinger himself, the historians of social conscience at last fully asserted themselves. In what is still the most highly regarded volume of the series, *The Rise of the City*, Schlesinger devoted considerable space and, it might be added, feeling to the subject of human welfare during the Gilded Age. He told of the increasing concern of Protestant as well as Catholic and Jewish clergymen in the fate of the immigrants pouring off the decks of the steamers from Europe. He pointed to the rise of the Institutional Church; the Christian Socialism of William Dwight Porter Bliss; the social zeal inspired by Charles Sheldon's

parable, *In His Steps*; and the efforts of Cardinal Gibbons of
Baltimore to ally the Roman Catholic Church with its poorer
communicants, the overwhelming majority, rather than with the
reactionary wing led by Archbishop Corrigan of New York.
Although the Church as such was 'slow to engage in works of
social amelioration', it had to be admitted that 'the humanitarian
leaders of the day were deeply imbued with the Christian spirit
and most of them were loyal church members'. The depression
which followed the Panic of 1873 intensified both the suffering
of many and the anxiety of others to serve them, so much so
that William Graham Sumner thought there were far too
many 'reformers, philanthropists, humanitarians, and would-be
managers-in-general of society'. James Bryce thought that Americans led the world in their care for the needy. Schlesinger's own
view was that 'Megalopolis, having crushed the human spirit with
its million iron hoofs, became suddenly sorry, wept from its
unnumerable eyes and strove ardently to make up for its careless-
ness and greed'.

Even when his criticisms of prevailing welfare agencies were not
altogether dissimilar from those of his predecessors, Schlesinger's
tone and the totality of his remarks placed him among the ranks of
those who believed in the obligation of society to help its needier
members. America's problem in social welfare, he asserted, was
not a lack of agencies, as much 'as a knowledge of how most wisely
to use them'.[35] He described the large number of public agencies
whose effectiveness was 'often marred by incompetent or wasteful
methods', resulting in poor care and duplication of almsgiving,
'thus indirectly encouraging duplicity and chronic improvidence
on the part of applicants'. He briefly, but realistically, sketched
the rise of state boards of charities and the charity organization
societies, whose plan, 'handicapped by a dearth of trained workers
and often by jealousy among the associated charities . . . richly
justified itself by the results'.[36]

The social historian was even more impressed by the 'migration
of resident colonies of social workers to the worst quarters of the
larger cities', as, following the lead of Stanton Coit and Jane
Addams, the settlements quickly spread across the land. It was
the settlement workers, he felt, who 'could not avoid seeing that
the social maladjustments with which they dealt were often

M

conditioned by forces and influences of which the individual was a hapless victim'. These workers responded to what they found by what Schlesinger called 'aggressive altruism'. They were led to support many ('all', he said) movements for improvement: better working conditions, abolition of child labour, sanitary housing, public health and penal reform; they campaigned against municipal corruption and particularly against 'the ubiquitous saloon'. They did not care whether poverty caused intemperance or the reverse, but they joined with the many forces 'which had long been battling against the evil'.[37] Here Schlesinger revealed himself a child of his age, for it must be recalled that the temperance and even the prohibition movements were reform movements, reform for the individual who drank too much, for his family deprived of the necessities which the money spent on drink could have bought, and against the corruption of political life intensified by the powers of the saloon-keeper, the brewer, and the distiller. (It must be noted that Schlesinger gave four and a half pages to social welfare reform and seven to the temperance movement.)

It is well here to observe another sidelight on attitudes of his age: in his generally sympathetic account of the plight of the American Indians, Schlesinger several times referred to them as 'savages' and to a young man as a 'buck'.[38]

On the condition of the Negro in the south, although he wished progress had been faster, the historian was optimistic, quoting, interestingly, 'a young Negro intellectual', W. E. B. Du Bois, to the effect that the first thirty years of freedom had 'changed the child of emancipation to the youth with dawning self-consciousness, self-realization, self-respect'.[39]

It would be impossible in a rapid survey such as this to explore the entire corpus of Schlesinger's work, but it is interesting, even informative, to look at a little book he published in 1922, a time not altogether different from our own when radical discontent led, occasionally, to bombings and the forces of the Right were reacting with equal violence. Much of the discontent of the age was laid to foreign agitators; Schlesinger agreed that the evils visited upon immigrants were sore indeed. He pointed out, however, that 'the modern programs for organized and scientific philanthropy had their origin very largely in the effort to cure these spreading social sores'. Another result, he wrote in *New Viewpoints in American History*, was the movement to restrict immigration and, although he did not approve of what would today be called 'racism', he did seem to feel that it was necessary to remove what he called the 'worst evils of indiscriminate immigration', especially the tendency of the new immigrants to crowd into the already overpopulated areas of the country.[40]

Of special interest today are some of Schlesinger's remarks about radicalism as he viewed it in 1922. Interest in reform, he asserted, has been a characteristic of American national development and it had invariably, as if in obedience to some law, followed a definite pattern, generally of three phases. It is impossible to summarize his thoughts without quoting directly at some length:

At the outset there occurs a period of violent propaganda conducted by a small group of agitators. These pioneers resort to picturesque and sensational methods of propaganda in order to awaken the apathetic public to the presence of evil conditions and the need for change. They constitute a flying wedge of protest and moral indignation. . . . These trumpeters of reform act irrationally according to the standards of the majority of the people, and must expect to suffer their ridicule or ostracism or persecution. In this advanced group may ordinarily be found the 'soapboxer', the 'muckraker', the idealist, the doctrinaire, the fanatic, the would-be revolutionist and, at times even in American history, the martyr. These agitators, irrespective of individual peculiarities, share a bitter disregard of existing public opinion, a passion for destructive criticism, and an emotional conviction that in their proposal is to be found panacea for human ills.

Some movements never advance beyond this first ultra-radical stage, for they fail to gain converts outside of the group immediately engaged in furthering the cause. The second stage arrives when the pioneer reformers succeed in arousing interest and approval among the soberer elements of the population. The ideas long regarded as 'queer' or 'dangerous' are now on the point of gaining the sanction of respectability; and the assurance of a growing popular favor enlists the support of some of the experienced leaders of the people—the 'practical statesmen'. These men possess the constructive ability, the organizing genius and the knowledge of political strategy which are necessary in order to carry into execution the ideas of the agitators. Less agile of imagination and frequently less pure of purpose, they know better the temper and limitations of the average man; and under their direction the new policies and doctrines, perhaps in modified form, become the law of the land. Thus the actual achievers of the reform are the liberals or progressives, aided perhaps by those moderates of the conservative camp who favor the proposed change as the best preventive of more basic changes. . . .

The third and final stage of the reform is reached when the new doctrines, having lost their air of strangeness and demonstrated either their utility or harmlessness, become imbedded in the conscience and philosophy of the people at large. The public becomes adjusted to practices and policies that were altogether unacceptable a few years earlier; indeed most of the people have already forgotten that these reforms were not always a part of the commonly accepted stock of ideas. The cycle of reform has about completed itself; for public opinion hardens into a new conservatism and forms a crust that toughly resists any further efforts for change. Advocates for new advances must employ the militant and fantastic methods which mark the 'lunatic fringe' of a new crusade for reform.[41]

The compassionate view of the American people enunciated by Schlesinger in *The Rise of the City* was echoed in the following volume, which had, in fact, been published earlier. Harold Faulkner described the advent of the war with Spain as a great relief to a nation wearied by a decade of panic, 'lengthening bread lines, the pitched battles between capital'. The war, however, provided only a respite and the nation faced, in the new century, the old unresolved problems and many new ones. America, Faulkner wrote, was at the turn of the century 'a land of curious contrasts', one of enormous but unevenly distributed wealth; an America whose true statistics of poverty were probably no better than those revealed in the then recent English studies; one with the most widespread system of education anywhere, but with six million illiterates; a land of great idealism and humanitarianism, with the greatest philanthropies, and the least protection from industrial accidents. 'In no nation was the status of the women higher or the lot of the child better, yet social legislation respecting women was far behind that of other progressive nations and child labor existed under conditions too horrible to believe.' Fortunately, America and its civilization were basically sound as the next fifteen years of social consciousness and reform were to show.[42]

The data reported by Robert Hunter in *Poverty* in 1904 were widely used by Faulkner, who evidently regarded them as eminently reliable. The use of the Hunter study by this economic historian is sufficiently significant to make further comment unnecessary. Reporting on the effectiveness of the Progressive movement, Faulkner wrote sympathetically of the improvement in the condition of women and the notable successes of efforts to improve the diet and health of children and reduce the appalling infant mortality rate. He described with relish the early endeavours to provide pure and cheap milk, visiting nurses and prenatal care centeres, and day nurseries for working mothers. It is ironic to realize how many of these goals of seventy years ago are still just that. He cheered the juvenile court movement and was optimistic, though cautiously so, about the struggle to eliminate child labour.[43] Curiously, he had not a word about the establishment of the Children's Bureau or the First White House Conference on Children. But how much stranger is the fact that nearly three-quarters of a century since Faulkner's starting date, the American rate of infant mortality ranks far down on the list of civilized nations.

When the series ended with Dixon Wecter's volume on the Great Depression and the New Deal, the issue, for most historians was settled. In words with which most historians of the age would agree, Wecter wrote that the crisis of the thirties had many causes but that most profoundly, it was 'selfish blindness to the bond between group welfare and the satisfactions of the individual'.[44] President Hoover was never able to recognize this bond and became possibly the most frustrated and the unhappiest president in American history. The New Dealers developed a vastly different approach to the problems of human need in a fantastically wealthy country:

What the citizen needed, rather than what he could afford to buy, became the determinant in the new social-service concept of government—a government which, having envisaged these needs, set out to meet them, not on the basis of cash in hand or calculations of ultimate profit, but with assurance that the bill would be paid by apportioning it among the taxpayers.[45]

In summarizing the social effects of the Depression and the New Deal, Wecter wrote, perhaps too sanguinely:

The Great Depression . . . fostered a tenderer social conscience, calling attention to a stratum of chronic misery—among slum dwellers, sweated labor, underprivileged children, submarginal farmers, share croppers and other classes—that long antedated the current emergency. . . .

Above all, the idea of social security took root in American life, seeking to protect the individual against hazards beyond his power to control, whether out-of-school youth in quest of his birthright or maturity facing the risks of illness, industrial accidents and technological unemployment, or old age confronting the ultimate joblessness.[46]

This somewhat overlong description of the *History of American Life* series epitomizes the changes among American historians to the issues of human welfare. By the 1940s there were few, if any, among them who questioned the obligation of the state to provide for the deprived and the unfortunate. Disagreement might exist as to whether or not the Roosevelt administrations had accomplished as much as they should have in these areas. Broadus Mitchell, whose hero of another era was Alexander Hamilton, criticized Roosevelt for his failure to develop a plan for the permanent cure of the ailments of the capitalist economy and to pursue that plan to its consummation, but as to the justice of making provision for the needy there was no question.[47]

It would be presumptuous, after Richard Hofstadter's thorough study of Turner, Parrington, and Beard to attempt more than a comment or two on these Progressive historians. Turner's concern, of course, was with the influence of what he conceived of as the freedom and democracy engendered by the west and the threats to those concepts produced by the closing of the frontier. Not only was wealth, and consequently power, being concentrated into a few hands in one or two eastern cities, but the end of free land meant that the huge numbers of immigrants coming now from eastern and southern Europe had no recourse save the urban slums, where they became prey to those feeding on their just resentment, furthering threatening the institutions upon which America had been built.[48]

To an age disillusioned by years of depression and war upon war, the essential optimism of Vernon Parrington may occasionally appear to be simplistic. The too-easy classification of political and literary figures of the American past into conservatives and liberals may bring approval from those eager for quick categorization, but others may long for less assurance. But Parrington's heart was in the right place, at least as far as a historian of social welfare is concerned. He wrote little enough directly about this subject but his intuition was reasonably good. His encomium of Benjamin Franklin was possibly a bit overdone, but who could not warm to these words about America's greatest polymath:

> All his life his sympathy went out to whoever suffered in person or fortune from the injustice of society: to the debtor who found himself pinched by the shrinking supply of currency; to the black slave who suffered the most elementary of wrongs; to impressed seamen; to the weak and wretched of earth. He was a part of that emerging humanitarian movement which, during the last half of the eighteenth century, was creating a new sense of social responsibility.[49]

In the third, uncompleted volume of his masterpiece, Parrington said of Henry George that he was 'still our most original economist' and the author of that 'noble study of social poverty'.[50] And Edward Bellamy who dreamed of a social order in which all men should be truly equal was 'an incorrigible optimist'.[51]

It is a curiosity of literary history that the two completed volumes of *Main Currents in American Thought* were published during the same year that saw the appearance of the first volume of Charles and Mary Beards' *The Rise of American Civilization*.

The sheer volume of the Beards' production is so formidable that the reader may well quail before the prospect either of reading it himself or having it all interpreted for him. It is proposed, therefore, that the few remarks to be made about Beard be limited to his most widely read work, *The Rise of American Civilization* and its two related later volumes, and *The Republic*. Although the attribution of the four volumes of the general history are to husband and wife, some comments will appear to be upon Charles alone. This approach is for the sake of simplicity only; no attempt is being made to belittle Mrs Beard's contribution!

It is surely no surprise that this student of the Populist, James Weaver, this young scholar who studied Bismarck's pioneer social insurance programme in Germany, who became an intimate of Britain's Christian Socialists, Fabians, and settlement leaders, and who admired the books of John Ruskin,[52] went far beyond the usual confines of political or even economic history. He recognized the importance of the old English poor law in populating the New World and in establishing such 'typically American' institutions as free public education.[53] Writing in the mid-twenties, moreover, Beard was enabled to preserve his essentially Whiggish optimism about the future of his country, so little was said directly in these volumes about social welfare. The chief exception was the tribute to the settlement movement, especially to Jane Addams and her friends at Hull House, which the authors linked effectively to the rise of social Christianity. It was the settlements which succeeded in focusing national attention upon the conditions of the poor, particularly the immigrant poor. 'Indeed, any search for the origins of social practice in the United States meets at some point the work of the settlement.'[54] The authors further cited the presence at the 1912 Bull Moose Convention among the reformers, idealists, and members of Roosevelt's 'lunatic fringe' of Jane Addams of 'Hull House, the famous social settlement of Chicago'.[55] The settlements and the scientific studies, such as Paul Kellog's *Pittsburgh Survey*, were to Beard, in 1928, examples of that American inventive genius which would solve the social and cultural problems of that age as surely as it was solving the industrial problems.

When *America in Midpassage* was published a decade later, the Great Depression and the New Deal lay between the authors and their earlier tome. The heralded 'inventive genius' of the twenties was now merely the producer of 'gadgets', the years before the crash were described as 'the summer solstice of Normalcy', and Calvin Coolidge had been the age incarnate. Although there was little to choose from between the two major parties in 1928, Alfred E. Smith was the preferable candidate as a friend of social legislation, a defender of civil liberties, a champion of public ownership of power sites and one who, 'with the help of expert advisers . . . had learned to clothe his natural sympathies for plain people in the language of social workers'.[56] (Fortunately no samples were offered!) Hoover, despite his intelligence and awareness of the persistence of poverty, even in 1928, and his desire to eliminate it, was unable to deal with depression on a grand scale other than through a hopeless 'trickle-down theory'.[57]

Although generally sympathetic to and finally almost enthusiastic about the New Deal anti-depression measures, Beard could never bring himself to accept any but the lowest and grossly inadequate estimates of unemployment, or to shake completely from his mind the assumption 'in the realm of gentility' that usually unemployment and poverty were due to 'defective minds or bodies or to congenital improvidence'. This was not true entirely in the thirties, but even then he could write about the preference of most Americans for work relief to what he persistently called 'doles'. 'Something frightful lurked in the prospect of ten million citizens sunk in the morass of permanent pauperism, sustained by meagre grants of money and commodities.'[58] So, in a series of statements which might today be seen as paradoxical, Beard pronounced general approval of the New Deal, despite the failure of its program to end the economic crisis, criticized it for not preparing plans to proceed further, and lamented the opportunities which 'chiselers' received through the reform measures.[59] In their peroration, the authors hailed what they saw as the final triumph of 'humanistic democracy' in the ascent to power of Franklin Roosevelt who had, by the beginning of this second term, abandoned his efforts to combine Hamiltonian and Jeffersonian ideals and gone over entirely to the latter. This was the school to which belonged, not only Jefferson, but Madison, and Lincoln. Roosevelt had, in brief, inherited the aspirations and the ideals of a multitude of reformers, including not merely those sanctified men, but such saints of social work as Jane Addams, Florence Kelley, Graham Taylor, Julia Lathrop, Edith Abbott, and Grace Abbott.[60] Finally, in the last volume of the general history, came a tribute to the economist Simon Patten, whose 1905 lectures at the New York School of Philanthropy had helped to set a new tone, indeed a revolution, against the poor relief concept which had been dominant since the early republic. The numerous schools of social work which appeared in the years following these lectures were 'concerned with private, community, and public interests, combining increasing technical knowledge with the spirit of Christianity and the Enlightenment, in a national campaign against poverty, in the interest of civilization'.[61]

If Beard's remarks in *The Republic* about general welfare and social welfare are to be taken as indicative, historians in the early 1940s, like the United States Supreme Court, had agreed that the general welfare clause of the Constitution was broad indeed. In that rather charming dialogue, Beard refused to be drawn into an argument about what the Founding Fathers would have thought about the New Deal. Instead, he placed himself squarely with Hamilton (note the ambivalence) in declaring that 'general welfare' could be interpreted to cover whatever the Congress construed it to be, provided only that it was neither expressly forbidden nor designed to apply to purely local situations. He quoted with approval Justice Benjamin Cardozo's opinion in the Social Security Case (*Helvering v. Davis*) that economic disaster had become, since 1787, a national problem and that Congress was completely within its rights in helping to provide against the exigencies of old age; indeed, Congress was obliged to act in such matters.

Beard went beyond generalities when he introduced into his dialogue a medical social worker who ardently defended the New Deal and all its works. She made a declaration about social work that could yet warm the heart of the devoted professional:

The practice of welfare calls for severe training, exact knowledge, and skills of many kinds. So that, whatever the word welfare may have meant in 1787, it now means, at least to people who study it instead of talking about or against it idly, the art and science of good working and living—individual and social, parts of the same thing—life worth living—American society civilized, from center to periphery. Under every form of government and economy, it is and will be necessary while the spirit of humanity lives.[62]

Our survey of the attitudes of some leading American historians towards social welfare is nearing its close. Many significant works by the authors examined here have gone unmentioned; even more serious, many exceedingly important historians who have displayed a keen interest in this topic have been ignored. It is essential, however, that at least two or three of them are mentioned: Ralph Henry Gabriel, whose *The Course of American Democratic Thought: An Intellectual History*[63] is really more about social than purely intellectual thought, and Merle Curti, the author of that staunchly New Dealing *The Growth of American Thought*.[64] Both of them hailed the emergence of the awareness of human need and the necessity to combat it. Today, with the recognition of the vital significance of urban history, thoughtful readers dare not overlook Carl Bridenbaugh who more than three decades ago examined the fledgling towns of the English colonies, paying particularly close attention to the provision—or lack of it—which those early settlements made for the poor and the aged, the sick and the insane, the victim of war, and the penniless immigrant.[65]

Today it would be unthinkable for a historian to write about the American past and to ignore these issues which so concern men today. From John Bach McMaster to Arthur Schlesinger Jr and William Leuchtenberg the progression has been reasonably recognizable. We now even have a growing coterie of scholars who have made welfare history their field of specialized study. It is quite unlikely that we shall ever again regard with composure historians whose view of the past is largely limited to presidential elections and military campaigns.

Notes

1. Richard Hofstadter, *The Progressive Historians: Turner, Beard, Parrington* (1968).
2. John Bach McMaster, *A History of the People of the United States from the Revolution to the Civil War* (1883), vol. I, p. 1.
3. *ibid.*, vol. I, pp. 1–2.
4. *ibid.*, vol. I, pp. 95–8.
5. *ibid.*, vol. I, pp. 98–102.
6. McMaster, *The Acquisition of Political, Social, and Industrial Rights of Man in America* (1961), p. 38.
7. *ibid.*, p. 41
8. McMaster, *History*, vol. I, p. 98.
9. *ibid.* vol. VIII, pp. 286–302
10. McMaster, *Acquisition of Rights*, pp. 122–23.
11. Hofstadter, *Progressive Historians*, p. 23.
12. John Fiske, 'Through Nature to God', *Studies in Religion* (1902), pp. 306–8.
13. *ibid.*, p. 318.
14. Letter from Fiske to William Lloyd Garrison, 1 February 1898, in Ethel F. Fiske (ed.), *The Letters of John Fiske* (1940), pp. 666–71.
15. Woodrow Wilson, *Division and Reunion, 1828–1889*—vol. III of *Epochs of American History*, ed. by A. B. Hart (1893), pp. 103–4.
16. A. B. Hart, *National Ideals Historically Traced, 1606–1907*—vol. XXVI of *The American Nation: A History*, ed. by A. B. Hart (1907), pp. xiii–xiv.
17. *ibid.*, pp. 250–2.
18. Frederic Austin Ogg, *National Progress, 1907–1917*—vol. XXVII of *The American Nation* (1918), pp. 91–4.
19. A. M. Simons, *Class Struggles in America* (1906), pp. 43–7.
20. John R. Commons, *Myself* (1934), pp. 43–4, 68; Allan G. Gruchy, *Modern Economic Thought: The American Contribution* (1947), pp. 135–243; Joseph Dorfman, *The Economic Mind in American Civilization* (1948), vol. III, pp. 276–94.
21. Commons, *The Distribution of Wealth* (1893), pp. 60–86; *Races and Immigrants in America* (1920), pp. 167–8.
22. Commons, 'Natural Selection, Social Selection, and Heredity', *The Arena*, XVIII (July 1897), pp. 90–7.
23. Edward Channing, *The War for Southern Independence*—vol. VI of *A History of the United States* (1927), pp. 197–201.
24. Carl Russell Fish, *The Development of American Nationality* (1913), p. 7.

25. *ibid.*, pp. 476–780.
26. Fish, *The Rise of the Common Man, 1830–1850*—vol. VI of *A History of American Life*, ed. by Arthur M. Schlesinger and Dixon Ryan Fox (1927), pp. 256–60.
27. Allen Nevins, *The Emergence of Modern America, 1865–1878*—vol. VIII of *A History of American Life* (1927), pp. 318–19.
28. *ibid.*, p. 327.
29. *ibid.*, pp. 316–17.
30. *ibid.*, pp. 328–35.
31. *ibid.*, pp. 346–7.
32. Ida M. Tarbell, *The Nationalizing of Business, 1878–1898*—vol. IX of *A History of American Life* (1936), pp. xv–xvi.
33. *ibid.*, pp. 222–7, 233–40.
34. *ibid.*, p. 262.
35. Arthur M. Schlesinger, *The Rise of the City, 1878–1898*—vol. X of *A History of American Life* (1933), pp. 338–44.
36. *ibid.*, pp. 349–51.
37. *ibid.*, pp. 351–3.
38. *ibid.*, pp. 369–73.
39. *ibid.*, pp. 385–6.
40. Schlesinger, *New Viewpoints in American History* (1922), pp. 18–19.
41. *ibid.*, pp. 110–12.
42. Harold U. Faulkner, *The Quest for Social Justice, 1898–1914*—vol. XI of *A History of American Life* (1931), pp. 1, 23–6.
43. *ibid.*, pp. 156–62, 177–88.
44. Dixon Wecter, *The Age of the Great Depression, 1929–1941*—vol. XIII of *A History of American Life* (1948), p. 24.
45. *ibid.*, p. 91.
46. *ibid.*, pp. 295–6.
47. Broadus Mitchell, *Depression Decade: From New Era through New Deal, 1929–1941*—vol. IX of *The Economic History of the United States* (1947).
48. Frederick Jackson Turner, *The Frontier in American History* (1920). See especially, 'Contributions of the West to American Democracy', pp. 243–68, written in 1903; and 'Social Forces in American History', pp. 311–34, his Presidential Address to the American Historical Association, delivered on 28 December 1910.
49. Vernon L. Parrington, *Main Currents in American Thought*, vol. I, 'The Colonial Mind 1620–1800' (1954), p. 180.
50. Parrington, *Main Currents in American Thought*, vol. III, 'The Beginnings of Critical Realism in America, 1860–1920' (1958), pp. 126, 314.
51. *ibid.*, p. 313.
52. Harvey Wish, *The American Historian: A Social-Intellectual History of the Writing of the American Past* (1960), pp. 269–70.
53. Charles A. and Mary R. Beard, *The Rise of American Civilization*, vol. I (1927), pp. 23–4, 178.
54. Beard and Beard, *The Rise of American Civilization*, vol. II (1928), pp. 421–3.

55. *ibid.*, vol. II, pp. 603–4.
56. *ibid.*, pp. 3–5, 38.
57. Beard and Beard, *America in Midpassage*—vol. III of *The Rise of American Civilization* (1939), pp. 3–5, 38–9, 88–93.
58. *ibid.*, pp. 223–6.
59. *ibid.*, p. 255.
60. *ibid.*, see esp. pp. 941–9.
61. Beard and Beard, *The American Spirit: A Study of the Idea of Civilization in the United States*—vol. IV of *Rise of American Civilization* (1942), p. 429.
62. Charles A. Beard, *The Republic: Conversations on Fundamentals* (1943), pp. 106–11.
63. Ralph Henry Gabriel, *The Course of American Democratic Thought: An Intellectual History since 1815* (1940).
64. Merle Curti, *The Growth of American Thought* (1943).
65. Carl Bridenbaugh, *Cities in the Wilderness: The First Century of Urban Life in America, 1625–1742* (1938).

7
Victorian Social Provision:
Central and Local Administration

E. C. MIDWINTER

Social provision is as socially determined as the problem it endeavours to solve. Typically, the medieval, in that he lived in more corporate terms than his modern descendant, worked out his social needs and obligations within his sociometric unit, such as the manor, the guild, the order of chivalry or the monastery. Ancient Rome, like other cities of antiquity, encountered a dreadful urban problem, and met it perforce within the civic frame of reference, with municipal efforts, such as 'bread and circuses' very much to the fore.

To throw the truism into absurd reversal, the welfare state was neither possible nor necessary for the prehistoric tribe, for its social problems were not those of a community able to construct such a political mechanism. Just as Goethe argued that he could define the nature of a society from a knowledge of its legal and military organization, so is a similar academic *legerdemain* possible with social welfare. People get the social provision as well as the governments they deserve, in the sense that problem and solution must emanate from the same socio-economic base.

It is also worth remembering that social deprivations are relative to this economic baseline or context. To be impoverished, there must be others richer; to be criminal, there must be others law-abiding; to be ignorant, there must be those more knowledgeable; even to be sick, it is necessary to compare one's lot with those healthier. Thus an American unemployed today does not judge his case against that of the Bombay beggar, still less against those of the ancient Egyptian slave or the Victorian pauper.

The perfect recluse cannot be poor, ignorant or criminally-inclined; theoretically, he can have no standard of wealth, knowledge or legality. Social ills imply inequalities and gradations within a particular community, and it is reasonable to suppose that generally they interconnect, so that the poorer, the sicker, the more ignorant and the more criminal tend to co-identify. Equally reasonably, one might suppose that, in the main, few societies attempt to eradicate these troubles completely (thereby creating social egality); rather do they try to keep in rein the excesses of inequality, often with a view to preserving it essentially. It is perhaps not too cynical to see the history of social provision as largely a story of social expediency.

These reminders are especially useful in an examination of Victorian attitudes and practice. Although they have mushroomed, alarmingly, the social issues we face are the same in kind as the Victorians tackled. The political and economic boundaries were already written in—the nation-state and the money economy—and the subsequent modifications, like shifts in the fount of sovereignty within the state or technical changes in the mechanics of the *geldwirtschaft*, were variations, still continuing, on those themes. What that interaction of explosive factors we term the industrial revolution wrought was, in the main, a social change. Demographic expansion, urbanization and the factory system conjoined to alter the social fabric, as more and more people crammed themselves into evermore cramped confines until the Liverpolitan's mean proximity in mid-nineteenth century was seven square yards. Herman Finer has coined the title 'congregation' to label this linked series of phenomena,[1] and it remains the key to the social difficulties, not only of the United Kingdom, but of much of the world besides.

'Congregation' radically altered the angle and scope of social distress. The four horsemen of the social worker's apocalypse—poverty, disease, crime and ignorance—were not novelties in nineteenth-century England. The newness lay in their mass incidence. People were poor by the thousand, as whole towns were thrown out of work by the ramifications of international trade. Diseases, like cholera and typhus, swifty struck down hundreds in the closely populated courts of the large towns. Mob action grew with the increasing density of urbanism, and the anonymous greyness of the towns, as well as the new lines of conveyance such as canals and railways, offered both loot and escape to the hordes of thieves. The entire social milieu made education more necessary even as it made it less possible, while, of course, the interrelation of these social evils rendered the problem a cumulative one. The odd vagrant thrown on the parish, the victim of fever to be strictly quarantined, the occasional thief probably known to most of his fellows in the village, and the child who could not, at very least, find a functional education in the home or in a trade—all these were truly banished to the past. Social trouble was now communal rather than individual; it was poverty, sickness, crime and ignorance en masse.

The Victorians responded, as indeed they had to, in their own terms, and, however described, these eventually boiled down to a wish to preserve the foundations of their society. Whether one opts for 'intolerability' or the more deliberate machinations of Benthamism as being behind Victorian social reform,[2] it eventually implied a desire to succour the regimen that existed. We in the twentieth century, then, are heirs not only to the same problems, but to the same solutions. The repairs we submit to the social weal are not often more than variants on Victorian practice. The danger is that we might fancy our goal to be a different one from theirs. For example, the factory, it is arguable, provided the social reformer with a ready-made formula. Consciously and unconsciously, he accepted its tenets and transferred them to the social services, using what Samuel Coleridge Taylor enthusiastically called 'the application of the steam-power principle'. The factory had its manager, its workshops, supervised by foremen and separated by function, and its artisans. The post-1834 union workhouse had its master, its dormitories, supervised by overseers and, in theory, rigorously segregated by typology, and its paupers. The new national prison, like Pentonville or Walton, had its governor, its wings, each guarded by a warder and divided according to type of crime, and its prisoners. The large general hospital, developed principally during the last century, had its matron, its wards, overlooked by sisters and separated by age, sex and category of illness, and its patients. The school (particularly on the model of E. Robson's central-hall schools planned initially for the London school board) had its headteacher, its classrooms or classes, with an assistant teacher in charge and segregated by age and ability, and its pupils.

This is not to suggest that such instances are not traceable in pre-industrial days, but that they became atypical in the nineteenth century. Alternately, the small-scale unit—the parish almshouse, the local lock-up, the cottage infirmary, the tiny charity class—became less characteristic, as alongside them in a causal relationship small-scale economic units sank into a decline. The advantage the Victorian reformer had over his modern counterpart was that he knew why the factory formula was adopted, whereas his successor sometimes believes that reformative or educational or medical reasons are much more intimately involved. The industrial almost military *regulo* that still exists now not only in prisons, but in hospitals, schools and welfare institutions bears painful testimony to this adherence to a tradition in constant need of reappraisal. This kind of perpetuation is physical, in that the original institutions are often still utilized or used as models for replacement, but it is also psychological, in so far as one's familiarity with the institutions makes it difficult to reconceive an alternative.

The chief administrative principle used to meet these social problems of 'congregation' was public intervention. There is no gainsaying the massive interference by civic agencies over the past hundred or so years. Possibly the three major waves of collectivism were the first and most successful of Gladstone's administrations in the early 1870s; the Liberal reforms, normally associated with Lloyd George, just prior to the first World War; and the so-called 'silent revolution' of the post-1945 Attlee ministry. The world wars, of course, made their own huge contribution to social legislation, and, more or less, the collectivist trend has been a continuing one. Eventually the core of this public expansion became the welfare state, with the individual protected at every turn and twist of his existence and thereby explicitly judged to be not the best assessor of his own actions. This was strictly contrary to the idealized *laissez-faire* state, in which the individual had complete freedom of action.

Basically, there is no argument about this. What has given rise to considerable academic controversy has been the seminal period before 1870 when the present administrative machinery originated. The older view was represented by A. V. Dicey.[3] He neatly clipped the century into three slots, with an early pre-Victorian period of 'legislative quiescence' and a later period of collectivism sandwiching an era of individualism from roughly 1830 to 1870. He argued that the legislation of these years was chiefly Benthamite in origin and that it was designed to free citizens from the shackles and restrictions of previous over-governance. In illustration, the new poor law of 1834 was, theoretically, an attempt to liberate the labour market by driving workers into jobs where hitherto they had been able to live off the parish. This was the 'artificial harmony of interests' branch of Benthamism, with laws deployed for the negative reason of 'keeping the ring clear' for *laissez-faire*. The administrative mechanisms so organized were, Dicey pointed out, later used for the construction of the collectivist state. Most commentators before the second World War were inclined, with varying emphases of criticism, to accept the high influence of Benthamism; the Webbs, the Hammonds and Halévy were among these.

Latterly, however, the pendulum has swung, as in historical controversy it will, the other way. These mid-century years have been seen as nothing less than an administrative transformation 'certainly as complete a break with older forms as had been the Tudor development of bureaucracy'. What one of the contenders termed 'an inherent momentum of administration' was forced on society by the gaping cracks of distress that appeared on its surface and the criss-cross pattern of executive government devloped by hard-working officers in the field. This accumulation of interference led to England being, it is suggested, a much-governed state by as early as 1854. Oliver MacDonagh, Royston Lambert and David Roberts have been among the keenest protagonists of this brilliantly held position, and emigration control and compulsory vaccination have been two of their leading instances.[4] In turn, this view has been challenged by Jennifer Hart, Henry Parris and one or two others. They have stressed the 'utility' as opposed to the 'individualism' of Benthamism in demonstrating the import of that creed on early Victorian politics and they have found 'intolerability' an unsatisfactory explanation of institutional change. All appear to agree that centralism was enlarged before the Diceyan watershed of about 1865. R. M. Gutchen, opposing Dicey's thesis, saw mid-century legislation as a 'trend towards uniformity', an almost Weber-like process of rationalization. J. B. Brebner, W. L. Burn and S. E. Finer, the last in a splendid appraisal of the work of Edwin Chadwick, most remorseless and active of Bentham's disciples, have, along with others, made equitable and balanced judgments on this fascinating contest.[5]

Put briefly and extremely, the major issue is whether classic Benthamite individualism or *ad hoc* governmental intervention proved the more significant. It is a question of, on balance, whether theory or practice was more influential. Did Victorian England fall or was it pushed into collectivism? It is worth noting, that, inevitably, the opposing schools of thought reflect their own climates of opinion. Dicey and his ilk wrote at a time academically strong on periodization and when large-scale viewpoints were more fashionable in and outside scholarship, than now. Oliver MacDonagh and his adherents are well attuned to the painstaking Namierian approach to research and they comment in an age of pragmatism and eschewal of sweeping overview. But all of them are concerned with the relation of the state and the individual. In Dicey's work, one watches the state legislate, through parliament. In his critics' writings, one watches servants of the state, albeit haphazardly and gradually, encroach on the privacy of the citizen. This almost neo-Platonic approach tends to omit the influence of possible intermediary 'associations' between state and self, and, of these factors, perhaps local government was the most important. And, in discussing this issue, it is intended to use Lancashire as the chief source of illustration throughout.[7]

To the legal theoretician, local government was no more than an adjunct of parliament, the fount of sovereignty, while the pragmatic commentator, although rehearsing the local field-work of executive officers, seems to see such efforts as eventually a prolongation of the state's arm. Local government, however, is as anomalous within this academic debate as it was in organizational practice. Was local government the ally and the projection of the state as it began to infringe private rights or was it defending the individualist cause by manning fortresses of municipal independence? When, for example, a reason for becoming incorporated —as in Oldham or Salford—was a desire to avoid involvement in the centrally supervised county constabulary, was this a blow for individualism or for collectivism? In 1842 Liverpool firmly set its face against the Poor Law Commission and went its separate way, with a vestry committee organizing the town's relief untroubled by central inspection or control. Wryly, it accomplished this by act of parliament. Again, was this nearer *laissez-faire* or state intervention?

Initially, the implication that the Victorian citizen was reduced from a state of civic grace by gradual interference is misleading. He had never been a free agent. Parochial and shire governance had prescribed systems of welfare for the poor, of law an order to a stringent degree and even of provision for health and other social problems. It is arguable that these were ineffective and cumulatively so as the years wore on, but they were, theoretically, anti-individualist. Few legislative chains have been more restrictive on the Englishman than the laws of settlement. Social reform was possibly to alter the pattern of intervention by expanding state supervision, but this did not automatically extend, let alone initiate, interference. Lord Brougham, speaking in the Lords' debate on the new poor law, expressed a hope echoed by many reformers of many kinds when he spoke of a streamlined, state-run agency reducing interference and thereby increasing liberty. The argument should properly be who should rather than whether one should interfere.

Another point concerns the feeble practical effect of state intervention. The difficulties of the four factory inspectorates, established by the first major factory act of 1833, are well known, but other central inspectorates had their troubles. In mid-century a number of state agencies were developed. The Home Office had some supervision of the county constabularies set up by the 1839 Rural Police Act, and it also demanded a quarterly return from the watch committees of the boroughs incorporated under the 1835 Municipal Corporations Act. Taking Lancashire as an example, few, if any, boroughs, complied with this request, and the formation of boroughs in the county had a strange consequence. In 1839 there had been four borough forces; in 1856 there were eleven—so that, despite the general rise in population, the numbers within the county régime actually dropped heavily, thus depriving thousands of the mixed blessings of state control. Not that such control was very formidable. No Home Office inspector or official ever visited the Lancashire police force prior to 1856, the year of the major police act, and, over nearly twenty years, only 118 communications—an average of half a dozen a year—were posted to the county authorities. In 1843 only one letter was mailed. Over a half were routine acknowledgements, returns and circulars, while nineteen were entirely negative, pointing out that the Home Secretary had 'no power to interfere'.

The General Board of Health, established in 1848, was built for a particular purpose and was not, like the Home Office, a consortium for residual affairs which often proved confusing to that department. But, except in extreme instances, it had to wait patiently for petitions to arrive from interested towns, whereupon the lengthy, often two-year, ritual of enquiry and order could be put in train. As with the factories, there were at first no more than six superintending inspectors to investigate and recommend, so that, apart from the preliminary enquiry and at times of crisis, the board's agents were rarely seen. The General Board of Health certainly posted 20,000 letters a year and more. The average Lancashire local board received from and dispatched to the General Board sixteen or seventeen missives a year, the vast majority a dulling round of returns and acknowledgements. Again, the formula of having 'no power whatever to interfere' was constantly used. In 1858, when the Local Government Act of that year superseded the Public Health Act, only one-fifth of Lancashire's two and a half millions lay within the puny grasp of the General Board. The loan sanction clause, which gave the board close control over local borrowing for large-scale sanitation and water supply schemes, was its chief weapon, and one wielded skilfully by Edwin Chadwick. It was only viable, nonetheless, when the local boards were moved to action. Granted their dilatoriness, the legal tangles and the clumsy and sometimes deceitful character of civil engineering, the lack of impact is scarcely surprising. Ormskirk was the only Lancastrian local board to have completed a comprehensive scheme of domestic water supply and water-driven sewerage in the mid-fifties.

Alternatively, some of the large towns, where the health

problem was urgent and pressing, had constructed their own administrative responses. Manchester, with a local act of 1844, and, more forcefully, Liverpool, with its 1846 Sanitary Act, led the way in this as in other respects. Once more parliamentary legislation was the key, but there was no overall state supervision as Dr Duncan became England's first properly constituted medical officer of health, as the aptly named Tom Fresh became Liverpool's first Borough Inspector of Nuisance and as John Newlands, the town's first Borough Engineer, embarked on his ambitious plans for watering and sewering the crowded port. When twenty thousand people were evicted from 7,000 Liverpudlian cellars in the late eighteen-forties, they must scarcely have pondered on the philosophic niceties of municipal as opposed to national intervention.

The Poor Law Commission (Board after 1847) was a much more vital agency than the Home Office or the Board of Health. Somerset House maintained a scrupulous and daunting level of office management, and its clerks sustained a devoted attachment to their welter of paperwork. The correspondence was, however, repetitious and mundane beyond belief. The normal Lancashire union and headquarters exchanged perhaps three dozen items each year, frequently including the demand for a return, the return itself, and a note of acknowledgement. As with other central bodies, there were grave restrictions on initiating action, of which the bar on the coercion of unions to build workhouses was the most serious. The Poor Law Commission received poor co-operation from many unions and it suffered diastrously from its own internal difficulties. It soon declined into a mechanically formal organization.

It was better served, numerically and probably qualitatively, than the General Board of Health in the question of inspection. Even so the function of an assistant commissioner was onerous in the extreme. Each of Chadwick's 'young crusaders' had some fifty unions, and the associated premises of each, to visit biannually, but this proved impossible. Alfred Power, a courageous proponent of the new poor law, a conscientious and assiduous worker and a friend of Edwin Chadwick, is a case in point. During his fifteen months as assistant commissioner in Lancashire and Yorkshire, he was unable to visit some boards of guardians at all. A main purpose of inspection was to check on finance, but, for many years, this proved to be no more than a casual confirmation of figures already entered, and was not a rigorous audit in any sense. Even, then, in Somerset House, that monument to the new creed of centralism, affairs were unsatisfactory and discouraging.

Ironically, it is conceivable that in education, constitutionally the weakest of the four principle social administrative structures at this time, interference paid, blow for blow, the best dividends. The inspectoral system, begun in 1839, gradually enabled the country's schools to be scoured annually. By 1870, Lancashire had over a thousand schools seeking grants in aid to the tune of nearly £300,000 per annum, and, according to their lights, the HMIs insisted on value for money. Although the state did not initiate educational provision before 1870, it would be false to say it did not control. There is no denying the significance of the fusion of inspection and grants in aid. It is also sometimes forgotten that other state agencies were involved in education. The poor law schools partook of public monies and were subject to poor law control. In 1850 Manchester had forty-eight and Liverpool ninety-four teachers in workhouse and industrial schools. There were also a number of works schools, many of them subject to the dictates of factory statutes and inspection. Greenbooth Mills Works, Rochdale; Haydock Colliery, near Warrington; and St Helens Crown Glass Works are but three of the dozens of factory schools in Lancashire in mid-century. In that the Home Office, the Poor Law Commission and the General Board of Health had decidedly limited powers of initiation, the activities of the Committee of the Privy Council for Education should not be relegated too far down any table of early Victorian state authority.

It is interesting that the central departments became of sharper and sturdier mettle when financial and compulsory weapons were added to their armour. The 1856 Police Act declared that all counties and boroughs were to be obliged to form police forces, that these would be submitted to annual inspection and that a satisfactory report would make the force eligible to substantial grant. The deathbed repentances were amusing. Wigan, a notorious backslider in policing, suddenly discovered a need for quadrupling its complement of six, and even then, at its first inspection, it was criticized for insufficient numbers. The 1856 Act proved to be, given time, one of the most effective of interventionist statutes, cleverly coupling compulsion and grants or, less prettily, fear and greed. It could also be argued that the giganitic programme of compulsory unionization, undertaken by the Poor Law Commission, was unsatisfactory until its successor, the Poor Law Board, grasped at the financial nettle. Parochial financing and rating survived the 1834 Poor Law Amendment Act, until the 1865 Union Chargeability Act made the union the proper fiscal unit and enabled the Board to establish viable audit districts and, subsequently, close supervision. Moreover, it was not until the famous public health legislation of 1866, 1872 and 1875 that widespread progress on that front was achieved. It was then that a comprehensive and obligatory pattern of public health authorities, with attendant financial provision, was constructed. Add the Education Act of 1870 and the Prisons Acts of 1865 and 1877 (the latter nationalizing the prison system), and the case for post-1865 collectivism looks quite sound.

In short, 'provincial prolongation' of central agencies was not highly influential before 1865, not because it did not exist but because it did not operate solidly. It might be observed that these middle years were Diceyan by accident, in that state intervention was present but dormant, unable to fulfil its potential until the last quarter of the century. This underlines the fallacy of confusing centralization with overgovernment. The reforms constituted not so much as an extension as a centripetal shift in public authority, but they did not bite deep for several years.

Active local government was the cause and the converse of relatively diffident state authority in this period. Its activities were not all, in a national sense, laudable. Boards of guardians, local boards of health and watch committees vied with one another in outwitting and outflanking their national mentors. With sins both of omission and commission, the unions, especially in the north, resisted and tempered efforts to enforce the thorough-going articles of the new poor law. Parochial influence was allowed to survive to an amazing degree, particularly with regard to rate collection and pauper treatment. As with the guardians, local board members were often elected purely to oppose acts legally enforceable, given the provisions of the 1848 Public Health Act. The 'shopocratic' corporations of the north were often in business to deny the encroachment of the state, and Manchesterism could be as scornful as Shaftesbury's 'meddling conservatism' as of Chadwick's 'meddling radicalism'. As J. Toulmin Smith, arch enemy of centralization, said, the establishment of a central board, with inspectors and the like, invades the first principle of local self-government'.

Herein lies the difficulty. On paper, the *ad hoc* provision of local bodies, like boards of guardians or local boards of health, seemed to identify them as servants of the state, but, in practice, they frequently defied their masters. Where government attempted to enact through the municipalities, the obstacles were sometimes greater, as in indirect defiance of the 1835 Municipal Reform Act, boroughs refused to police their domains efficiently. As two instances among many, the incorporation of Ashton-under-Lyne and Warrington led indeed to the formation of a borough police force; but, on closer examination, they turn out to be exactly the same personnel as in the purportedly defunct township watch. This regular continuum of personnel—policemen, prison officers, poor law overseers and relieving officers, workhouse masters, nuisance inspectors and so on—is in itself a meaningful element. Acts of Parliament did not overnight produce new men to fill the novel administrative bills, and, over and over, old faces took on new labels.

The school boards, some permissive, some compulsory, were established after 1870, but, although they postdate the mainstream of *ad hoc* local agencies, they may most lucidly be examined as of a series with the boards of guardians and the local boards of health. Like them, many school boards fought a last-ditch struggle against the incursions of the state, twisting and turning sophistically to avoid the expense of constructing new schools, leaning over backwards to accommodate less children than the central department agreed in more places that the central department accepted. This was frequently the case both in large boards, like Manchester and Liverpool, and small ones. A popular assumption is that school boards were locked in rivalry with church schools. Often nothing could have been further from the truth.

The electorate by and large was Christian and not atheistical and churchmen very frequently ran the boards. The concentration of many boards, certainly those in Lancashire, on attendance and the marked preference, especially again in Lancashire, to the cheapter (because no provision had to be found) school attendance committees of Sandon's 1876 Education Act favoured the church school. Attendance was enforced by the boards and committees at the voluntary schools, and, as state grants were assessed by attendance and by that rote-learning only attendance could obtain, the churchmen, whatever their outbursts at 'Godless' boards, could afford some secret pleasure in the 1870 and 1876 Acts.

Liverpool illustrates some of this tendency. In 1870 the Education Department of the Privy Council issued its precept for the election of a school board in Liverpool, but 'every prospect of a warmly-contested election' alarmed rather than excited the Liverpolitan politicians. 'A large number of gentlemen' agreed the then famous 'Liverpool Platform', aimed at healing religious breaches by a latitudinarian statement of intent. A public meeting approved the proposition, and a committee was formed to select fifteen candidates for uncontested election. The committee decided on seven Anglicans, four Roman Catholics and four Non-Conformists, all nominated by the respective church organizations, and 'the remaining candidates were prevailed upon to ultimately withdraw'. The board was thus elected 'at a cost to the rate payers of only £32 12s 4d'.

This oligarchic proceeding was not untypical, nor was the drawn-out controversy over accommodation that followed. It is not without meaning that, in Lancashire by 1902, the established church, despite several closures, had contrived to open more schools over all that the fifty Lancastrian boards *in toto*, and that, in 1902, the Roman Catholics still had more schools than the school boards. This was in spite of the fact that most of the sizeable boroughs had established school boards. It was, of course, because the school boards could levy rates that their attempts at providing accommodation were occasionally timorous and even non-existent. School board members, as representatives of the rate-payers, were not anxious to overdo the privilege afforded them by the 1870 legislation.

Once more the sordid issue of finance must be faced. In all aspects of Victorian local social administration, money is central. The municipal corporations, the local boards of health (later to become urban santiary authorities), the boards of guardians and the other bits and pieces of local organization, like the burial boards and the highway boards and the still surviving improvement commissions—they all managed, roughly or smoothly, to identify themselves with the ratepayers. People, it has been said, pay taxes in sorrow and rates in anger. The Victorian ratepayer was not as attuned as ourselves to the astronomical designs of public spending, but he was learning the hard way. The county rate and the parish poor rate began to grow, to be joined by the special and general district rates of boards of health or the heavy rating of the municipality. Even before the school boards joined battle for the rate levies, municipal activity in a number of fields, like libraries and parks, began to develop. With each turn of the fiscal screw, the ratepayer had to be persuaded that expenditure was an investment or that, in Asa Brigg's succinct phrase, the long run was worth worrying about. Without financial wherewithal, ambitious social plans were doomed to remain on the drawing board.

Much has been written of the 'utility' and 'laissez-faire' elements in Benthamism, but, in either case, economic criteria abounded. Both 'tutelage' and 'self-help' were closely linked with monetary considerations and the need for a careful watch on public expenditure along with the desired growth of private income. Edwin Chadwick, as the chief proponent of the 'artificial' or 'tutelary' school of Benthamism, identified the greatest happiness for the greatest number with a maximization of the gross national product. In this sense Benthamism had an obvious local manifestation, or, at least, municipal leaders turned to its formulas to support cases for low or selective expenditure. The preventive principle was invoked time and again in the council chambers and board meetings of England. A preventive police would preserve the local economy and social fabric from the 'depredations' of that constant, niggling theft which so irritated Victorian commercial life. The effect of this on police reform has been undeployed, usually because the spectacular drama of Chartism and mass disorder has been deemed crucial. An intimate examination of police origins suggests that humdrum theft was more critical than normally has been assumed. In the words of an early meeting of Liverpool watch committee in 1836:

the establishment of an efficient preventive police (would) by diminishing crime, prove a saving in contingent expenses . . . which little addition to the sum now expended upon a system which has been found to be totally inadequate.

In 1831, 233 attested convicts from Lancashire lay in England's eight convict hulks. Practically all were convicted of forms of theft. In 1849 there were 409 in the two national prisons and twelve hulks. These, too, were almost all thieves. Not one was a rioter, a Chartist or a political prisoner of any kind. Twelve-year-old Christopher Hall, sentenced at Preston to seven years for stealing a currant pie, or William Naylor, the same age, serving life transportation for stealing a cow—these were apparently more feared than the temporary aberration of mass demonstration, which (whether police existed or not) required military treatment.

Public health was mooted as an investment to rid the economy of the huge losses consequent on 'preventable' death and illness. The reports which preceded the formation of local boards were, in their day, minor best-sellers, and each included a sample of felicific calculus worthy of the master himself. For instance, Robert Rawlinson, the famous civil engineer, calculated that, in Rusholme, over a $6\frac{1}{2}$-year period, there had been 40 preventable deaths and 1,200 preventable sicknesses, costing, at £5 per funeral and £1 per patient, some £1,400. He added another £1,500 for the five years' extra production by each such premature death, and showed an annual loss to the community of £446. This equalled the annual interest repayable on a capital loan of £8,920 at 5 per cent, being the sum necessary to provide a scheme 'which would drain the whole township' and prevent much of this ill-health. Rusholme, with its celebrated 'dung-mountains', one of them 30,000 tons in size, could ill afford to miss such a golden opportunity.

The austerities of the new poor law were similarly designed to prevent obstructions on the labour market by the application of the workhouse test. That it proved to be 'a dam not a sieve', and

205

that it was based on a mistaking of the symptoms of poverty for its causes, does not alter this. Its main hope of success was a reduction of the poor rate, and, initially, this was achieved, for the *per capita* cost nationally dropped from 10s 2d in 1832 to 5s 6d in 1852. It is interesting to note that opposition in the north was partially due to the low costs hitherto obtaining being increased after 1834. The old poor law in Lancashire cost roughly 3s 3d a head; by 1848 it had risen to 6s 11d. The Poor Law Commission could be accused of failing in its own objectives in Lancashire.

When fear and caution were in balance the ratepayers saw the point. Dread of cholera, of theft and of vagrancy and an appreciation of their interrelatedness combined with a consideration of shrewd investment. 'It was a secret', Thomas Carlyle coolly remarked, 'known to all rat-catchers.' Here is one reason why educational reform was a little later in the day, for the local businessman or owner-occupier was not so directly concerned. That bane of the Victorian social workers' life, for example, the common lodging house, acted as 'flash-house' and brothel, it was a locus for disease and it attracted the unemployed and the unemployable. Its dangers could be hedged in by police, sanitary control and the workhouse. It took some time for the interconnectedness of education to be realized. Two factors helped. One was the growing need for an adult literate working force, to man the evermore sophisticated economy, and, with it, a decline in the necessity for child-labour. In the 1860s the large towns were suffering from the impasse of thousands of children roaming the streets for whom there was neither work nor school available. The second was the requirements of civic literacy in an equally more complex society. When Liverpool sent out its thousands of cellar eviction orders, most of the recipients could not read them! The Victorian debate on whether literacy would lead to the lower orders studying the bible and other standard works on British moral practice or conning scabrous revolutionary rags was partly settled by this twin need for economic and social literacy.

This analysis of the role of local expediency in social reform is not as pleasant to record as the outbreak of active humanitarianism in the nineteenth century. It is not intended to deny this its place. It is hoped to restore a balance marred by an overexposure of the happy tales spun of humanitarianism and its attractive personalities.

The abrasive style of Chadwick, and the repugnant nature of much of his chosen work, have not earned him a place in the pantheon of English social reformers, in the long line of Wilberforce and Shaftesbury. Humanitarian fervour was as vital as it is encouraging, but the starker facts of committee life have been a little too frequently forgotten. Two other aspects deserve notice. First, there is no doubt that the benefits of industrialism slowly began to permeate downwards, so that the general populace were able to participate in the bounty of the industrial revolution, either through personal improvement or through the broader margin allowed in the political economy for social welfare. Second, an improved administrative technology was a prerequisite of major social reform. At all levels, from national structure to office mechanics, social progress waited on organizational change.

Large-scale administrative realignment was slowly developed to meet this requirement, and the replication of the same institutional formula is indeed compelling. Chadwick's ideal *tutelle* comprised a central supervisory department, with itinerant inspectors, local elective boards, with (in the old Benthamite slogan) the interests of governed and governors identified, an accent on expertise, and an acute awareness of cost-accounting and strict audit. General Board of Health, Poor Law Commission, Home Office and Committee of Council for Education; superintending inspectors, assistant poor law commissioners, inspectors of constabulary and HMIs; local boards, boards of guardians and watch committees; medical officers and sanitary inspectors, relieving officers, police constables and qualified teachers; each aspect with its own fiscal interpretation of 'less eligibility' or 'payment by results'. Slowly the Benthamite formula was evolved. The major gap before 1870 was the absence of a local elective committee for education. It is not always realized that the establishment of the school board was, in effect, a closing of this gap. This manifestatation of Benthamism was more than coincidence. The contenders for piecemeal reform too often forget that dozens of proposals were made to answer the social problems of the Victorian era. With crime, for example, preliminary inquiry, pursuit by private persons, vigilante as well as township watches, the grouping of civil police around a stipendiary magistracy, bounty-hunting, parochial bands of policemen, insurance companies, a simple doubling of watch salaries, pensioned ex-soldiers as a rural force, a *gens d'armerie* on the continental pattern; these and other modes were proposed and some of them tried, but, eventually, it was the Benthamite mould that was adopted.

Just as the central departments turned out to be weak, so did the other elements in the format prove to be unsound or unreliable on occasion. The Chadwickian 'expertise' in practice might be no more than drunken constables, deceitful relieving officers, or incompetent workhouse masters. Oliver MacDonagh's strictures on administrative procreation are certainly valid. The 'considerable reduction of officers employed' desired by the Poor Law Commission, for example, was soon seen to be chimerical. By 1850 the Lancashire unions employed over a thousand officials at a cost of £50,000 per year, while, there was, Alfred Power noted, 'the continuance in office of the old paid officers'. The expense of pauperism began to creep upwards again; the death rate and the crime rate stayed constant, and all the local committees, from boards of guardians to the school boards, proved frequently to be obstructive.

In terms of future development, however, the scene was set for that familiar bipartite character of English administration. Possibly the very suspicion and awkwardness of the local agencies preserved their autonomy against any overwhelming tendencies of the central departments. It is not automatic. Some states have developed much more heavily centralized and others as deeply devolved administrations. The uneasy balance of Whitehall and town hall is peculiarly English, and foursquare with nineteenth-century theory and practice. Many other similar traditions obtain. The difficulties of watering conurbations (Manchester versus the Lake District for instance) stem from water supply beng placed on a local and not a national footing in Victorian times. The problems of present-day police amalgamation are partly the consequence of borough forces preceding, by four years, county forces, so that the picture of a county police area dotted with municipal forces is still with us.

The delicately balanced dichotomy of central and local control is here the main concern. It might be said that local government maintained a more secure line of administrative continuity than is sometimes thought. Local government was active before, during, and after the social reforms of mid-century. Individualism was always contravened by local government; state action at first hardly altered the balance.

Unluckily, local government did not alter fundamentally to meet new circumstances, and, of course, none of the problems stood still long enough to be solved, as the mounting population of the century indicates. Rather were additions of kind or function made, until the whole fabric did amount (as Dicey's critics are right to affirm) to an unholy mess. The vertical stratification of central office and local board was neat enough, but, viewed horizontally, it was untidy and confused. A thousand years of local government had left a county like Lancashire in a bewildering condition by 1870. As time flowed over medieval institutionalism and early ecclesiastical settlement, bits and pieces were added, but very little was erased. The six hundreds, two of them subdivided, had existed since before 1066, and, through the magistrates, who sometimes met in hundred groups, shire-governance was controlled. The Lord Lieutenant reigned over the magistracy, and his dominions were divided into sixteen sub-lieutenancies. These did not correspond to other juridicial divisions. There was one court of quarter sessions, based on Lancaster, with four branches in other leading towns. These four and nine others had separate commissions of the peace, leaving, illogically, six other boroughs without their own magistracies. Beyond this, the county was divided into twenty-three petty sessional districts and the country police area was composed of eighteen divisions. Apart from these, there were thirteen borough police forces, although another five boroughs had not established their own force.

The ecclesiastical history of Lancashire contributed to the mishmash. The county fell into four dioceses, and, by an act of 1874, its handful of parishes had gradually been fragmented for administrative purposes into 455 civil parishes, variously known as chapelries and townships. These enjoyed a definitive legal identity, and were the key local government units of their age. Under the Poor Law Amendment Act, they were unionized for poor law purposes, although this took until 1869 in Lancashire and parochial influence was strongly perpetuated in the new regime. In 1870 Lancashire boasted twenty-nine unions. The institutional merry-go-round did not stop there. There were eighty-nine local boards, twenty-seven registration districts (normally associated with the unions), nine highway districts and a number of improvement commissions and other bodies. To this baffling jigsaw, the education acts of 1870 and 1876 were about to add fifty-odd school boards and eighty-odd school attendance committees, and public health legislation was moving towards the urban or rural sanitary authority. Sometimes the function was made the responsibility of an existing authority. In Lancashire, for example, in 1880, there were thirty of the nation's sixty-nine bodies rejoicing under the unwieldly title of urban sanitary authority school attendance committee. A sanitary board being responsible for truancy demonstrates the tortuous situation into which local government had twisted itself!

It was little wonder that local government reforms were mooted toward the end of the nineteenth century, and, by the acts of 1888 and 1894, the familiar pattern of counties, county boroughs as well as municipal boroughs, urban and rural district councils and parish councils emerged. Slowly, the multi-purpose local authority was created. After 1902 education was taken under the wing of the counties and county boroughs and, after 1929, welfare services were transferred to the counties from the now defunct poor law unions. Police control began its still busy activity of rationalization, and public health areas were aligned with the new pattern of local responsibility. As part of the collectivist trend, the functions of municipalization were extended to an extraordinary degree. The characteristic bipartite construct of local and central departments remained and was expanded, albeit with the balance of power (education is a good example) tending more and more in favour of the latter. It is interesting to note that although the local body became multipurpose, the same was obviously not true of the central administration. The purportedly integrated local departments were related to national departments which still remained as separatist as of old.

The local government reforms contrived to jump ahead, stand and backtrack all at the same time. They were progressive in that they ironed out anomalies, filled gaps and erected a comprehensive regimen of local authority. Everyone lived, basically, in either a county or a county borough, with the former offering within its pale only two or three alternatives of sub-county allegiance. The rating confusion was tidied up with eminent simplicity, and certain other rational steps were taken. Behind the facade of forward-looking uniformity, however, there was the solid brickwork of continuity. The shires and large towns already existed; so did the smaller boroughs, the parishes and the sanitary authorities which were to become district councils. Because of this kind of momentum, much of the change was a rewriting of labels; that contradiction in terms 'the county borough' is an indication of this. It is noteworthy how often one can trace the continuum. Parish becomes local board of health becomes urban sanitary authority becomes urban district council; at sometime it might have also become school board or school attendance committee and thus become Part III Authority become divisional executive. This enforcement of a previous impetus made so-called uniformity misleading. The school boards had been criticized for being both frighteningly large and ludicruously small, but, today, both Birmingham and the Isles of Scilly run their own education services.

The reforms also put the clock back. Chadwick and his successors had hoped to move away from the outmoded shire concept, with many of the relevant boundaries formulated by vague medieval requirements. The local government reforms were conservative measures, and they included some measure of concern for the rural areas. They tried to invigorate the county system and presumably retrieve some power for the traditional county hierarchies. This was to shore up some rather flimsy structures which no longer had much reality. It also effectively stopped the conurbations from spreading their administrative tendrils and left many cities with still unresolved border disputes about districts palpably part of but politically distinct from the conurbation. Worse perhaps of all, by concentrating a plenitude of responsibility in frequently remote county towns, the promising elements of local participation in the Victorian *ad hoc* boards were often lost.

In the event, the outcome has been that major local functions are operated on the large scale, either through the sizeable yet often abruptly circumscribed town and city or the frequently bizarre-shaped shire. Apart from both being open to objections of unreal form, both have been, in differing ways, criticized for becoming faceless and aloof. The English, like so many others, have never found the secret of combining the advantages of large-scale enterprise with the social benefits of small-scale identification One indication of this is the pathetically low level of active interest in local government. Commentators severely castigate the public for its apathy, but this is possibly unfair. There could be thousands of sincere, positive and genuinely convinced 'don't knows' in the electorate. One of the saddest points, for instance, is the actual lack of (as opposed to the theoretical presence of) integration in the multi-purpose authority. Partly due to a corresponding lack of central togetherness, local departments overlap and fail to dovetail in the field. Action is slowed by the stately quadrille of a complex committee structure, councillors move uneasily from cemeteries to wash-houses to art galleries, and the public are subject to an amalgam of services, administratively tiered from state to parish, which not infrequently appear inefficient and impersonal. Briefly, coordination at field level—the only major purpose of the multi-purpose authority—is rarely experienced, except, thankfully, in the financial sphere, where a single rate, whatever its several other faults, is preferable to several different ratings.

Has the twentieth century any lessons to learn from the *ad hoc* single-purpose body of Victorian times ? These are usually berated for being overweeningly pompous, ultracautious and static, unduly severe in attitude, extremely bourgeois and patronizingly smug. This, however, is to condemn them for being Victorian. Their character was coloured by their epoch. It would be unfair to expect them to have been matey and generous of spirit in a contemporary manner. The issue lies in the viability of their administrative form, and here there were some hopeful signs. In studying local boards of health and small school boards one is sometimes impressed by the recognition of peculiar needs and the deployment of especial responses. Sometimes they were eccentric and amusing, but they often appear to have been wholeheartedly searching to adapt national legislative norms to their own require-ments, however one might retrospectively object to their particular commitment. Occasionally a local pride and sense of community breathes through the arid pages of minute books and files of correspondence. In some respects, then, they allowed for what now fashionably might be called 'participation'. It is interesting to muse on this small-time elective principle imbued with the twentieth instead of the nineteenth-century personality: the popularly elected school board running the neighbourhood school; the democratic board of health making decisions for the local housing estate about refuse collection, the public wash-house, the clinic, the neighbouring playground and so on.

Certainly the hundred-year-old tendency towards centralism seems a dwindling force. The comparative failure of the purportedly radical Wilson administration to intervene decisively, as against the definitive triumphs of Gladstone, Lloyd George and Attlee, is as indicative as the *cri de coeur* for devolution and anti-authoritarianism or the apathetic malaise affecting municipal government. One might recall that all the nineteenth-century socialist doctrines, including Marxism, were anti-state, and, in this, paralleled English *laissez-faire* and the Jeffersonian concept of 'frugal government'. In practice, circumstances dictated that *laissez-faire* and Jeffersonianism as well as communism, became state-oriented, and Engels' prophecy of the state withering away looked nonsensical. The anocratic dreams of much nineteenth-century political thought are now rehearsed in modern times, although, of course, few are willing to sacrifice the amenities of contemporary existence that only, it seems, large-scale enterprise can provide. The dilemma is a considerable one. How can the unit, tiny enough for participation be matched with the service, gigantic enough for competent provision?

In the 1870s, a writer calling himself 'A Liverpool Shipwright' published a series of articles in the Liverpool weekly journal *Porcupine* criticizing the town's new school board. In one of them, he proposed that the problem of schooling needed 'an educational Rowland Hill' to put it to rights on the same basis as the GPO. It is, a fascinating thought. Assuredly the GPO, possibly more than any other institution, managed normally to combine the massive and the minute smoothly. It operates an international telecommunications agency at one pole, and, at the other, there is a friendly neighbourhood postman and the old age pensioner collecting her weekly shillings at the corner shop. Perhaps the 'corporation' idea might be extended. For instance, the main

213

difficulty with the school boards was that they were sporadic, so that an alternative to abolishing them in favour of the multi-purpose county authorities might have been to complete the pattern. Then school boards of varied types and sizes might have turned for large-scale installation and maintenance to the national department. Instead of this, we have usually an undifferentiated and abstract treatment by a unit not strong enough to challenge the uniform regimen of the state nor organic enough to tap the feelings of the public. The fact that the areas and the services are neither uniform nor identical aggravates the situation. The principle of equity is not met when wildly disparate areas are treated with a chilling standardization, and when the confused overlapping of public facilities makes a mockery of the multi-purpose principle.

Perhaps the roles of state and locality should be simply defined, with the former as a contracting and providing agency and the latter as an articulate, decision-making consumer body. The local community could make policy according to its own priorities, and then negotiate and consult with the educational corporation for its school, the public health corporation for its hospital and so forth. We should not pretend that decisions on social administration can be meaningful when made nationally. There is no point in everyone having the same kind of police, of health service, of school or of welfare amenity, if it is unsuitable for the consumer. There was something in the Victorian notion that the state would expand to destroy local autonomy, and there was point in the obstructionist tactics of local committees. Conditions somehow led to overwhelming intervenism from centre, and middle-range local governmental units came more and more to act as executive sub-offices of the state. But the balance has never completely been lost. The dichotomy of state and locality, the uneasy partnership of Whitehall and town hall, created by the social reforms of the last century, still remain intact. Perhaps it is time to reweigh that balance a little, emasculating the state of much of its policy consideration and giving powers of decision directly to the consumer in his natural locale. The state would more become a storehouse or emporium to fit out the bespoke needs of the local communities, and could become their servant as opposed to their master.

This rose-coloured excursion into a sort of sociological fantasy world was prompted by an intuitive appreciation of fruitful growth-points of Victorian local social administration, some of which were destroyed. It could be that the Victorians gave both central and local government momentum which, had it not become ill-directed, might have offered the twentieth century a happier solution than it seems capable of finding from scratch.

Notes

1. H. Finer, *The Theory and Practice of Modern Government* (1950).
2. O. MacDonagh, 'Nineteenth Century Revolution in Government', *Historical Journal* II (1958); D. Roberts, 'Jeremy Bentham and the Victorian Administrative State', *Victorian Studies* II (1959); J. Hart, 'Nineteenth Century Social Reform: A Tory Interpretation of History', *Past and Present* 31 (1965); *et al.*
3. A. V. Dicey, *Law and Public Opinion in England* (1914).
4. O. MacDonagh, *A Pattern of Government Growth* (1961); R. J. Lambert, 'A Victorian National Health Service; State Vaccination, 1855–71', *Historical Journal* V (1962); and D. Roberts, *Victorian Origins of the British Welfare State* 1960).
5. J. Hart, 'Nineteenth Century Social Reform', *op. cit.*; H. Parris, 'Nineteenth Century Revolution in Government: A Reappraisal Reappraised', *Historical Journal* III (1960); R. M. Gutchen, 'Local Improvements and Centralization in Nineteenth Century England,' *Historical Journal* IV (1961); J. B. Brebner, 'Laissez-faire and State Intervention,' *Journal of Economic History* VIII (1948); W. L. Burn, *The Age of Equipoise* (1964); and S. E. Finer, *The Life and Times of Sir Edwin Chadwick* (1952).
6. Much of the illustration quoted hereafter is drawn from E. C. Midwinter, *Social Administration in Lancashire, 1830–1860* (1969); and the same author's *The Administration of Public Education in Late Victorian Lancashire* (forthcoming).

Bibliography

Standard Works
F. Adams, *The History of the Elementary School Contest in England* (1882).
W. H. G. Armytage, *Four Hundred Years of English Education* (1965).

T. S. Ashton, *The Industrial Revolution* (1948).
H. C. Barnard, *A Short History of English Education, 1760–1944*.
A. Briggs, *Victorian Cities* (1963).
W. H. L. Burn, *The Age of Equipoise* (1964).
J. J. Clarke, *History of the Local Government of the United Kingdom* (1955).
W. F. Connell, *The Foundations of Education* (1963).
A. V. Dicey, *Law and Public Opinion in England* (1914).
E. J. R. Eaglesham, *From School Board to Local Authority* (1956).
H. Finer, *The Theory and Practice of Modern Government* (1950).
S. E. Finer, *The Life and Times of Sir Edwin Chadwick* (1952).
W. M. Frazer, *Duncan of Liverpool.*
W. M. Frazer, *A History of Medicine* (1945).
A. L. Goodhart, *English Contributions to the Philosophy of Law* (1948).
Major Greenwood, *Some British Pioneers of Social Medicine* (1948).
D. C. Guthrie, *A History of Medicine* (1945).
E. Havley, *The Growth of Philosophic Radicalism* (1928).
J. L. and B. Hammond, *The Bleak Age* (1934).
J. Hart, *The British Police* (1951).
B. L. Hutchins, *Public Health Agitation, 1833–1848* (1909).
C. W. Hutt and H. H. Thompson, *The Principles and Practice of Preventive Medicine* (1935).
A. V. Judges (ed.), *Pioneers of English Education* (1952).
G. Kitson-Clark, *The Making of Victorian England* (1962).
R. J. Lambert, *Sir John Simon* (1964).
H. Laski *et al.*, *A Century of Municipal Progress* (1935).
R. A. Lewis, *Edwin Chadwick and the Public Health Movement, 1832–1854* (1952).
S. Leff, *Social Medicine* (1953).
V. D. Lipmann, *Local Government Areas, 1834–1945* (1949).
G. A. N. Lowndes, *The Silent Social Revolution* (1937).
O. MacDonagh, *A Pattern of Government Growth* (1961).
J. D. Marshall, *The Old Poor Law, 1745–1834* (1968).
E. W. Martin, *Where London Ends* (1958).
W. L. Melville-Lee, *A History of Police in England* (1901).
E. C. Midwinter, *Social Administration in Lancashire, 1830–1860* (1969).
E. C. Midwinter, *Victorian Social Reform* (1968).
J. Murphy, *The Religious Problem in English Education; the Crucial Experiment* (1959).
G. Nicholls, *The History of the English Poor Law* (1899).
K. Polyani, *Origins of Our Time; the Great Transformation* (1945).
P. Pringle, *The Thief* (1958).
L. Radzinowicz, *A History of English Criminal Law* (1956).
A. Reford, *The History of Local Government in Manchester* (1940).
C. Reith, *The Blind Eye of History* (1952).
C. Reith, *British Police and the Democratic Ideal* (1943).
C. Reith, *A New Study of Police History* (1956).
D. Roberts, *Victorian Origins of the British Welfare State* (1960).

Sir J. Simon, *English Sanitary Institutions* (1890).
B. Simon, *Studies in the History of Education*, vol. i, 1780–1870 (1960); vol. ii, 1870–1921 (1965).
F. Smith, *Life of Sir James Kay-Shuttleworth* (1923).
J. R. Somers Vine, *The English Municipalities* (1879).
E. Troop, *The Home Office* (1925).
S. B. Webb, *English Local Government* (1929).
E. G. West, *Education and the State* (1965).
B. D. White, *A History of the Corporation of Liverpool* (1951).
R. Williams, *The Long Revolution* (1961).
S. M. Young, *Victorian England; Portrait of an Age* (1936).
Articles
J. B. Brebner, 'Laissez-faire and State Intervention', *Journal of Economic History* VIII, (1948).
H. L. Beales, 'The New Poor Law', *History* (1931).
M. Blaug, 'The Myth of the Old Poor Law and the Making of the New', *Journal of Economic History* XXIII, (1963).
M. Blaug, 'The Poor Law Report Re-examined, *ibid.* XXIV (1964).
R. Boyson, 'The New Poor Law in North-east Lancashire', *Lancs. & Ches. Historical Society* (1960).
F. Brockington, 'Public Health at the Privy Council 1831–34', *Journal of the History of Medicine* XVI (1961).
E. J. R. Eaglesham, 'Planning the Education Bill of 1902', *British Journal of Educational Studies* IX, i (1960).
R. M. Gutchen, 'Local Improvements and Centralization in Nineteenth Century England', *Historical Journal* IV (1961).
J. Hart, 'Reform of the Borough Police, 1835–1856', *English Historical Review* 70 (1955).
J. Hart, 'Nineteenth Century Century Social Reform: A Tory Interpretation of History', *Past and Present* 31 (1965).
S. W. F. Holloway, 'Medical Education in England, 1830–1858', *History* (1964).
R. J. Lambert, 'A Victorian National Health Service: State Vaccination, 1855–1871', *Historical Journal* V (1962).
O. MacDonagh, 'Nineteenth Century Revolution in Government', *Historical Journal* (1958).
O. MacDonagh, 'Relegated Legislation and Administrative Devolutions in the Eighteen-Fifties', *Victorian Studies* II (1959).
E. C. Midwinter, 'The Administration of Public Education in Late Victorian Lancashire', *Northern History* IV (1969).
E. C. Midwinter, 'Central and Local Government in Mid-Nineteenth Century Lancashire', *Northern History* III (1968).
E. C. Midwinter, 'Law and Order in Early Victorian Lancashire' (1968).
E. C. Midwinter, 'Local Boards of Health in Lancashire, 1848–1858', *Lancs. & Ches. Historic Society* (1965).
E. C. Midwinter, 'Non-events in the History of Education', *Education for Teaching* (1965).

E. C. Midwinter, 'State Intervention at the Local Level: the New Poor Law in Lancashire', *Historical Journal* X (1967).

E. C. Midwinter, 'A Tory Interpretation of History: Some Comments', *Past and Present* 34 (1966).

J. Murphy, 'The Rise of Elementary Education in Liverpool, 1784–1818', *Lancs. and Ches. Historic Society* (1964).

H. Parris, 'Nineteenth Century Revolution in Government: A Reappraisal Reappraised', *Historical Journal* III (1960).

H. J. Perkin, 'Middle-class Education and Employment in the 19th Century: A Critical Note', *Economic History Review* XIV (1961).

D. Roberts, 'How Cruel was the New Poor Law?' *Historical Journal* V (1963).

D. Roberts, Jeremy Bentham and the Victorian Administrative state', *Victorian Studies* II (1959).

M. Sanderson, 'Social Change and Elementary Education in Industrial Lancashire, 1780–1840', *Northern History* III (1968).

G. Ward, 'Education of Factory Child-workers, 1833–1850', *Economic History* III (1935).

E. G. West, 'Private versus Public Education—A Classical Economic Dispute', *Journal of Political Economy* (1964).

8
The History of Medical Care

BRIAN ABEL-SMITH

There are extraordinarily few countries in the world where there has been less public control in the medical care market than in the United States. The phrase 'public control' as distinct from 'public regulation' is used here to cover two separate developments. The first is the ownership of medical care facilities by public authorities. The second is the use of tax or compulsory insurance financing.

Data collected by WHO shows the pattern of ownership of hospital facilities in different countries of the world. Though there may be occasional exceptions, I am confident that the data from Africa, Asia, Australasia and Europe as a whole will show that well over half the hospital beds for the physically sick are publicly owned. Among the high-income countries of Europe, with which the United States can most readily be compared, only the Netherlands has less than half its beds (about 30 per cent) owned by public authorities. While public authorities in the United States pay for the bulk of mental hospitals and offer services to the armed forces, veterans, Presidents and other categories, there is no compulsory health insurance. The vast majority of other high-income countries have some form of compulsory health insurance, and taxation pays for a considerable proportion, and usually a majority, of medical care services in the United Kingdom, Scandinavia, Eastern Europe, Africa and south-east Asia.

Why are the patterns of financing and organizing medical care services so different in the United States from those in other countries? It is only in recent years that this question has begun to be studied. And the answer is beginning to emerge from detailed studies of the history of medical care organization. Most of my examples are drawn from high-income countries (particularly those in Europe) as it is thought that this experience is most relevant to the problems now facing the United States.

The philosophies which underlie systems of medical care organization cannot be understood without a knowledge of the history both of medical care and of wider social and political developments in each country. There is a danger of attributing systems of medical care organization to political ideologies of relatively recent origin—particularly to socialism or communism. Such notions can be dispelled only by a careful study of developments during the past two centuries and even earlier. This point can be made most forcibly by giving three quotations. They come from the same book.

> The majority of the population in England consider it not only not a disgrace, but the most natural thing in the world, when they fall ill, to demand and receive free treatment without question or delay.[1]
>
> Americans hold rightly that no person is entitled to occupy a free bed unless or until he can prove beyond dispute that he is unable to pay something for the treatment he receives in the hospital ward.[2]
>
> There is relatively little free medical relief anywhere in America.[3]
>
> The entire hospital system in Russia is now under the control of the State and municipal corporations.[4]

The quotations seem platitudinous until the date of publication is appreciated. They all come from a book published in 1893.

When comparing the history of medical care in the United States with that of Europe, it should be appreciated that for centuries it has been regarded as a public responsibility in Europe to make provision for the sick poor. And poverty has been interpreted generously. Just as the poor needed schools, so it was believed, to an extent varying in different countries and at different times, that the poor needed hospitals and medical care. In medieval Europe provisions were made by the Catholic Church. But gradually, or suddenly in the case of the French Revolution, many continental hospitals were transferred into the hands of public authorities either because of mismanagement, misappropriation of funds, or just the absence of adequate financial backing.[5] In both Denmark and Sweden it had by 1870 been made the duty of local authorities to provide hospitals.[6] Thus, in Scandinavia, the hospital services grew up almost entirely as a public service like the education service in the United States. In Britain up to 1948 charitable bodies provided the more costly acute hospitals, but this private sector was supplemented by public provision for the mentally ill, the chronic sick and cases of infectious disease. And where provision for the acute sick by charitable effort was inadequate to provide for all who needed care, the acute sector of hospital care was, from 1870 onwards, gradually supplemented by public authorities. For over a century the majority of the physically sick in institutional care in Britain have been in publicly owned institutions.[7]

Both charity and public authority hospitals set out to provide a service to the public—but mainly to the low-income public. The criterion for admission was medical need. The question of payment was not normally raised until after the patient had been admitted. If figures were available, I suggest that they would show that patient's direct payments unaided by insurance, have never contributed much to the running costs of European hospitals. In Britain, it was not until 1881 that any major hospital accommodated any paying patients at all. And even in 1938, paying patients were substantially less than 5 per cent of all hospital patients. In America hospitals have tended to be run on different lines. In 1893 Burdett reported that the majority of hospital beds were occupied by paying patients and that the managers would authorize a stated number of beds for the use of free patients, and this number could not be exceeded.[8]

The extensive development of public hospitals in Europe treating poor persons who made little or no payment for their care led to the employment of physicians on a whole-time or part-time salaried basis to look after them. Patients who had no physician could not be expected to be treated by their own physician when they entered hospital. Thus there emerged a separate class of hospital-based physicians who had every opportunity to specialize. This system became established before medical professions were effectively organized. And in the early days, few of the hospital patients could have paid much for any sort of medical services.

In Britain, the division between physicians working in the main voluntary hospitals and physicians working outside corresponded with an ancient class distinction within the medical profession. Similar traditional distinctions can be found in France, Sweden and Italy. While in the United States all purpose doctors preceded specialist doctors, in Britain specialists in the form of internists and surgeons preceded the emergence of general practioners out of the class of apothecary-tradesmen.

Indeed, I imagine that physician emigrants to the United States up to 1900 and beyond almost entirely consisted of general practitioners rather than the higher class of specialist. In Britain, the latter had a university education—an advantage not shared by general practitioners until much later. The internists and surgeons also charged much higher fees. It was this group of physicians who obtained a virtual monopoly of the principal hospital appointments. Having acquired it so early, the internists and surgeons have retained their hold over appointments in the principal hospitals in Britain. In the voluntary hospital days they did their hospital work for virtually no direct payment, supporting themselves by private consultations, for which they charged about ten times more than a general practitioner. This system of charging and the etiquette of cases being referred by general practitioners to specialists helped to preserve a fairly sharp distinction between specialists and general practitioners in the main towns.[9] It also meant that specialist services to those who were not wealthy have always been given at hospital departments where no payment is made to the doctor.

It was not only free hospital care which was made available to the poor, almost as a right. As part of the development of 'poor law' or public assistance services, doctors were paid to give medical care to the poor either on a part-time or wholetime salaried basis. Such care was provided in London in dispensaries in the nineteenth century. Similarly, salaried doctors were employed to work in the outlying parts of Sweden, Norway and Switzerland. In the poorer parts of Europe at the end of the nineteenth century, salaried community doctors were engaged on a considerable scale to supervise the public health and give medical services to the poor. The system was extensively used in Poland and, similarly, 'zemstvo' doctors were employed in the rural communities of Tzarist Russia.[10] Such doctors were often based upon dispensaries or polyclinics—a natural corollary of their salaried status. Any extensive use of home visiting would have been wasteful of scarce doctors' time. The polyclinic system was extended by the Russians after the communist revolution under their system of compulsory insurance. It was similarly used in neighbouring Poland and Czechoslovakia,[12] which were not under communist domination. The Eastern European system of poly-cylinics was adopted in the sick fund started by the Jewish immigrants to Palestine. It is still used in Israel today.

Thus, in Europe, salaried physicians were paid by government authorities to give service to the poor both in hospitals and dispensaries. When Europeans developed colonies in the even poorer countries of Asia and Africa, they introduced the same system. Originally the services were for the colonists themselves. In the same way as armed forces take with them their own medical services, so did the colonial services. But these services were gradually extended for the use of the local population, before and after independence. The physicians were paid by salary. These services were supplemented in some countries (e.g. India) by indigenous charitable effort and in all countries by medical missionaries. Thus, the low-income countries have developed a high proportion of publicly owned hospitals and salaried physicians.

Thus, government and charity played a much larger role, and indeed a different role, outside the United States, and this role was affected by the pattern of development of the medical and allied professions. In Europe, home-nursing services grew up alongside home medical services. For example, district nursing was organized as a charitable movement in Britain from 1859[13] and in time came to be heavily subsidized by or transferred to local authorities. Obstetric nursing developed in Britain, the Netherlands, France, Belgium[14] and some other countries as a separate independent profession which still takes a major responsibility for normal home confinements in Britain and the Netherlands. The experience of the United States has been different in this respect.

In the United States provisions by public authorities for both the poor as a whole and for the sick poor in particular have tended to be less developed than in Europe. Several reasons can be suggested for this. First, the 'poor' were often Negroes and new immigrants with whose needs older white settlers did not readily identify. Secondly, until relatively recently, land was available where it was thought the 'poor' could settle and make a living. Thirdly, unmet need is more obvious in the large urban communities of a heavily industrialized nation: the latter were a later development in the United States than in Europe. Fourthly, there were many fewer hospital beds in nineteenth century America than in Europe and the general standard of medical care was lower. As few people received good medical care, it is not surprising that little was done for the poor. And finally, the more developed European countries (with the possible exception of France) developed strong working-class movements which became an important political force. Such a force came much later in the United States and has never been of the same character as in Europe.

It was the working-class movements, developing often out of earlier guilds, which pioneered the voluntary insurance movement out of which compulsory insurance was later to develop. In 1804, about thirty years before the British Medical Association was founded, there were about a million members of friendly societies in Britain, though systematic information about their activities in the health insurance field is not available. By 1900, there were, in Britain, seven million members of friendly societies—most of them entitled to invalidity cash benefits, the services of a doctor and the drugs he prescribed. The voluntary sickness insurance movement was also developed extensively in the Netherlands, Germany, Austria, Switzerland and Scandinavia during the nineteenth century. In the earlier schemes, it was common for physicians to be paid by capitation or salary as this simplified budgeting and administration for these somewhat amateur organizations which depended, during their early years at least, on the voluntary work undertaken by the members.

In Britain and Scandinavia,[15] the sickness insurance movement was primarily a movement run by consumers for their mutual

benefit. In Britain it was a general and local working-class movement among the more skilled. Contributions were the same for all,
though there were variations according to benefits provided. In
Holland, Austria and Germany, it had more of an occupational
bais. It was promoted in Germany by paternalist employers, and
benefits were often related to wages. In some countries, prepayment systems were developed by individual physicians among
their patients as a means of restricting the number of bad debts.
This system of 'provider-sponsored' pre-payment was to be
found in the Netherlands, in Spain[16] and among middle-class
patients in Britain, but consumer-sponsored prepayment was by
far the larger sector.

The voluntary health insurance societies generally provided
service benefits. In Sweden and France, however, benefits were
mostly or exclusively given in cash. Thus, in many countries the
consumers of medical care came to be organized before the
physicians were effectively organized and they were in a position
to dictate the terms of service of physicians who were engaged to
provide services. There were many aspects of these terms of
service which caused resentment among the physicians. The
societies tended to appoint some physicians and not others to
work for the fund: this damaged the practices of those excluded.
Disciplinary matters were handled by lay committees which thus
decided professional matters. And, finally, the level of remuneration fixed by the societies was held to be grossly inadequate. The
societies were exploiting their quasimonopolistic position in each
area. The resentment of doctors led to the development of medical
organizations whose main activity was to fight the societies.[17]

The insurance of doctors' services came to Europe before
hospital insurance. This was partly because hospitalization was
much rarer than it is today and partly because both charity and
public hospitals adjusted charges to means, thus making insurance
unnecessary. The insurers adopted capitation and salary systems
of paying doctors, whatever their advantages or disadvantages for
securing good medical care, because they had the overwhelming
advantage of enabling them to control and predict their expenditures. It was not long before this system of voluntary insurance
was made compulsory for certain sections of the population. When
legislation of this kind was passed in Germany, in 1883, and

Britain, in 1911, it involved the extension of an existing system rather than the creation of a new one. It also brought the government into the disputes, which continued concerning levels and methods of remuneration, the control of medical services and other matters.

Often, the providers of services could persuade the government to force upon the insurers changes which they had refused to accept before they worked within a statutory framework.

In Germany, the administration of compulsory health insurance was left in the hands of local sick funds, and there were major protests from doctors about the 'closed panel' restrictions extensively operated by them. Opposition was directed also at the capitation and salary systems of payment which were associated with the 'closed panels'. The universalization of fee-for-service systems of payment, which the German profession fought for and eventually won, was a means of establishing open competition between all physicians who wished to take part in the health insurance scheme.

In Britain the disputes which accompanied the establishment of compulsory health insurance in 1911 concerned, partly, levels of remuneration and, partly, the issue of who was to administer the system of medical benefit—the government, the friendly societies or the doctors.[18] Eventually *ad hoc* statutory bodies were set up in each locality in which all three took part and the principle was accepted that every doctor could participate in the scheme who chose to do so. The capitation system of payment was adopted and has retained the support of the profession. This might not have happened if the right of every doctor to take part in the scheme had not been conceded from the start. In a sense, the intervention of government in Britain had the effect of rescuing physicians from the control of friendly societies, while in Germany it initially enhanced the power which sick funds could exercise over the profession.

The capitation system, and the closed panels which were usually associated with it, have now been eliminated in Norway as well as in Germany, and their role has been substantially reduced in Denmark, Italy and Austria. In the latter, payment per three-monthly case—a modified capitation system—remains the most common way of paying general practitioners.[19] Capitation is still used in the towns of Denmark and in the rural areas of Italy and remains the sole way of paying physicians under the compulsory health insurance schemes of Spain and the Netherlands and in the British National Health Service. Where it exists, it has had the effect of protecting, promoting and crystallizing the concept of the general practitioner as the personal physician to whom the patient goes in the first instance whenever he needs medical care. The patient can, in fact, obtain 'free' medical care only by approaching first of all the particular doctor with whom he has chosen to register for the time being. He cannot 'shop around' among different physicians according to the particular disease he thinks he is suffering from. Thus, specialising within general practice does not give any obvious advantage to a physician hoping to attract patients from within the scheme. Specialists are seen on referral from a general practitioner who has to decide whether a specialist's opinion is required and, if so, what specialist. These decisions are much more likely to be taken by the patients themselves under fee-for-service systems of paying physicians. Specialization can, therefore, be used as a means of attracting additional consultations.

Thus, the trend toward fee-for-service systems of paying physicians under compulsory insurance has had the effect of fragmenting medical care at the point at which the patient originally consults the physician. Fewer patients have one personal physician who knows their whole medical history from having participated in its management—at least in its initial stages. This process has not occurred in those parts of Denmark where physicians are paid on a fee-for-service basis as there is an entrenched tradition of referral from general practititioner to specialist, which has been incorporated in the compulsory insurance regulations.[20] Fragmentation has gone furthest in Switzerland, where 53 per cent of practitioners in independent practice are 'specialists'.[21] It is also widespread in Stockholm and Oslo.[22] The trend has been the same in the United States, where compulsory health insurance does not exist.

All the insurance schemes established before the medical profession became effectively organized give service benefits. In other words, the scheme pays the physician directly for his services to beneficiaries. This is presumably what the consumers of medical care wanted. Systems of reimbursing patients for their medical care costs are to be found in those countries which were late in developing their insurance schemes. And in each case lobbying by the medical profession, often accompanied by 'strikes' or threats of 'strikes' has played an important role. Switzerland, which has little compulsory but considerable voluntary health insurance, is half one and half the other—representing a transitional stage in the history of health insurance. In France, voluntary insurance appears to have been restricted historically to cash benefits. Compulsory insurance was not introduced until 1930 and the reimbursement plan was adopted. New Zealand followed in 1938, Australia in 1950 and Sweden in 1956. In all these countries governments had originally tried to institute a service plan but were foiled by the profession. The option of a reimbursement system was eventually accepted by the Saskatchewan government after the stormy battles of 1962. Under most reimbursement plans, the physicians can negotiate levels of reimbursement and then charge patients additional sums if they wish to do so.

The 'freedom of medicine' movement was influenced greatly by the desire to avoid the experiences of Germany which have been briefly described above. It crystallized in France in the twenties and in French-speaking Switzerland and had an important influence on the thinking of the profession in the United States at the same period. The opposition to 'third parties' was essentially opposition to the German sick funds and generated the drive towards reimbursement systems of paying physicians. While reimbursement systems have given medical professions who operate under them more control of their economic destiny, they have not freed them from all controls. Indeed, reimbursement plans and straight fee-for-service plans have led to more interference with the clinical freedom of physicians than capitation plans because of the much larger possibilities of abuse at the expense of insurance funds. Thus, in France, 900 full-time control physicians and further part-time physicians are employed to check on the actions of individual physicians.[23] In Germany, the control of 'abuse' is in the hands of the local medical profession. It involves extensive administrative work and discussions with individual physicians.[24]

Pharmaceutical benefits are normally included in compulsory

228

insurance and public service health schemes. The usual system is for them to be purchased through local pharmacists, and either the pharmacist or the patient claims reimbursement from the sick fund or government. In the main sick fund of Israel, the drugs are issued through the sick fund. In the USSR patients have to purchase their own drugs for use at home. In Britain any drug may be prescribed for patients, though individual doctors may be required to account for their actions to their colleagues in the area, if their prescribing appears to be 'excessive'. The patient pays a standard charge of 20p for each preparation. In Australia, defined 'life-saving' drugs are available free to the bulk of the population, with a more extensive list for pensioners.[25] There is a similar limitation to 'essential' drugs in Sweden.[26] In the Netherlands doctors may not prescribe medicines which are in the experimental stage, or for which there is a less costly substitute of equal therapeutic value.[27]

The development of health insurance inevitably raised the question of whether hospital services should be included among the benefits. In countries where hospitals made substantial charges for the higher classes of accommodation, and the means tests and treatment of indigents were regarded as humiliating, there was a strong incentive for hospital benefits to be included. Thus they are found among the benefits in most countries of Europe with compulsory or voluntary health insurance schemes. Where contributions are wage related and where the employer also pays substantial contributions, a much higher proportion of hospital costs can be, and has been, shifted on to the insurance scheme. Thus, a substantial part of hospital costs is paid for by social security funds in France, Belgium, Germany and Holland. In these countries the government also participates in hospital financing in some form. Either it adds a contribution to the social security funds or it meets the deficits of hospitals, as in Belgium and many cantons of Switzerland, or else it gives grants for capital construction, as in Germany.[28] In Sweden, Norway, Switzerland and Denmark the bulk of hospital costs are met by the local authorities which run them:[29] in the latter case the insurance funds pay only about a tenth of the cost of hospitals.

In Britain, when compulsory insurance with flat-rate contributions was introduced in 1911, it was rare for in-patients to pay anything for treatment and there was no obvious crisis in hospital financing. Thus, the case for a hospital benefit was not given priority: a restricted benefit for the treatment of tuberculosis was, however, introduced for a short period. When the whole system of health insurance was reviewed by a Royal Commission in the middle 1920s, it was decided that the contribution required would be more than wage earners could afford.[30] Potential increases in revenue from social insurance contributions were reserved for the extension of cash benefits for widows and old people. Instead of compulsory hospital insurance there developed in Britain a system of voluntary contributory schemes which did not pretend to be run on an actuarial basis. Workers contributed what they could afford—usually about a quarter of the actuarial cost of the risk of hospitalization—and the money collected was handed over to the voluntary hospitals in the locality. By 1938 these schemes raised about a third of the revenue of the voluntary hospitals and covered about ten million persons. Contributing bestowed no legal right to care in hospital. Some full-cost insurance of the 'Blue Cross' type did, however, develop on a very small scale in the inter-war years among those who were comfortably off.

Thus, hospital insurance developed much earlier in Europe than in the United States and it took a completely different form. 'Blue Cross' was a movement which was promoted by the providers of services.[31] The hospitals needed to have more 'semi-private' patients who could pay the whole cost of the services they needed. Prepayment had, therefore, to begin among those with better than average incomes, and spread down the income scale as the country became more affluent.[32] In Europe, hospital insurance was part of the movement of mutual aid among the working classes. It was designed for those with 'blue collar' incomes and often specifically excluded those who were more comfortably placed. The level of benefit was thus determined by the level of contributions which 'blue collar' workers could afford, and not by the cost of providing the service. Any difference had to be made up by deductibles, charity and grants from public authorities: the latter subsidized hospital budgets directly, met deficits and often paid the deductibles of the indigent. The ultimate duty of society, to see that those who needed hospital treatment received it, had been tacitly accepted long before hospital insurance was started. It was this philosophy and the ability to pay contributions which have together determined the role which hospital insurance plays in different systems of medical care in Europe.

Once one accepts the citizen's right to receive medical care as a broad philosophy underlying a century or more of European history, the considerable difference in financing systems between the different countries become matters primarily of detail. The role of deductibles and national charges certainly varies greatly. So also does the role of insurance contributions. But it was not so wildly out of line with the arrangements of neighbouring countries for Russia to substitute a public service plan for the insurance method of financing in 1937, and for Britain to do the same in 1948. Lest it be supposed that there was some common political ideology shared by these two countries, it should be mentioned that the insurance method of financing is still retained in communist Poland and that in Scandinavia the bulk of hospital costs are in fact met on a public service basis without adopting the grandiloquent title of a National Health Service. The transition to a public service system usually involves extending the coverage of pre-paid health services to include the whole population. A high proportion of the population of European countries is, in fact, already entitled to pre-paid medical care under existing plans. The Norwegian insurance plan covers the whole population:[33] in Germany 85 per cent of the population is covered, and about three-quarters of the population is covered in Austria, Italy, the Netherlands and Switzerland.[34] In view of these figures and the early development of non-profit voluntary insurance, out of which compulsory insurance emerged, there has never been much room for profit-making insurance companies in the financing of medical costs. They play hardly any role in Europe.

The creation of Britain's National Health Service involved both an extension of the coverage of prepaid medical care from approximately one half to the whole population and also an extension of the range of benefits to include free hospitalization and dental, ophthalmic, home nursing and other services. A further major step was taken at the same time: the hospitals were nationalized. This was the solution chosen to deal with the problem of planning the size, function and location of hospitals. In Scandinavia, most of the hospitals were built by the large local authorities. Their siting has, therefore, always been planned. Similarly, continental local authorities have generally planned the development of the main hospital services in their area. Where they have not, hospital authorities have generally been powerful religious bodies of varying denominations. In Britain, the voluntary sector was large, uncoordinated and secular. Many haphazard influences had affected the size and location of the various units. Hospital beds were spread most unevenly round the country. Most hospitals were far too small to meet the needs of efficient modern medicine. The case for some system of planning was recognized first in London in the early eighteen-nineties,[35] just as it was recognized first in New York after the First World War. It was recognized as a national problem in Britain during the thirties,[36] just as it has become recognized as a national problem in the United States in the fifties and sixties.[37] Neither the voluntary hospitals nor the medical profession were prepared to accept a hospital system controlled by the local authorities. Both preferred national ownership. Britain's nationalized hospitals are not run on the pattern of the veterans' hospitals of the United States. Instead, they have been handed on to a battery of planning boards and management boards, to which are appointed representatives of the medical profession, ex-voluntary hospital trustees, local authority councillors and other persons drawn from the local community. Nationalization, paradoxically, has therefore led to an extension in the scope for voluntary work. Some five to ten thousand unpaid committee men and women meet at least once a month to control the affairs of their local hospitals.

Many aspects of the European pattern of organizing health services can be traced to developments which occurred long before compulsory insurance was invented, doctors were highly organized or commercial insurance had entered the field of financing health costs. For example, the split between hospital-based doctors and home-based doctors arose because hospitals developed apart from the private medical care market. It means that normally the European patient is looked after by a different physician when he is admitted to hospital. Those Americans who are used to a different system may see this as an undesirable break in continuity of care. Defenders of the European system would, however, argue that most admissions to hospitals require the services of a specialist and that physicians with hospital facilities are tempted to undertake more specialist work than their training warrants.[38] And as most illnesses do not require hospitalization, continuity of care in out-of-hospital treatment is more important than continuity between home care and hospital care.

While much of European medical care is the product of long tradition, the schemes of pre-payment found in different countries have affected the patterns of organizing health services. Countries with capitation systems of paying physicians have managed to combine the principle of free choice of physician with the principle of the personal physician who arranges all treatment, though he does not always provide it, and who has the advantage of continuity of relationships with particular patients and families. Protagonists of the system argue that the family doctor can practise better medicine in view of this continuity of relationship. It is true, however, that many patients in Europe, as in America, seem to like to choose their physician according to their diagnosis of their illness when they have the opportunity to do so within a compulsory health insurance scheme. Is the free choice of patients necessarily the best choice in this highly technical field? Similarly, private patients in Europe, as in the United States, like to have their own physician treat them in hospital. Will physicians always give the best advice about whether a specialist should be brought in when they have a financial interest in providing all the care themselves?

The principle of free choice of family physician is accepted in every Western European health scheme except that of Spain. In Eastern Europe, polyclinic physicians are given districts, as has been the practice since long before the communist revolutions. Special arrangements can be made for a particular patient to be attached to the physician responsible for another district, but this is seldom done. While this system may restrict the confidence of the patient in his physician, it has both epidemiological and economic advantages. And preventive medicine can be more systematically promoted in a salaried service. It may also be encouraged to some extent under the capitation system of paying physicians with the continuity of relationships it engenders. It is less likely to be encouraged when patients can shop around between different physicians for different illnesses. On the other hand, such a system clearly keeps physicians keen to attract and hold custom. But one means of doing so may be an excessive use of drugs.

Payment systems can affect or be deliberately used to influence the way in which medicine is practised. Thus, loading of the capitation fee and maximum list sizes can be used, as is the practice in both the Netherlands and Britain, to reduce the financial incentives of physicians to take on more patients than they can manage. Loading is also used in Britain to encourage physicians to work together in groups. This is, however, discouraged in Germany, where doctors are paid on a fee-for-service basis, because of the opportunities it would offer physicans to increase fees by passing patients around among the partners. It would be hard to draw the line between legitimate consultations and undesirable abuses. Teamwork, though desirable in modern medicine, is hard to accommodate in a pre-paid scheme where physicians are paid on a fee-for-service basis. The fee structures of both Germany and Sweden encourage the use of scientific diagnostic tests. There is not the same incentive for such tests where physicians are paid on a capitation basis. Fee structures can also be used to encourage referral in particular cases if a specialist is paid much more for a particular procedure than a non-specialist —particularly if the fee given to the latter barely compensates him for the time involved. Similarly, home calls and night calls can be encouraged if extra payment is given for them. All these features have been built into different health schemes.

How far physicians and patients respond to particular financial incentives, or become apathetic in the absence of them, is hard to assess. One might expect the number of times the average patient sees his physician to vary according to the system of payment. Thus, there would be a higher consultation rate under a fee-for-service system of payment than under a capitation or salaried system of paying doctors. The highest consultation rates reported in a recent international study were found in countries with a fee-for service system—Germany with 10 consultations a year and Japan with 15 consultations a year.[39]

The lowest consultation rates (about 2 a year) were found in France and Sweden with their reimbursement systems. Belgium and Switzerland were about average (5 a year). The Netherlands with its capitation scheme of paying doctors had $5\frac{1}{2}$ consultations a year, though pensioners are excluded from these figures. Spain, also a capitation scheme, had 7 consultations a year. Austria, with partly a fee-for-service scheme and partly a modified capitation scheme, had nearly 10 consultations a year, and Israel, with its salaried scheme, had about 8 consultations a year. Some of these variations may be explained by differences in the ratio of physicians in the countries studied and by differences in the level of health. For example, Israel is much more generously stocked with doctors than Sweden, but it makes it hard to generalize about the 'inevitable' effects of remuneration systems. It may be that tradition, culture and medical education play the major roles. The subject deserves careful study. Such a study would have to take account of cost-sharing regulations and the availability of 'free' drugs in the various schemes and the use of private consultations outside it.

The development and extension of systems of prepaying medical care have normally led to extensions in the use of services, but it does not follow that the countries where pre-payment systems or public health services are most developed spend the highest proportion of their national incomes on health services. The development of pre-payment not only makes medical care more readily available, it also introduces a third party which is in a position to bargain about the standards of care, particularly in its 'amenity' aspects, which are thought to be reasonable: it can also negotiate collectively about levels of remuneration. The extent to which a 'third party' performs its function depends on how far it is really representative of consumers and how far it needs to compromise when faced with the wishes and bargaining power of providers of services. The proportion of gross national expenditure devoted to health services (public and private, capital and current) was 4·7 per cent in Sweden (1956) and England and Wales (1960–1), 5·1 per cent in Israel (1959–60) and 5·2 per cent in the United States (1957–8).[40] An earlier and less through study estimated that public and private expenditure on medical care as a proportion of national income was 3·7 per cent in Denmark (1952–3), 3·8 per cent in the Netherlands (1953),

4·1 per cent in Belgium (1954) and in England and Wales (1953–4), 4·4 per cent in Canada (1953) and in France (1952), and 4·5 per cent in Norway (1955) and the United States (1953) and 4·6 per cent in New Zealand (1953).[41]

Thus when one looks around the high-income world, one can distinguish three essentially different patterns of providing medical care services. The first is the *American system*, where typically the patient chooses the physician for his illness, be he general practitioner or specialist, and that physician continues responsibility for that patient's care should hospitalization be necessary. This pattern is to be found extensively for *private* patients in Portugal and France and some other continental European countries, though the hospital to which such a patient is admitted in continental Europe is often owned and operated by the physician concerned, while in the United States the hospital is typically a non-profit and independent institution. Of course there is a growing number of closed hospitals and salaried physicians in the United States, but the general pattern is as I have described.

The second system is what I will call the *Western European system*, where physicians retain their private offices as in the United States but hospital care is normally the responsibility of a separate group of salaried physicians working mainly in governmental hospitals (usually local units of government). The compulsory insurance system pays the physician or reimburses the patient and pays the whole or part of the cost of the drugs which the physician prescribes. In many countries there are also home nursing services provided by local units of government. In Britain, these services are particularly well developed. For each general practitioner in the National Health Service there is a quarter of a health visitor (a public health nurse who devotes most of her time to preventive services among children and old people), a quarter of an obstetric nurse (midwife) and one-third of a qualified home-care nurse who provides basic and technical nursing services to patients sick in their own homes.

The third system I will call the *Eastern European system*, though it is to be found in Israel under the main sick fund and throughout the low-income countries of Africa and Asia. Here the physician is salaried and operates from an office (polyclinic, dispensary or health centre) which is provided by the service. This office is often sited beside the hospital, as is the growing pattern in North America. The district doctor, to whom patients are normally assigned, refers cases requiring hospitalization to a separate group of salaried physicians. A district doctor can be 'promoted' to this group on passing the appropriate examinations. The epidemiological and preventive services work in close association with the other health services.

Thus, the major difference between the Eastern European and Western European systems is to be found in the independence of 'out of hospital' physicians. They are private contractors in Western Europe and salaried officials in Eastern Europe. In other respects the services are more similar though there is much more centralized control and national planning in Eastern Europe than Western Europe. In the latter systems the planning of hospital services tends to be the responsibility of local rather than central government. In Eastern Europe 'posting' of physicians and especially high salaries for the less-popular posts are used to try and secure even coverage of the country with physicians. In Western Europe basic salaries and systems of mileage allowances and loading of remuneration systems are used to attract physicians to work in the less populous areas. Britain also uses a system of *negative* control over the location of general practitioners: a physician cannot get a contract under the national health service in certain scheduled 'over-doctored' areas unless he has some special family or other claim to work there. Britain's hospital service is more like that of Eastern Europe in so far as it is centrally and regionally planned, but no posting of physicians occurs and both the planning and management of hospitals is done by bodies which are composed of both local lay and local medical representatives.

I have argued that the fundamental differences in the organization and financing of medical care between the United States and other high income countries have been greatly influenced by long-established differences in attitudes to medical care. In Europe the provision of medical care has always been regarded more as a collective responsibility and different institutions have been developed to undertake it. Hospitals were started to serve the needs of the poor rather than to meet the needs of paying patients. In most European countries hospitals started in the hands of mainly religious charitable bodies but have been increasingly transferred to public authorities. American short-stay hospitals have remained primarily non-profit community services. They always took paying patients and the role of charitable support has gradually declined.

In America prepayment has been primarily a movement generated by providers of services, though particularly in the last ten years the field has been entered by the profit-making insurance organizations. In Europe prepayment has always been primarily a non-profit movement sponsored and controlled by consumers. When government has entered the field it has usually been to extend by compulsion the membership of these consumers' organizations rather than to supersede them. Thus it has found itself cast in the role of mediator in what previously had been the private disputes between producers and consumers. And the sick funds of Europe and particularly of Israel are powerful bodies. In the United States there have hardly ever been any consumers' organizations in this field. With the possible exception of the unions, whose interests are large and diffused, there is virtually no organized countervailing power to balance the demands of providers of services—of the hospitals and the physicians. Thus, when government has intervened in the medical care market, it has had to initiate, not to mediate. And there is never much incentive for a government to challenge organized and articulate interests on behalf of less articulate and largely unorganized opinion, unless it is compelled to do so.

In any review of the emergence of medical-care systems throughout the world, there is a danger of over-emphasizing the extent to which each country has been a slave to its own culture and tradition. It is so much easier to detect after the event the forces which have led to particular developments. The alternative courses which history might have taken are much harder to identify. Governments and consumers' organizations can influence and have deliberately influenced patterns of health care, not only in Britain and Eastern Europe but throughout the world.

The fact that usually intervention has been slow and gradual has perhaps been largely because we know so little about what constitutes good medical care. Governments act and, in a democracy, the public demands action more readily when indisputable facts are available to support the need for action. Each country tends to shroud its medical system in complacent praise. In an age when tools of research have never been so readily available, argument by assertion can no longer be tolerated. Instead, we need facts. In particular we need to measure the quality of medical care under different systems of financing and organization.

Notes

1. Henry C. Burdett, *Hospitals and Asylums of the World* (1893), vol. 3, p. 56.
2. *ibid.*
3. *ibid.*, p. 55.
4. *ibid.*, p. 613. The author makes two relatively minor exceptions to this general statement.
5. *ibid.*, pp. 76, 423, 454, 618.
6. *ibid.*, pp. 448–57, 662.
7. Brian Abel-Smith, *Hospitals 1800–1948* (1964).
8. Burdett, p. 56.
9. Abel-Smith, *op. cit.*
10. Mark G. Field, *Doctor and Patient in Soviet Russia* (1957).
11. Sir Arthur Newsholme, *International Studies on the Relations between the Private and Official Practice of Medicine* (1931), vol. 2, p. 216.
12. *ibid.*, p. 241.
13. Mary Stocks, *A Hundred Years of District Nursing* (1960).
14. Newsholme, p. 31, vol. 2, pp. 26, 57.
15. James Hogarth, *The Payment of the General Practitioner* (1962), p. 392.
16. Newsholme, Vol. 1, p. 24.
17. Brain Abel-Smith, 'Paying the Family Doctor', *Medical Care*, 1 (1963), p. 30.
18. R. M. Titmuss, 'Health' in *Law and Opinion in England in the Twentieth Century*, ed. M. Ginsberg (1959). Reprinted in *Commitment to Welfare*, London 1968.
19. Hogarth, p. 346.
20. *op. cit.*, p. 401.

21. *op. cit.*, p. 282.
22. *op. cit.*, p. 62, 100.
23. *op. cit.*, p. 149.
24. *op. cit.*, pp. 243–8.
25. Ministry of Health, *Final Report of the Committee on Cost of Prescribing* (1959), p. 38.
26. International Social Security Association, *Volume and Cost of Benefits in Kind and Cash* (1961), p. 382.
27. Ministry of Health, *op. cit.*, p. 38.
28. Abel-Smith, 'Changing methods of financing hospital care', *The Changing Role of the Hospital in a Changing World*, published by the International Hospital Federation (1963).
29. Hogarth, *op. cit.*, pp. 52, 94, 272, 389.
30. Abel-Smith, *Hospitals 1800–1948*.
31. H. and Ann Somers, *Doctors Patients and Health Insurance* (1961), p. 292.
32. *ibid.*, p. 291.
33. Hogarth, *op. cit.*, p. 94.
34. *ibid.*, p. 328.
35. Abel-Smith, *Hospitals 1800–1948, op. cit.*
36. *ibid.*
37. Somer, *op. cit.*, pp. 83–90.
38. See, for example, Ray Trussell, *The Quantity, Quality and Costs of Medical and Hospital Care Secured by a Sample of Teamster Families in the New York Area* (undated).
39. The figures quoted in this paragraph come from International Social Security Association, *op. cit.*, p. 392.
40. Abel-Smith, (1963), 'Health Expenditure in Seven Countries', *The Times Review of Industry and Technology* (March 1963), p. vi. The final report appeared in *An International Study of Health Expenditure*, Public Health Papers No. 32, W.H.O. (1967).
41. International Labour Office, *The Cost of Medical Care* (1959), pp. 76–7.

Notes on Contributors

Brian Abel-Smith is Professor of Social Administration in the London School of Economics. He is the author of many books and articles on aspects of poverty and mental health including *The Hospitals 1800–1948* and *In Search of Justice*.

Asa Briggs is Vice-Chancellor and Professor of History at the University of Sussex. He is an established authority on nineteenth-century British Social History and his most recent book is the third volume of *The History of Broadcasting in the United Kingdom*.

Blanche Coll is a historian in the Social and Rehabilitation Service, US Department of Health, Education and Welfare. Her most recent book is *Perspectives in Public Welfare*.

E. W. Martin is well known as a social historian with special concern for the problems and institutions of the rural poor. He was awarded a Leverhulme Research Fellowship at Sussex University from 1965 to 1967.

E. C. Midwinter is Director of the Liverpool Educational Priority Area Project and has a special interest in Victorian social administration. His recent publications include *Victorian Social Reform* and *Social Administration in Lancashire 1830–1860*.

Mark Neuman, Associate Professor of History at Bucknell University, wrote his doctoral thesis on Berkshire and the Speenhamland system. He has co-operated with Ashley Montague in presenting a new edition of J. Townsend's *A Dissertation on the Poor Laws*.

Milton Speizman is Professor of Social Work and Social Research at Bryn Mawr University, Pennsylvania and has been engaged in social work education with a special interest in social welfare history since 1959.

James S. Taylor is Associate Professor of History, Wells College, New York. He has written a thesis on 'Poverty in Rural Devon 1780–1840'.

Index

Abbott, Edith and Grace, 186
Abel-Smith, Brian, 239–40n
Acts of Parliament, Education (1870), 201, 208, 210; (1876), 203, 210; (1902), 18, 23; 5, Eliz, I c. 4, (1563), 86–7; 39, Eliz, I c. 3, (1597–8), 29, 51, 76n, 120n; 43, Eliz, I c. 2. (1601), 29, 40, 45, 48, 76n, 120n; General Workhouse (1722), 60; 22, George III c. 83 (Gilbert's Act (1782)) and localism, 35–4, 60, 120n; 59, George III c. 12 (Sturges Bourne's Act (1819), 59n; Liverpool Sanitary (1846), 199; Local, 29, 31, 77n, 199; Municipal Corporations (1835), 197, 202; Of Settlement and Removal (1622), 32, 52n, 130; Police (1866), 200: Poor Law Amendment (1834), 28, 32, 40, 45, 47, 64, 93, 140, 201, 209; Prisons (1865 and 1867), 201; Public Health (1858), 198, 202; Union Chargeability (1835), 28, 47, 201; Workhouse Test, 32
Addams, Jane, 177n, 184
Agriculture, Board of, 127n
Aiyer, S. P., 22n
Alcock, Thomas, 48, 56n
Apprentice(s) and Apprenticeship, 29, 31, 37–8, 54n, 65, 71, 78–9n
Ashby, A. W., 120n
Ashley, Sir Wm., 50n
Ashton-under-Lyne, 202

Baker, J., 51n
Baltimore, 129, 135–7, 141, 144, 156n, 170–1
Beales, H. L. 21, 24n, 51n
Beard, Charles and Mary, 183–7, 189–90
Bellamy, Edward, 183

Bellers, John, 32
Bentham, Jeremy, 39, 47, 54n; on pauperism and management, 56n; and Benthamism, 195, 204, 207–8
Bergh, Henry, 175
Berkshire, 85, 89, 96, 98–101, 107–118, 118–19n, 125–7n
Bernstein, B., 16, 23n
Beveridge, Senator, 169
Bicheno, J. E., 90, 111, 120–1n
Blaug, Mark, 55–56n, 75n, 77n, 94–5, 97–9, 121–3n
Bliss, W. D. P., 176
Blomfield, Bishop, 39, 54n
Bloombergh, W., 24n
Blythe, Ronald, 127n
Body, G. A., 54n, 79n, 98, 120n
Bois, W. E. B. Du, 178
Boston, 129, 133, 142–4
Booth, Charles, 13
Brace, C. L. 175
Brebner, J. B., 196, 215n
Breckenridge, S. P., 156n
Brereton, C. D., 57, 75n
Bridenbaugh, Carl, 187, 190n
Briggs, Asa, 22–3, 204
Bristol, 32, 61, 78n, 84
Britain, 24n, 221–6, 231–2, 234, 236–8
Brooke, Sir John, 52n, 127n
Brooklyn, 175
Brougham, Lord, 197
Bruce, Maurice, 20, 29, 51n
Bruchey, Stuart, 129, 155n
Bruges, 27
Bryce, James, 177
Buckinghamshire, 36, 53n, 120
Budd, William, 112–13, 119n
Bunbury, S. H. N., 24n
Burdett, H., 239n
Burke, Edmund, 53n
Burn, Rev. R., 51n, 59, 79n

Burn, W. L., 23n, 196, 215n
Butcher, E. E., 52n

Cabell, J. C. and J. L., 156n
Cambridgeshire, 70, 75n, 79–80n, 90
'Captain Swing,' 92, 113
Cannan, Edwin, 126n
Carey, M., 147–8
Carlyle, Thomas, 206
Cary, J., 32
Chadwick, Edwin, on administration, 42–4, 55n, 202; activities, 54n, 196, 211; and poor rates, 46–7; and Poor Law Commission, 199; and sanitation, 198; and Benthamism, 204
Chalmers, Rev. Thomas, 'brutal optimism' of, 39; and poor laws, 48; works and influence of, 54–5n
Channing, Edward, 172–3, 188n
Charity, (philanthropy), 'indiscriminate', 15, 26; decline of personal, 27–8; utilitarianism and, 40; and social welfare, 50n; Defoe and, 32, 52n; comparison with public relief, 55n, 117; in U.S.A., 131, 133–140, 145–55, 156n, 165–70, 173–5, 177–8; in modern Britain, 221–2; in Europe, 225
Chartism, 204–5
Chatham, Earl of, 119n
Christie, I. R., 52n
Churchill, W. S., 23n
Clapham, Sir John, 32, 52n, 92, 95, 99, 120–1n
Cleveland, President, 173
Club, Political Economy, 48
Coats, A. W., 52n, 75n
Cobbett, William, on the new poor law, 46, 56n
Coit, Stanton, 177
Commons, John, and labour history, 170–2, 188n
Coode, George, and settlement, 32, 52n
Cornwall, 33
Corrigan, Archbishop, 177
Cowell, J. W., 48
Crabbe, George, 57, 73, 75n, 83–4n
Cumberland, 59, 76n
Cunningham, William, 91, 121n
Curti, Merle, 187, 190n

Darwin, Charles, 168–9
Defoe, Daniel, 32, 52n
Devon, 31–8, 54n, 59, 76n, 78n, 80–3n, 98
Dicey, A. V., 195–6, 201, 209, 215n
Dix, Dorothea, 151, 156n, 175
Dobbs, Sir Richard, 50n
Dodd, Theodore, 51n
Dorfman, J., 188n
Dorset, 31, 33, 38, 54n, 98, 120n
Downs, A., 24n
Dugdale, R. L., 175
Duncan, Dr., 199
Dundas, Charles, 86, 112–16, 118, 126–27n
Durrell, Dr., 127n
Dyos, H. J., 22n

Eden, Sir F. M., 52–3n; his survey of evidence, 59; and workhouse earnings, 78–9n, and deaths in, 81–2n; and Speenhamland, 90–1, 95, 119–21, 124n
Edmonds, E. L. and O. P., 23n
Education, 14, 18, 27–32, 100; Woodard Schools and, 14, 23n; *Robbins Report* and, 22n; Committee of Privy Council for, 203, 207; Department of Privy Council for, 203; and School Boards, 202–3, 211–14
Eliot, George, 15–6
Ellwood, C. A., 55n
Elton, G. R., 29
Ely, R. T., 170
Emmison, F. G., 84n
England and English, 9–17, 26–9, 33, 48, 59–63, 74, 77n, 85–6, 94–6, 110, 123n, 125n 131, 140, 167, 171, 187, 192, 197, 204–5, 212–3
Ernle, Lord, 93–4, 121n
Essex, 83n
Europe, 10, 183, 219 *passim*

Faulkner, Harold H., 180–1, 189n
Fay, C. R., 52n, 100
Field, M., 239n
Finer, H., 192, 215n
Finer, S. E., 54n, 196, 215n
Fish, C. R., 173, 175, 188–9n

Fiske, E. F., 188n
Fiske, John, 165–7, 188n
Fitch, J., 22n
Flick, A. C., 155n
Fowle, Rev. F. C., 126n
Fox, D. R., 173
Franklin, Benjamin, 183
Fresh, Tom, 199

Gabriel, R. H., 187, 190n
Garrison, W. L., 160, 188n
George, Henry, 183
Germany, 13, 23n
Gibbons, Cardinal, 177
Gilbert, B.S., 13, 23n
Gilbert, Thomas, and provincial work-
    houses 32; effects of his work, 33;
    and localism, 33–4; pamphlets and,
    52n; influence on policy, 78n;
    and unions, 81n
Gilboy, E., 75n
Ginsberg, M., 24n, 239n
Goldman, Emma, 167
Goodlake, T., 127n
Goodman, P. H., 120n
Graham, J. Q., 23n
Gray, B. Kirkham, 39, 54n
Green, J. R., 161
Gursslin, O. R., 49n
Gutchen, R. M., 196, 215n

Halévy, Elie, 80n, 195
Hamilton, Alexander, 182
Hamilton, R. W., 10, 22n
Hammond, J. L. and B., 118, 120–1;
    Speenhamland, 53n, 91–2, 96; and
    Benthamism, 195
Hampson, E. M., 75n, 89, 120n
Handcock, W. D., 55n
Hanway, Jonas, 65
Harrison, W., 50n
Hart, A. B., 168–9, 188n
Hart, J., 195, 215n
Health, General Board of, 198–9;
    insurance, voluntary societies and,
    224–225; compulsory insurance,
    226–8; and hospital services, 229–
    33; expenditure on, 234–6
Henderson, C. R., 55n
Henderson, D., 23n

Hill, Christopher, 51n
Hinden, R., 24n
Hobsbawn, E. J., 121n
Hofstadter, R., 165, 182, 188n
Hogarth, J., 239–40n
Home Office, 197–99
Hopkins, N. D., 98, 122n
Hunter, R., 181
Inglis, Brian, 23n
International Labour Organization, 11

Jackson, Andrew, 152, 156n
Jay, John, 161
Jernegan, Marcus, 129, 155n
Johnson, P. A., 24n
Johnson, R., 23n
Jones, E. L., 123n
Jordan, W. K., 76n

Kelley, Florence, 186
Kellog, P., 184
Kelso, R. W., 56n
Kent, 77n
Krieger, L., 24n

Lambert, R. J., 23n, 215n
Lambert, Royston, 195
Lampard, Wm., 51n
Lancashire, 76–7n, 197–200, 205–6,
    208–9
Landes, D. S., 23n
Lawton, D., 23n
Lee, I., 175
Leonard, E. M., 51n
Levy, S. L., 54n
Lewis, Oscar, 49n
Lewis, Sir T. F., 39, 55n
Lington, J., 51n
Lipson, E. E., 52n
Liverpool, 15, 61, 197, 203, 205
London, 27, 61, 65, 175
Lousley, J., 113, 126n
Lowe, Rev., 96
Lubove, R., 55n, 156
Luther, Martin, 26

MacDonagh, O., 22n, 195–6, 208, 215
Macfie, A. L., 49n

Mackay, T., 51n
Machworth, Humphrey, 52n,
Magistrates and Counties, 68–9, 81n, 88–9, 101, 106–8, 112–18, 209, 126–7n
Malthus, Rev. R. T., 39, 43; his influence, 47–8, 115
Marryott, M., 32
Marshall, Alfred, 49n
Marshall, Dorothy, 51n, 57, 75n, 78n, 120–22n
Marshall, J. D., 98, 121–2n
Marshall, T. H., 20
Martin, E. W., 127n
Marwick, A., 24n
Marx, Karl, on Bentham and parsons, 39; on Malthus, 54n
Masterman, C. F. G., 13
Mavor, W., 119–20n, 123n, 125n, 127n
McMaster, J. B., 120–5, 187–8n
Medical care, 219–21, 224–26; systems of, 236–7; differences in Europe and U.S.A., 237–8
Melling, E., 82n, 84n
Midwinter, E. C., 215n
Mill, J. S., 25, 49n
Mingay, G. E., 125n
Mitchell, Broadus, 182, 189n
Mitchelson, N., 82n
Morris, Pauline, 79n
Moseley, Henry, 16–17

Namier, L., 52n, 127n
Neuman, Mark, 54n
Nevins, Allen, 174–5, 189n
Newlands, John, 199
Newsholme, Sir A., 239n
New York, 129, 133–4, 137–9, 141–7, 149, 151, 156n, 163, 174–5, 219
Nicholls, Sir G., 91, 96
Northumberland, 96
Nottinghamshire, 48, 96

Ogg, F. A., 169, 188n
Oldham, C. R., 82n
Osborne, B., 51n
Owen, D., 23n
Oxfordshire, 77n, 120n

Pack, L., 76n
Page, F., 87, 90, 95, 106–7, 119, 121n, 126–7n
Parish Officers, 31–5, 109–12; and apprenticeship, 37–8, 58, 79; and workhouses, 32, 40, 70, 82n, 107
Parrington, Vernon, 182–3
Parris, H., 195, 215n
Pashley, R., 45
Paupers and pauperism, 28, 31–3, 40, 44, 49n, 74, 83n, 117, 146–7, 150, 155–6n, 162–3, 166, 171, 191; in the U.S.A., 150–3
Peabody, G., 175
Perkin, H., 22n
Philadelphia, 129, 137, 142–4, 147–8, 156, 174
Pierce, Franklin, 152
Pitt, William, 192n
Polanyi, Karl, 18, 24n, 54n, 96–7, 119n, 121n
Poole, Thomas, 75n
Poor Law Commission (1832–4), Report of, 38–42, 44–5, 57–9, 72–3n, 91, 111; and the Elizabethan Act, 29–30; and rural and town queries, 41, 59, 65–8, 73, 76–7n, 80–3, 95, 126n
Relief, (Allowance System), 36–7, 41–2, 44, 53–4n, 71–2n, 85–118, 118–27n; in South Eastern Counties, 63; and the parish, 101–5; and bread scales, 36–7, 87–91, 95–6, 100–7, 109, 112–13
Workhouses, experiments in, 27, 31–2; definition of, 58–61; governorship of, 65–9; post-1834, 75n; outdoor relief, 44, 62, 71–3, 77–8n, 91–4, 134, 140–1, 144, 163, 170–1
Poverty, 12–3, 25, 28, 119, 165, 167; controversy in the U.S.A. and Britain, 17, 24n; culture of, 49n; rural, 35; Elizabethan code and, 26; Chalmers on 55n
Power, A., 199
Power, W., 137
Poynter, J. R., 23n, 76–8n, 83n, 98, 120n, 122n
Pretyman, J. R., 55n
Price, J. M., 23n
Pumphrey, R. E., and M. W., 155–7

Quincy, J., 205

Rawlinson, R., 205
Reader, W. J., 23n
Rex, John, 18, 24n
Rickman, John, 58
Ridley, Bishop, 27, 50–1n
Roach, J., 49n
Robbins' Report, 22n
Roberts, D., 22–3, 75n, 83n, 195, 215
Romilly, Sir Samuel, 29, 51n
Roosevelt, F. D., 151, 182, 185
Roosevelt, Theodore, 168–9
Rowney, D. K., 23n
Rowntree, S., 13, 23n
Rudé, George, 121n
Runciman, W. G., 24n
Ruskin, John, 184
Russell, Henry, 123n
Russell, Lord John, 42
Rutland, 61

Salter, F. R., 50–1n
Sandford, H., 75n
Schlesinger, A. M., 176–7, 189n
Schmandt, H. J., 24n
Schweinitz, Karl de, 29, 51n
Scott, R., 24n
Select Committee on, Labourers' Wages (1824), 90, 97, 99
  Old Age Pension (1899), 19
  Poor Laws (1817), 53n
  „   „   (1828, Lords), 56n
  „   „   (1831, Lords), 76n
Senior, Nassau, 39, 54n; 1834 Report and poor laws, 42–4; and labourers wages, 43–4 54–5n
Settlement, Law of, condemnation of, 32, 47; report on, 52n; in U.S.A. 130–3
Shaftesbury, Lord, 202
Shaw, J., 23n
Sheldon, Charles, 176
Shropshire, 76n
Simey, Margaret, 15, 23n
Simey, T. S., 24n
Simpson, N., 55n
Smith, Adam, 87, 119n
Smith, Alfred E., 185
Smith, J. Toulmin, 202

Smith, Sydney, 75n
Social policy, 11, 13, 17–8, 20–22, 24n
Somerset, 31, 37, 41
Somers, H. and A., 240
Staffordshire, 33
Steiner, G. Y., 24n
Stern, W. M., 118n
Stocks, Mary, 239n
Stokes, Rev. Dr R., 82n
Sturges Bourne, Rt. Hon. W., 53–5n
Suffolk, 75n, 82n
Sumner, W. Graham, 177–80
Sussex, 59

Tarbell, Ida, 175–6, 189n
Tate, W. E., 36, 51n, 53n
Tawney, R. H., 21, 37, 50n, 56n
Taylor, J. S., 35, 53n, 98, 122n
Thomas, M. W., 23n
Thompson, F. M. L., 125, 127
Thropp, E. T., 138
Tierney, Brian, 50n
Tilly, C., 23n
Titmuss, Richard, 17, 20–1, 24n, 239n
Tooke, Thomas, 119
Townsend, Peter, 24n
Toynbee, Arnold, 91
Troeltsch, Ernst, 50n
Turner, Frederick, J., 189n
Twistleton, E. B., 29–30, 51n

Ullman, W., 50n
United States, 13, 17; adoption of English poor law system, 128, 130–1; almshouses in, 138–9, 152–4; Association for Improving Conditions of the Poor, 149–51; Children's Bureau, 169, 181; Civil Rights Movement in, 159; Civil War in, 167, 181; education service in, 221; 'eligibility', 153, 155; First White House Conference on Children, 181; Great Depression, 151, 159, 181–2, 184; Keating-Owen's Child Labour Law, 169; National Child Labour Committee in, 169; New Deal in, 181–2, 184–5, 187; no compulsory health insurance in, 219, 221; outdoor relief in, 140–5, 154–5; Roman Catholics in, 177; settlements in, 184; Social Science

Research Council, 155; State Board for Charity, 167; Wisconsin Conference of Social Work in, 170; Women's Christian Temperance Union, 174
University of California, 50n
Utilitarianism, 16

Vancouver, J., 49n
Vestry, 31; select 37, 107; open, 67–8
Victorian, voluntary action, 12, 14; public health, 15; administration, 191–213; bibliography of social provision, 215–18
Villiers, C. P. and Union Chargeability Act, 46–8, 71, 100–1
Virginia, 129, 141, 156
Vives, J. L., 26–7

Wales, 61, 77n
Walter, John, 126n
Waterloo, 90, 112
Watts, Rev., G., 101
Weaver, James, 184

Webb, S. and B., 18, 27, 32, 35, 50n; 56n; on workhouses, 57, 61–3, 75–6n 78–9, 89, 96, 114, 120–2n, 195
Weber, Max, 196
Wecter, Dixon, 181–2, 189n
Westmorland, 76n
Weston, Charles, 32, 52n, 96, 121, 123n, 125n, 127n
Wilson, Rev., Edward, 87–8, 199n
Wilson, Woodrow, 167–9, 188n
Wiltshire, 31, 39, 41, 76, 79
Windsor, Justin, 157n
Wish, Harvey, 189n
Woodard, Nathaniel, 14

Ximenes, Morris, 113, 126n

Yates, J. V. N., 133–4
Yorkshire, 76n, 98, 199
Young, Arthur, 90, 120n
Young, G. M., 55n

Zurich, 50n
Zwingli, Ulrich, 26, 50n